THE FEDERAL COURTS

THE FEDERAL COURTS

Robert A. Carp
University of Houston

Ronald Stidham
Lamar University

A division of Congressional Quarterly Inc.
1414 22nd Street N.W., Washington, D.C. 20037

Printed in the United States of America

Second Printing

Library of Congress Cataloging in Publication Data

Carp, Robert A., 1943-
    The federal courts.

    Bibliography: p. 239
    Includes index.
    1. Courts—United States.   I. Stidham, Ronald,
1940-   .   II. Title.
KF8719.C33   1985   347.73′2   85-17095
ISBN 0-87187-349-4   347.3071

To my remarkable and much-loved grandparents: my maternal grandmother, Mrs. Florence Schmidt, and my paternal grandfather, Mr. Arthur Carp.

R.A.C.

To four very important people in my life: my wife, Laquita, and sons Tony, Todd, and Sam.

R.S.

Contents

Preface   ix

1 History, Function, and
  Organization of the Federal Judiciary   1

  The Historical Context   1
  The U.S. Supreme Court   3
  The U.S. Courts of Appeals   13
  U.S. District Courts   23
  Constitutional Courts and Legislative Courts   28
  The Federal Courts in the American Political System   30
  Summary   33

2 Jurisdiction, Workload, and
  Policy-Making Boundaries   37

  U.S. District Courts   37
  U.S. Courts of Appeals   41
  U.S. Supreme Court   43
  Jurisdiction and Congressional Politics   45
  Judicial Self-Restraint   47
  Summary   58

3 Administrative and Staff Support
  in the Federal Judiciary   61

  A Brief History of the Judicial Administration Movement   62
  Major Administrative Support Structures   65
  Personnel Support   74
  Summary   86

Contents

4 The Federal Judges   89

Background Characteristics   89
Formal and Informal Qualifications   98
The Selection Process and Its Participants   102
Policy Links Between the Citizenry, the President,
and the Federal Judiciary   111
The Judicial Socialization Process   121
The Retirement and Removal of Federal Judges   125
Summary   129

5 The Decision-Making Process   133

The Decision-Making Environment   133
The Legal Subculture   135
The Democratic Subculture   141
The Subcultures as Predictors   161
Summary   166

6 Decision Making: The Special Case
of Collegial Courts   173

Cue Theory   174
Small-Group Analysis   176
Attitude Theory and Bloc-Formation Analysis   189
Fact Pattern Analysis   193
Summary   195

7 Implementation and Impact
of Federal Judicial Policies   199

The Impact of Upper-Court Decisions on Lower Courts   200
Congressional Influences on the Implementation Process   207
Executive Influences on the Implementation Process   209
Other Implementors   212
The Impact of Judicial Policies   214
Summary   220

8 Policy Making by Federal Judges:
An Attempt at Synthesis   225

The Nature of the Case or Issue   226
The Values and Orientations of the Judges   228
The Nature of the Judicial Decision-Making Process   232
The Impact of Extraneous Influences   235

Selected Bibliography   239

Index   247

Preface

We have sought to prepare a readable, comprehensive textbook about the federal judiciary and its impact on our daily lives. It is designed primarily for students in courses in judicial process and behavior, constitutional law, American government, and law and society. We have written the book with minimal resort to the jargon and theoretical vocabulary of political science and the law. While at times it is necessary and useful to use some technical terms and evoke some theoretical concepts in our look at U.S. courts, we address the basic questions on a level that is meaningful to an educated layperson. For those who may desire more specialized explanations or who wish to explore more deeply some of the issues we touch on, the footnotes and selected bibliography contain ample resources for such quests. Readers will find the contributions of historians, political scientists, legal scholars, court administrators, journalists, and psychologists in the pages that follow. Those interested in behavioralism will find much material of interest to them and so will those who favor a more traditional approach to studying the federal judiciary.

Throughout the text we are constantly mindful of the interrelation between the courts and public policy. We have worked with the premise that significant portions of our lives—as individuals and as a nation—are affected by what our federal judges choose to do and refrain from doing. We reject the often-held assumption that only liberals make public policy while conservatives practice restraint; rather, we believe that to some degree all judges engage in this normal and inevitable activity. Liberals on the bench may well hand down rulings that advance the policy goals of their particular interests (civil rights or environmental protection, for example), and conservatives can be expected to act in ways consistent with their policy interests, such as a tough stand on law-and-order or advancing the cause of states' rights. The question then, as we see it, is not whether U.S. courts make policy but rather which direction the policy decisions will take. In the chapters that follow we shall explain why this has come to be, how it works, and what the consequences are for America today.

Chapter 1 provides a brief sketch of the organizational structure of the federal judiciary, placed in historical perspective. As we shall see, much of the reason why our judges have the powers they do is a function of historical quirks, pragmatic compromises made during now-forgotten political duels, and haphazard factors quite unintended by the founders of the Republic. Our federal judicial system did not appear one day out of whole cloth but is the product of two centuries of evolution, trial and error, and a pinch of serendipity. The distinction between routine norm enforcement and policy making by federal judges is first addressed in this chapter.

The second chapter outlines the jurisdiction of the three levels of the U.S. courts and provides current data about the workload of these tribunals. Besides a discussion of what judges are authorized to do in the federal system, there is an in-depth look at judicial self-restraint. We believe that a full understanding of how judges affect our daily lives also requires us to outline those many substantive areas into which the federal jurists may *not* roam and where they are not free to make public policy.

Chapter 3 underscores the theme that "judging" is more and more a team effort. This chapter describes the duties and contributions of the staff and administrative agencies that support the federal courts today, such as law clerks, magistrates, and the Administrative Office of the U.S. Courts.

In Chapter 4 we take a close look at the men and women who wear the black robe in the United States. What are their background characteristics and their qualifications for office? What are their values and how do these values manifest themselves in the subsequent behavior of the judges and justices? In this chapter we also explore the process of judicial selection and who the major participants are. We strongly emphasize that there is a discernible policy link between the values of a majority of voters in a presidential election, the values of the appointing president, and the subsequent policy content of decisions made by judges nominated by the chief executive.

Chapter 5 is the first of two on judicial decision making. Here we outline those aspects of the decision-making process that are characteristic of *all* judges, and we do this in the context of the "legal subculture" and the "democratic subculture." Under the former we emphasize the importance of the traditional legal reasoning model for explaining judges' decisions—a model that still accounts for the lion's share of most routine, norm enforcement decision making. Using the lens of the democratic subculture, we look at a number of extralegal factors that appear to be associated with judges' policy decisions: political party affiliation, local customs and traditions, environmental influences such as public opinion, and pressures from Congress and the president. We also take a look at role theory.

The sixth chapter examines the special case of decision making in collegial, appellate courts. We explore the assumptions and contributions of small-group theory, attitude and bloc analysis, and the fact pattern approach to our understanding of the behavior of multijudge tribunals.

Chapter 7 explores the policy impact of federal court decisions and discusses the process by which judicial rulings are implemented—or why some are *not* implemented. We look at the conditions that must prevail if court decisions are to be carried out efficiently and meaningfully, and we also examine the various individuals and institutions that play such a vital role in this process.

In the final chapter we discuss some factors that determine whether judges will engage in policy making and that also predict the substantive direction of policy decisions.

Many people contributed to the writing of this book, and to all of them we offer our sincere thanks. Charles Johnson of Texas A & M University read the entire manuscript and provided us with many useful criticisms and suggestions. Lawrence Baum of Ohio State University, Beverly Cook of the University of Wisconsin, and David Neubauer of the University of New Orleans also offered helpful criticisms and suggestions. For any errors that may remain, we assume responsibility.

Our relationship with CQ Press has been a most pleasant one. Joanne Daniels, director of CQ Press, offered encouragement, sound advice, and helpful suggestions at crucial stages of the project. We also appreciate the fine work of our editor, Susan Joseph.

Four persons had the unenviable task of transforming our work into a final product. The typing chores were handled most efficiently by Jenny McConnell, Pamela Claiborne, and Theresa Caldwell at the University of Houston and by Laquita Stidham at Lamar University. We thank them for an excellent job.

Several students helped by providing research assistance. In this regard, our thanks go to Anthony LaPoint and Greg Orvis at the University of Houston and Mitzi Angelle, Davis Brinson, Richard Huang, Anna Mannich, Sue Nelson, Van Wiggington, and Bernie Wiseman at Lamar University.

Stidham was aided by a faculty development leave during the fall 1984 semester, which provided valuable research and writing time. For this he expresses his appreciation to the Board of Regents of Lamar University.

THE FEDERAL COURTS

History, Function, and Organization of the Federal Judiciary

1

Because a knowledge of the historical events that helped shape the national court system can shed light on the present judicial structure, our study of the federal judiciary begins with a description of the court system as it has evolved over nearly 200 years. We will examine the three levels of the federal court system in the order in which they were established: the Supreme Court, the courts of appeals, and the district courts. The emphasis in our discussion of each level will be on historical development, policy-making roles, and decision-making procedures.

In a brief look at other federal courts we will focus on the distinction between constitutional and legislative courts, using the example of bankruptcy courts to illustrate a major difference in the two types. Our overview discussion will conclude with an examination of the role of the federal courts in the American political system. We will be particularly interested in comparing the courts' role in public policy making with that of the president and the Congress.

The Historical Context

Prior to the adoption of the Constitution, the country was governed by the Articles of Confederation. Under the Articles, practically all functions of government were vested in a single-chamber legislature called a Congress. There was no separation of executive and legislative powers.

The absence of a national judiciary was considered a major weakness of the Articles of Confederation. Both James Madison and Alexander Hamilton, for example, saw a need for a separate judicial branch.

Consequently, the delegates gathered at the Constitutional Convention in Philadelphia in 1787 expressed widespread agreement that a national judiciary should be established. There was a good deal of disagreement, however, on the specific form that the judicial branch should take.

The Constitutional Convention and Article III

The first proposal presented to the Constitutional Convention was the Randolph, or Virginia, Plan, which would have set up both a Supreme Court and inferior federal courts. Opponents of the Virginia Plan responded with the Paterson, or New Jersey, Plan, which called for the creation of a single federal supreme tribunal. Supporters of the New Jersey Plan were especially disturbed by the idea of lower federal courts. They argued that the state courts could hear all cases in the first instance and that a right of appeal to the Supreme Court would be sufficient to protect national rights and provide uniform judgments throughout the country.

The conflict between the states' rights advocates and the nationalists was resolved by one of the many compromises that characterized the Constitutional Convention. The compromise is found in Article III of the Constitution which states, in part, "The judicial power of the United States, shall be vested in one Supreme Court, and in such inferior Courts as the Congress may from time to time ordain and establish." Thus the conflict would be postponed until the new government was in operation.

The Judiciary Act of 1789

Once the Constitution was ratified, action on the federal judiciary came quickly. When the new Congress convened in 1789, its first major concern was judicial organization. Discussions of Senate Bill Number One involved many of the same participants and arguments that were involved in the Constitutional Convention's debates on the judiciary. Once again, the question was whether lower federal courts should be created at all or whether federal claims should first be heard in state courts. Attempts to resolve this controversy split Congress into two distinct groups.

One group, which believed that federal law should be adjudicated first in the state courts and by the United States Supreme Court only on appeal, expressed the fear that the new government would destroy the rights of the states. Other legislators, suspicious of the parochial prejudice of state courts, feared that litigants from other states and other countries would be dealt with unjustly. This latter group naturally favored a judicial system that included lower federal courts. The law that emerged from this debate, the Judiciary Act of 1789, set up a judicial system composed of a Supreme Court, consisting of a chief justice and five associate justices; three circuit courts, each comprising two justices of the Supreme Court and a district judge; and thirteen district courts, each presided over by one district judge. The power to create inferior federal courts, then, was immediately exercised. In fact, Congress created not one but two sets of lower courts. The next three sections will be devoted to the Supreme Court and the two lower-court systems.

The U.S. Supreme Court

A First Look

A famous jurist once said, "The Supreme Court of the United States is distinctly American in conception and function, and owes little to prior judicial institutions." [1] To understand what the framers of the Constitution envisioned for the Court, we must consider another American concept: the federal form of government. The founders provided for both a national government and state governments. Article VI states, in part, "This Constitution, and the Laws of the United States which shall be made in Pursuance thereof . . . shall be the supreme Law of the Land; and the Judges in every State shall be bound thereby." In other words, the framers established a system whereby state courts were to be bound by federal laws. However, final interpretation of federal laws simply could not be left to a state court, and certainly not to several state tribunals, whose judgments might disagree. Thus, the Supreme Court must interpret federal legislation. Another of the founders' intentions was for the federal government to act directly upon individual citizens as well as upon the states. The Supreme Court's function in the federal system may be summarized as follows:

> In the most natural way, as the result of the creation of Federal law under a written constitution conferring limited powers, the Supreme Court of the United States came into being with its unique function. That court maintains the balance between State and Nation through the maintenance of the rights and duties of individuals. [2]

Given the High Court's importance to our system of government, it was perhaps inevitable that the Court would evoke great controversy. A leading student of the Supreme Court says:

> Nothing in the Court's history is more striking than the fact that, while its significant and necessary place in the Federal form of Government has always been recognized by thoughtful and patriotic men, nevertheless, no branch of the Government and no institution under the

Constitution has sustained more continuous attack or reached its present position after more vigorous opposition.[3]

The Court's First Decade

George Washington, in appointing the first Supreme Court justices, established two important traditions. First, he began the practice of naming to the Court those with whom he was politically compatible. Washington, the only president ever to have an opportunity to appoint the entire federal judiciary, did a good job of filling federal judgeships with party bedfellows. Without exception, the federal judgeships went to faithful Federalists.

The second tradition established by Washington was that of roughly equal geographic representation on the federal courts. His first six appointees to the Supreme Court included three northerners and three southerners. On the basis of ability and legal reputation, only three or four of Washington's original appointees actually merited their justiceships. Many able men were either passed over or declined to serve.

The chief justiceship was the most important appointment Washington made. The president felt that the man to head the first Supreme Court should be an eminent lawyer, statesman, executive, and leader. Many names were presented to Washington, and at least one person, James Wilson, formally applied for the position. Ultimately, Washington settled upon John Jay of New York. Although only 44 years old, Jay had experience as a lawyer, a judge, and a diplomat. In addition, he was the main drafter of his state's first constitution. Concerning the selection of Jay as chief justice, it has been said:

> That Washington picked Jay over his top two rivals for the post, James Wilson and John Rutledge, was either fortuitous or inspired—for it would scarcely have added to the fledgling Supreme Court's popular prestige to have its Chief Justice go insane, as Rutledge later did, or spend his last days jumping from one state to another to avoid being arrested for a debt, as did Wilson.[4]

Washington did, however, appoint both Wilson and Rutledge to the Court as associate justices. Neither man contributed significantly to the Court as a government institution. Thus, Washington became the first of many presidents to misjudge an appointee to the Court.

The remaining three associate justices who served on the original Supreme Court were William Cushing, John Blair, and James Iredell. Cushing remained on the Court for 20 years, more than twice as long as any of the other original justices, although senility affected his competency in later years. Blair was a close personal friend of Washington's, and

Iredell was a strong Federalist from North Carolina who was instrumental in getting that state to join the Union. The appointments of Blair and Iredell, then, have been seen as sheer political rewards. Despite the generally mediocre quality of the original six appointees, though, they were held in somewhat higher esteem by their contemporaries, according to studies of letters and correspondence written during that early era.[5]

The Supreme Court met for the first time on Monday, February 1, 1790, in the Royal Exchange, a building located in the Wall Street section of New York City. Compared to today's Supreme Court, that first session was certainly unimpressive. Tongue in cheek, one Court historian noted: "The first President immediately on taking office settled down to the pressing business of being President. The first Congress enacted the first laws. *The first Supreme Court adjourned.*" [Emphasis added.][6]

Only Jay, Wilson, and Cushing, the three northern justices, were present on opening day. Justice Blair arrived from Virginia for the second day, while Rutledge and Iredell, the other southerners did not appear at all during the opening session.

The Supreme Court's first session lasted just 10 days. During this period the Court selected a clerk, chose a seal, and admitted several lawyers to practice before it in the future. There were, of course, no cases to be decided. In fact, the Court did not rule on a single case during its first three years. In spite of this insignificant and abbreviated beginning,

the New York and the Philadelphia newspapers described the proceedings of this first session of the Court more fully than any other event connected with the new Government; and their accounts were reproduced in the leading papers of all the States.[7]

The minor role the Supreme Court played continued throughout its first decade of existence. The 1790-1799 period saw several individuals decline their nomination to the Court and one, Robert H. Harrison, refuse appointment even though the Senate had confirmed him. Harrison chose to accept a *state* position rather than a Supreme Court justiceship.

During its first decade the Court decided only about 50 cases. However, one of these, *Chisholm v. Georgia*, involved the Court in considerable controversy.[8] In *Chisholm* the justices held that a citizen of one state could sue another state in a federal court. That decision was vigorously attacked by states' rights forces and was ultimately overturned by ratification of the Eleventh Amendment in 1798.

The Impact of Chief Justice Marshall

John Marshall served as chief justice from 1801 to 1835 and dominated the Court to a degree unmatched by any other justice. In effect,

Marshall *was* the Court—perhaps because, in the words of one scholar, he "brought a first-class mind and a thoroughly engaging personality into second-class company." [9]

Marshall's dominance of the Court enabled him to initiate some major changes in the way opinions were presented. Prior to his tenure, the justices ordinarily wrote separate opinions (called *seriatim* opinions) in major cases. Under Marshall's stewardship, the Court adopted the practice of handing down a single opinion. As one might expect, the evidence shows that, from 1801 to 1835, Marshall himself wrote almost half the opinions. [10]

It was Marshall's goal to keep dissension to a minimum. Arguing that dissent undermined the Court's authority, he tried to persuade the justices to settle their differences privately and then present a united front to the public. No doubt his first-class mind and engaging personality aided him in this endeavor. As strange as it may sound, so did the cozy living arrangements of the time. The justices lived in the same Washington, D.C., boarding house while the Court was in session. Thus, they were together before, during, and after work in a pleasant, comfortable routine that discouraged deep disagreements. Can you imagine having breakfast, lunch, and dinner every day with a fellow justice whom you have sharply criticized in a public opinion? Human nature, it would seem, was on Marshall's side in keeping dissension to a low level.

In addition to bringing about changes in opinion-writing practices, Marshall used his powers to involve the Court in the policy-making process. Early in his tenure as chief justice, the Court asserted its power to declare an act of Congress unconstitutional, in *Marbury v. Madison* (1803). [11]

This case had its beginnings in the presidential election of 1800, when Thomas Jefferson defeated John Adams in his bid for reelection. Before leaving office in March 1801, however, Adams and the lame-duck Federalist Congress combined efforts to create several new federal judgeships. To fill these new positions Adams nominated, and the Senate confirmed, loyal Federalists. In addition, Adams named his outgoing secretary of state, John Marshall, to be the new chief justice of the Supreme Court.

As secretary of state it had been Marshall's job to deliver the commissions of the newly appointed judges. Time ran out, however, and 17 of the commissions were not delivered before Jefferson's inauguration. The new president ordered *his* secretary of state, James Madison, not to deliver the remaining commissions.

One of the disappointed nominees was William Marbury. He and three of his colleagues, all confirmed as justices of the peace for the

District of Columbia, decided to ask the Supreme Court to force Madison to deliver their commissions. They relied upon Section 13 of the Judiciary Act of 1789, which granted the Supreme Court the authority to issue *writs of mandamus*—court orders commanding a public official to perform an official, nondiscretionary duty.

The case placed Marshall in an uncomfortable predicament. Some suggested that he disqualify himself because of his earlier involvement as secretary of state. There was also the question of the Court's power. If Marshall were to grant the writ, Madison (under Jefferson's orders) was almost certain to refuse to deliver the commissions. The Supreme Court would then be powerless to enforce its order. On the other hand, if Marshall refused to grant the writ, Jefferson would win by default.

The decision Marshall fashioned from this seemingly impossible predicament was sheer genius. He declared Section 13 of the Judiciary Act of 1789 unconstitutional because it granted original jurisdiction to the Supreme Court in excess of that specified in Article III of the Constitution. Thus the Court's power to review and determine the constitutionality of acts of Congress was established. This decision is rightly seen as one of the single most important decisions the Supreme Court ever handed down. A few years later the Court also claimed the right of judicial review over actions of state legislatures; during Marshall's tenure it overturned more than a dozen state laws on constitutional grounds.[12]

The Changing Issue Emphasis of the Supreme Court

We complete our brief historical review of the Supreme Court by looking at the major issue areas that have occupied the Court's attention. Up to approximately 1865 the legal relationship between the national and state governments, or cases of federalism, dominated the Court's docket. John Marshall believed in a strong national government and was not hesitant to restrict state policies that interfered with its activities. A case in point is *Gibbons v. Ogden* (1824), in which the Court overturned a state monopoly over steamboat transportation on the ground that it interfered with national control over interstate commerce.[13] Another good example of Marshall's use of the Court to expand the federal government's powers came in *McCulloch v. Maryland* (1819), in which the chief justice held that the necessary-and-proper clause of the Constitution permitted Congress to establish a national bank.[14] The Court also ruled that the state could not tax a nationally chartered bank. The Court's insistence on a strong government in Washington did not significantly diminish after Marshall's death. Roger Taney, who succeeded Marshall as chief justice, served from 1836 to 1864. Although the Court's position during this period was not as uniformly favorable to the federal government, the Taney Court did not reverse the Marshall Court's direction.

During the 1865 to 1937 period issues of economic regulation dominated the Court's docket. The shift in emphasis from federalism to economic regulation was brought on by a growing number of national and state laws aimed at monitoring business activities. As such laws increased, so did the number of cases challenging their constitutionality. Early in this period the Court's position on regulation was mixed, but by the 1920s the bench had become quite hostile toward government regulatory policy. Federal regulations were generally overturned on the ground that they were unsupported by constitutional grants of power to Congress, while state laws were thrown out mainly as violations of economic rights protected by the Fourteenth Amendment.

Matters came to a head in the mid-1930s as a result of the Court's conflict with President Franklin D. Roosevelt, whose New Deal program to combat the effects of the Depression included broad measures to control the economy. However, "in the 16 months starting in January 1935, the Supreme Court heard cases involving ten major New Deal measures or actions; eight of them were declared unconstitutional by the Court." [15] Following his overwhelming reelection in 1936, Roosevelt fought back against the Court. On February 5, 1937, he proposed a plan whereby an additional justice could be added to the Court for each sitting justice over the age of 70. The result of FDR's "Court-packing" plan would have been to increase the Court's size temporarily to 15 justices.

While Roosevelt's proposal was being debated in Congress, the Court made an about-face and began to uphold New Deal legislation and similar state legislation.[16] This "switch in time that saved nine," as it has been called, came about because Chief Justice Charles Evans Hughes and Justice Owen Roberts changed their votes to establish majority support for the New Deal legislation. As a result, the Court-packing plan became a moot issue and quietly died in Congress.

Since 1937 the Supreme Court has focused on civil liberties concerns—in particular, the constitutional guarantees of freedom of expression and freedom of religion. In addition, an increasing number of cases have dealt with procedural rights of criminal defendants. Finally, the Court has decided a great number of cases involving equal treatment by the government of racial minorities and other disadvantaged groups.

The Supreme Court's position on civil liberties and civil rights has varied a good deal over the years. Without doubt, it gave its strongest and most active support for civil liberties and civil rights during the 1953 to 1969 period, when Earl Warren served as chief justice. Perhaps the best known decision of the period was *Brown v. Board of Education* (1954), which ordered desegregation of the public schools.[17] Other notable decisions guaranteed the right to counsel in state trials, limited police search and seizure practices, required that police inform suspects of their rights, mandated legislatures to be apportioned according to population, and prohibited state-written and state-required prayer in public schools.[18] These and many other controversial decisions led to heavy criticism of the Warren Court.

During his 1968 presidential campaign Richard Nixon pledged that, if elected, he would appoint more conservative individuals to the Court. In 1969 he took the first step toward making good on that promise by naming Warren Burger to replace the retiring Earl Warren as chief justice. Over the next two years Nixon appointed three other justices and did indeed produce a Court whose aggregate viewpoint has been more conservative.

We next turn our attention to the various roles played by the Supreme Court. First, we examine its policy-making function.

The Supreme Court as a Policy Maker

The Supreme Court's role as a policy maker derives from the fact that it interprets the law. Public policy issues come before the Court in the form of legal disputes that must be resolved, as one scholar has explained:

> Courts in any political system participate to some degree in the policymaking process because it is their job. Any judge faced with a choice between two or more interpretations and applications of a legislative act, executive order, or constitutional provision must choose among them because the controversy must be decided. And when the judge chooses, his or her interpretation becomes policy for the specific litigants. If the interpretation is accepted by the other judges, the judge has made policy for all jurisdictions in which that view prevails.[19]

An excellent example may be found in the area of racial equality. In the late 1880s many states enacted laws requiring the separation of blacks and whites in public facilities. In 1890, for instance, Louisiana enacted a law requiring separate but equal railroad accommodations for blacks and whites.

A challenge came two years later. Homer Plessy, who was one-eighth black, protested against the Louisiana law by refusing to move from a seat in the white car of a train traveling from New Orleans to Covington, Louisiana. Arrested and charged with violating the statute, Plessy contended that the law was unconstitutional. The United States Supreme Court, in *Plessy v. Ferguson* (1896), upheld the Louisiana statute.[20] Thus the Court established the *separate-but-equal* policy that was to reign for about 60 years. During this period many states required that the races sit in different areas of buses, trains, terminals, and theaters; to use different restrooms; and to drink from different water fountains. Blacks were sometimes excluded from restaurants and public libraries. Perhaps most important, the separate-but-equal policy often meant that black students had to attend inferior schools.

Separation of the races in public schools was contested in the famous *Brown v. Board of Education* case. Black schoolchildren claimed that state laws requiring or permitting segregation deprived them of equal protection of the laws under the Fourteenth Amendment. The Supreme Court ruled that separate educational facilities are inherently unequal and, therefore, segregation constitutes a denial of equal protection. In the *Brown* decision the Court laid to rest the separate-but-equal doctrine and established a policy of desegregated public schools.

In an average year the Court decides, with full opinions, only about 150 cases. Thousands of other cases are disposed of with less than the full treatment. Thus the Court deals at length with a very select set of policy issues that, as noted, have varied throughout the Court's history.

In a democracy broad matters of public policy are, in theory at least, presumed to be left to the elected representatives of the people—not to judicial appointees with life terms. Thus, in principle, U.S. judges are not supposed to make policy. However, as we shall demonstrate when we discuss decision making in Chapters 5 and 6, in practice judges cannot help but make policy to some extent.

It should be noted that the Supreme Court differs from legislative and executive policy makers. Especially important is the fact that the Court has no self-starting device. The justices must wait for problems to be brought to them; there can be no judicial policy making if there is no litigation. The president and members of Congress have no such constraints. Moreover, even the most assertive Supreme Court is limited to some extent by the actions of other policy makers, such as lower-court judges, Congress, and the president. The Court depends upon others to implement or carry out its decisions. This process of implementation will be discussed in detail in Chapter 7.

The Supreme Court as Final Arbiter

The Supreme Court has both original and appellate jurisdiction. The two types of jurisdiction will be discussed in detail in Chapter 2, but a brief definition of each will be helpful at this point. In *original jurisdiction* a court has the power to hear a case for the first time. In *appellate jurisdiction,* on the other hand, a higher court has the authority to review cases originally decided by a lower court.

The Supreme Court is primarily an appellate court since most of its time is devoted to reviewing decisions of lower courts. Regardless of whether its decisions are seen as correct, it is the highest appellate tribunal in the country. As such, it has the final word in the interpretation of the Constitution, acts of legislative bodies, and treaties—unless the Court's decision is altered by a constitutional amendment or, in some instances, by an act of Congress.

Since 1925 a device known as *certiorari* has allowed the High Court to exercise discretion in deciding which cases it should review. Under this method a person may *request* Supreme Court review of a lower-court decision; it is then up to the justices to determine whether the request should be granted. If review is granted, the Court issues a *writ of certiorari*, which is an order to the lower court to send up a complete record of the case. When certiorari is denied, the decision of the lower court stands.

The Supreme Court at Work

The formal session of the Supreme Court lasts 36 weeks annually—from the first Monday in October until the end of June. Occasionally the tribunal will meet in special session or extend its formal session.

Since 1935 the Supreme Court has had its own building in Washington. The building, constructed of marble with the words "Equal Justice Under Law" carved above the entrance, is five stories tall and covers a square block across from the Capitol. Formal sessions of the Court are held in a large courtroom that seats 300 people. At the front of the courtroom is the bench where the justices are seated. When the Court is in session, the chief justice, followed by the eight associate justices in order of seniority, (length of continuous service on the Court) enters through the purple draperies behind the bench and takes a seat. Seats are arranged according to seniority, with the chief justice in the center, the senior associate justice on the chief justice's right, the second-ranking associate justice on the left, and continuing alternately in declining order of seniority. Near the courtroom are the conference room, where the justices decide cases, and the chambers that contain offices for the justices and their staff.

The Court's term is divided into *sittings,* of approximately two weeks each, during which it meets in open session and holds internal conferences, and *recesses,* during which the justices work behind closed doors as they consider cases and write opinions. The 150 or so cases per term that receive the Court's full treatment follow a fairly routine pattern, which is described below.

Oral Argument. Oral arguments are generally scheduled on Monday through Wednesday during the sittings. The sessions run from 10:00 a.m. until noon and from 1:00 until 3:00 p.m. Since the procedure is not a trial or the original hearing of a case, no jury is assembled and no witnesses are called. Instead, the two opposing attorneys present their arguments to the justices. The general practice is to allow thirty minutes for each side, although the Court may decide that additional time is necessary. The Court can normally hear four cases in one day. Attorneys presenting oral arguments are frequently interrupted with probing questions from the justices. The oral argument is considered very important by both attorneys and justices because it is the only stage in the process that allows such personal exchanges.

The Conference. During sittings the Court holds conferences on Wednesday afternoons and all day on Fridays. At the Wednesday meeting the justices discuss the cases argued on Tuesday and Wednesday plus any other matters that need to be considered—in particular, appeals from lower courts.

Prior to the Friday conference each justice is given a list of the cases that will be discussed. The conference begins about 9:30 or 10:00 a.m. and runs until 5:30 or 6:00 p.m. As the justices enter the conference room they shake hands with each other and take their seats around a rectangular table. They meet in secret behind locked doors, with no official record being kept of the discussions. The chief justice presides over the conference and offers an opinion first in each case. The other justices follow in descending order of seniority. At one time a formal vote was then taken in reverse order (with the junior justice voting first); however, today the justices usually indicate their view during the discussion, making a formal vote unnecessary.[21]

A quorum for a decision on a case is six members, but there is seldom any difficulty in obtaining a quorum. Cases are sometimes decided by less than nine justices because of vacancies, illnesses, or nonparticipation because of possible conflicts of interest. Supreme Court decisions are made by a majority vote. In case of a tie the lower-court decision is upheld.

Opinion Writing. After a tentative decision has been reached in conference, the next step is to assign the Court's opinion to an individual justice. Chief justices in the majority assign the opinion, either to themselves or to another justice who voted with the majority. When the chief justice votes with the minority, then the most senior justice in the majority makes the assignment.

After the conference the justice who will write the Court's opinion begins work on an initial draft. Other justices may work on the case by writing alternative opinions. The completed opinion is circulated to justices in both the majority and minority groups. The writer seeks to persuade justices originally in the minority to change their votes, and to keep his or her majority group intact. A bargaining process occurs and the wording of the opinion may be changed in order to satisfy other justices or obtain their support. A deeply divided Court makes it difficult to achieve a clear, coherent opinion and may even result in a shift in votes or in another justice's opinion becoming the Court's official ruling.

In most cases a single opinion does obtain majority support, although only a few rulings are unanimous. Those who disagree with the opinion of the Court are said to *dissent*. A dissent does not have to be accompanied by an opinion; in recent years, however, it usually is. Whenever more than one justice dissents, each may write an opinion or they may join in a single opinion.

On occasion a justice will agree with the Court's decision but differ in his or her reason for reaching that conclusion. Such a justice may write what is called a *concurring opinion*. A good example may be found in Justice Potter Stewart's concurring opinion in *Stanley v. Georgia* (1969).[22] In that case an investigation of Stanley's alleged bookmaking activities led to the issuance of a search warrant for his home. Federal and state agents conducting the search found three reels of film, a projector, and a screen. After viewing the films, the state officers seized them as pornographic. Stanley was convicted of "knowingly having possession of obscene matter" in violation of Georgia law. The Supreme Court overturned the Georgia trial court's decision on the ground that mere private possession of lewd material could not constitutionally be made a crime. Justice Stewart agreed that the lower court decision should be overturned, but he did so for quite a different reason; he felt that the films had been seized unlawfully in violation of the Fourth and Fourteenth Amendments.

An opinion labeled *concurring and dissenting* agrees with part of a Court ruling but disagrees with other parts. Finally, the Court occasionally issues a *per curiam opinion*—an unsigned opinion that is usually quite brief. Table 1-1 shows the types of opinions written by the individual justices for the 1981, 1982, and 1983 terms of the Supreme Court.

The U.S. Courts of Appeals

The courts of appeals have been described as "perhaps the least-noticed of the regular constitutional courts."[23] They receive less media coverage than the Supreme Court, in part because their activities are simply not as dramatic. However, one should not assume that the courts of

Table 1-1 Types of Opinions Written by Supreme Court Justices: 1981, 1982, 1983 Terms

Justice	Opinions of the Court			Concurring opinions			Dissenting opinions			Total		
	1981	1982	1983	1981	1982	1983	1981	1982	1983	1981	1982	1983
Blackmun	14	15	16	18	12	6	12	17	9	44	44	31
Brennan	16	15	16	11	13	10	17	18	29	44	46	55
Burger	16	16	16	6	3	2	12	5	0	34	24	18
Marshall	15	17	15	5	3	2	4	27	16	24	47	33
O'Connor	13	16	17	12	7	10	10	11	9	35	34	36
Powell	16	18	18	13	9	11	22	8	7	51	35	36
Rehnquist	17	20	19	7	5	3	15	16	14	39	41	36
Stevens	15	15	16	15	12	18	26	27	34	56	54	68
White	19	19	18	8	6	6	17	11	9	44	36	33
Per curiam	26	11	12	–	–	–	–	–	–	26	11	12
Total	167	162	163	95	70	68	135	140	127	397	372	358

Source: "The Supreme Court, 1981 Term," *Harvard Law Review* 96 (November 1982): 304; "The Supreme Court, 1982 Term," *Harvard Law Review* 97 (November 1983): 295; and "The Supreme Court, 1983 Term," *Harvard Law Review* 98 (November 1984): 307. Copyright © 1982, 1983, 1984 by the Harvard Law Review Association. Reprinted by permission.

appeals are unimportant to the judicial system. As we shall see, their role has increased significantly over the years.

Circuit Courts: 1789-1801

As noted earlier, the Judiciary Act of 1789 created three circuit courts—the southern, middle, and eastern circuits—each composed of two justices of the Supreme Court and a district judge. The circuit court was to hold two sessions each year in each district within the circuit.

It was the district judge who became primarily responsible for establishing the circuit court's workload. The two Supreme Court justices then came into the local area and participated in the cases. This practice tended to give a local rather than national focus to the circuit courts.

The circuit court system was regarded from the beginning as unsatisfactory, especially by Supreme Court justices, who objected to the traveling imposed upon them. As early as September 1790, Chief Justice Jay wrote to the president urging changes in the circuit-riding duties prescribed by the Judiciary Act of 1789. Justice Iredell, who resided in North Carolina, was particularly hard pressed; in addition to some 2,000 miles of travel between his home and Philadelphia (where Supreme Court sessions were held), he was required to tour the states of Georgia, North Carolina, and South Carolina twice annually. It is no wonder Iredell referred to his life as that of a "travelling postboy." [24]

Supreme Court justices were not the only ones who objected to the circuit-riding duties. Attorney General Edmund Randolph and President Washington also urged relief for the Supreme Court justices. Congress made a slight change in 1793 by altering the circuit court organization to include only one Supreme Court justice and one district judge. The Randolph proposal for separate circuit court judgeships to replace Supreme Court participation was not implemented, however. The circuit courts had become the center of a political controversy, with the Federalists urging passage of Randolph's proposal for separate circuit judges, while the Antifederalist leaders saw the Randolph proposal as an attempt to enlarge the federal judiciary and remove it from state surveillance.

Circuit Courts: 1801-1891

In the closing days of President Adams's administration in 1801, Congress passed the "midnight judges" act, which eliminated circuit riding by the Supreme Court justices, authorized the appointment of sixteen new circuit judges, and greatly extended the jurisdiction of the lower courts.

Some saw the Judiciary Act of 1801 as the Federalists' last-ditch effort to prolong their domination of government, while others viewed it as an extension of federal jurisdiction to suits that previously had been tried only in state courts. Certainly the Federalists were interested in federal judgeships, and they wanted to protect the judiciary from Antifederalists. The act of 1801, however, was not a last-minute effort. As we have seen, efforts to change the circuit courts had been going on for over ten years.

The new administration of Thomas Jefferson strongly opposed the "midnight judges" act, and Congress wasted little time in repealing it. The Circuit Court Act of 1802 restored circuit riding by Supreme Court justices and expanded the number of circuits. However, the 1802 legislation allowed the circuit court to be held by a single district judge. At first glance, such a change may seem slight, but it proved to be of great importance. Increasingly, the district judges began to assume responsibility for both the district and circuit courts. In practice, then, original and appellate jurisdiction were both in the hands of the district judges.

The next major step in the development of the courts of appeals did not come until 1869, although there had been a growing recognition that some form of judicial reorganization was necessary. The pro-state and pronationalist interests disagreed on the exact form of judicial relief that should be enacted. The pronationalists did not want a plan that would transfer power from the national government to the states. They favored shifting many conflicts to the lower federal courts under the supervision of the Supreme Court. Thus, "reorganization of the circuit courts continued to be the key to the nationalists' strategy." [25] Expansion of the circuit courts with greater control over appeals would free the Supreme Court to concentrate on the key cases as well as to formulate policy. The pro-state interests also wanted to lessen the High Court's burden, but by reducing its power. Unable to do so, they were willing to accept only minor changes in the basic judicial structure established in 1789.

The political stalemate prevented any major reorganization between 1802 and 1869. Consequently, the courts simply were unable to handle the flood of litigation. Then, in 1869, Congress approved a measure that authorized the appointment of nine new circuit judges and reduced the Supreme Court justices' circuit court duty to one term every two years. Still, the High Court was flooded with cases because there were no limitations on the right of appeal to the Supreme Court. Six years later Congress broadened the jurisdiction of the circuit courts. The workload of the Supreme Court was not significantly decreased, however, since there was still an automatic right of appeal to the High Court. A more drastic revision of the federal judicial system was to come in 1891.

The Courts of Appeals: 1891 to the Present

On March 3, 1891, the Evarts Act was signed into law, creating new courts known as circuit courts of appeals. These new tribunals were to hear most of the appeals from district courts. The old circuit courts, which had existed since 1789, also remained—a situation surely confusing to all but the most serious students of the judicial system. The new circuit court of appeals was to consist of one circuit judge, one circuit court of appeals judge, one district judge, and a Supreme Court justice. Two judges constituted a quorum in these new courts.

Let us briefly summarize the situation that existed following passage of the Evarts Act. There were two trial tribunals in the federal judiciary: district courts and circuit courts. There were also two appellate tribunals: circuit courts of appeals and the Supreme Court. Most appeals of trial decisions were to go to the circuit court of appeals, although the act also allowed direct review in some instances by the Supreme Court. In short, creation of the circuit courts of appeals released the Supreme Court from many petty types of cases. There would still be appeals, but the High Court would now have much greater control over its own workload. Much of its former caseload was thus shifted to the two lower levels of the federal judiciary.

The next step in the evolution of the courts of appeals came in 1911. In that year Congress passed legislation abolishing the old circuit courts, which had no appellate jurisdiction and frequently duplicated the functions of district courts.

Today, as a result of a name change implemented in the 1948 Judicial Code, the intermediate tribunals are officially known as courts of appeals. Nine regional courts of appeals, covering several states, were created in 1891. Another, covering the District of Columbia, was absorbed into the system after 1893. The Court of Appeals for the Tenth Circuit was carved from the Eighth Circuit in 1929, and the Court of Appeals for the Eleventh Circuit was carved from the Fifth in 1981. Figure 1-1 shows the boundaries of each circuit and indicates the states contained in each.

On April 2, 1982, President Ronald Reagan signed the Federal Courts Improvement Act, which created a thirteenth circuit court. The act, which took effect on October 1, 1982, created the United States Court of Appeals for the Federal Circuit. This newest appellate court consolidated the Court of Claims and the Court of Customs and Patent Appeals (types of courts which will be described later in this chapter).

The Review Function of the Courts of Appeals

As one modern-day student of our judiciary has noted:

Figure 1-1 District and Appellate Court Boundaries

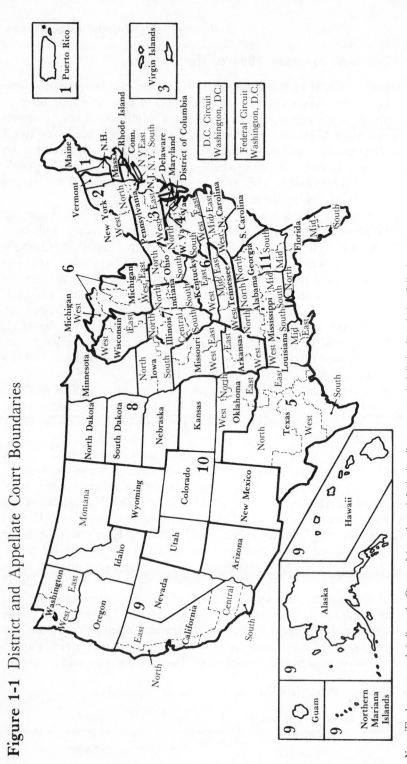

Note: The large numerals indicate the Courts of Appeals, and the broken lines represent jurisdiction boundaries of district courts.

Source: Administrative Office of the U.S. Courts.

The distribution of labor among the Supreme Court and the Courts of Appeals, implicit in the Judiciary Act of 1925, has matured into fully differentiated functions for federal appellate courts. Substantively, the Supreme Court has become more and more a constitutional tribunal. Courts of Appeals concentrate on statutory interpretation, administrative review, and error correction in masses of routine adjudications.[26]

Although the Supreme Court has had discretionary control of its docket since 1925, the Courts of Appeals still have no such luxury. Instead, their docket depends on how many and what types of cases are appealed to them.

Most of the cases reviewed by the courts of appeals originate in the federal district courts. Litigants disappointed with the lower court decision may appeal the case to the court of appeals of the circuit in which the federal district court is located. The appellate courts have also been given authority to review the decisions of certain administrative agencies. This type of case enters the federal judicial system at the court of appeals level rather than at the federal district court level.

Since the courts of appeals have no control over which cases are brought to them, they deal with both highly important and routine matters. Scholars identify five general types of appeals that the circuit judges consider:

1. Ritualistic appeals—petitions that are expected or demanded even though the odds of winning are very low. Such appeals were quite common following the school desegregation decision (*Brown v. Board of Education*) in 1954. Those favoring the continuance of segregated schools routinely appealed their cases from the federal district courts to the Court of Appeals for the southern-oriented Fourth or Fifth Circuit. Although they were almost certain to lose, they were able to shift the burden for defeat outside the local area and, at the same time, convince their supporters they had done everything possible under the law to defend segregationist interests.

2. Frivolous appeals—cases and claims that have no substance and little or no chance for success. Many of these appeals come from prisoners who have everything to gain and nothing to lose. Occasionally a claim is successful, however, and then other prisoners become motivated to appeal.

3. Bureaucratic appeals—challenges of federal agencies and commissions. Outright reversal of agency decisions is rare, but modification of administrative orders is not uncommon.

4. Consensual appeals—cases in which there is substantial agreement as to how the issue should be resolved. Petitioners who have lost, however, hope to change the original verdict. In other words, the litigants seek modifications of the lower-court monetary awards. Such appeals,

called the "bread and butter" issues of the appellate docket, include income tax, corporate activity, and eminent domain cases.

5. Nonconsensual appeals—cases that raise major questions of public policy and evoke strong disagreement. Decisions by the courts of appeals are likely to establish policy for society as a whole, not just for the specific litigants. Civil liberties, reapportionment, religion, and education cases provide good examples of the kinds of disputes that may affect us all.

So far we have focused on the sources and types of appeals. Let us now turn our attention to the purpose of review in the courts of appeals. The first is *error correction*. Judges in the various circuits are called upon to monitor the performance of federal district courts and federal agencies and to supervise their application and interpretation of national and state laws. In doing so, the courts of appeals do not seek out new factual evidence, but instead examine the record of the lower court for errors. In the process of correcting errors the courts of appeals also settle disputes and enforce national law. Since the Supreme Court intervenes so infrequently, the courts of appeals become the last resort in the overwhelming majority of cases.

Since, of course, some cases do find their way to the High Court, the courts of appeals perform a second function: sorting out and developing those few cases worthy of Supreme Court review. The circuit judges tackle the legal issues earlier than the Supreme Court justices and may help shape what they consider review-worthy claims. Judicial scholars have found that appealed cases often differ in their second hearing from their first. An analysis of cases that raised civil liberties issues when taken from district courts to Courts of Appeals for the Third, Fifth, and Eighth Circuits during the 1956-1961 period revealed that only about one-third had had a civil liberties content in the trial court.[27] In other words, the substance of the case shifted on appeal, and routine cases were given greater political significance. More recently, however, a study of Courts of Appeals in the Second, Fifth, and District of Columbia Circuits showed that in only 7 percent of the opinions had circuit judges reformulated the issues.[28]

The Courts of Appeals as Policy Makers

We noted earlier that the Supreme Court's role as a policy maker derives from the fact that it interprets the law; the same holds true for the courts of appeals. The scope of the courts of appeals' policy-making role takes on added importance when we recall that they are the courts of last resort in the vast majority of cases. Let us look at a couple of examples to illustrate the far-reaching impact of the circuit judges.

In 1966 the Court of Appeals for the District of Columbia Circuit decided a case involving an application for a license renewal by televison station WLBT in Jackson, Mississippi.[29] Complaints against WLBT included charges of racial and religious discrimination and excessive use of commercials. The first major complaint dated back to 1955, when it was alleged that WLBT had deliberately cut off a network program about race relations on which the general counsel of the National Association for the Advancement of Colored People was appearing; according to the complaint, the station flashed on the screen a "Sorry, Cable Trouble" sign. In 1957 WLBT was accused of presenting a program that urged the maintenance of racial segregation and then of refusing requests for time to offer an opposing view point. When WLBT applied for its license renewal in the mid-1960s, the Office of Communications of the United Church of Christ asked the Federal Communications Commission (FCC) for permission to present arguments and evidence in opposition to the renewal application. The FCC dismissed the Church of Christ's petition and took the unusual step of granting a conditional license to WLBT for one year instead of the usual three. Speaking for the court of appeals, Judge Warren Burger (now chief justice of the United States) held that the granting of WLBT's license was erroneous and ordered the FCC to hold hearings allowing opponents of the license renewal to present their arguments.

The second example involves a case that began in the small town of Shaw, Mississippi.[30] Shaw's population of about 2,500 included 1,500 blacks and 1,000 whites. Blacks complained they were being discriminated against because of disparities in municipal services. The evidence showed that nearly 98 percent of all homes fronting on unpaved streets were occupied by blacks, 97 percent of the homes not served by sanitary sewers were in black neighborhoods, and that all the new mercury vapor street lighting fixtures had been installed in white neighborhoods. The Court of Appeals for the Fifth Circuit held on January 23, 1971, that these practices resulted in a denial of equal protection for the town's black citizens. The town was ordered to submit, for the court's approval, a plan detailing how it proposed to cure the results of a long history of discrimination.

A major difference in policy making by the Supreme Court and by the courts of appeals should be noted. While there is one High Court for the entire country, each court of appeals covers only a specific region. Thus, the courts of appeals are more likely to make policy on a regional basis. Still, they are a part of the federal judicial system and "participate in both national and local policy networks, their decisions becoming regional law unless intolerable to the Justices." [31]

The Courts of Appeals at Work

As we noted earlier, the courts of appeals do not have the same degree of discretion as the Supreme Court to decide whether to accept a case for review. Still, as we shall see, circuit judges have developed methods for using their time as efficiently as possible.

Screening. During the screening stage the judges decide whether to give an appeal a full review or to dispose of it in some other way. The docket may be reduced to some extent by consolidating similar claims into single cases, a process that also results in a uniform decision. In deciding which cases can be disposed of without oral argument, the courts of appeals increasingly rely on law clerks or staff attorneys. These court personnel (discussed in greater detail in Chapter 3) read petitions and briefs and then submit recommendations to the judges. The screening process is very effective. According to Chief Judge Charles Clark of the Fifth Circuit, in fact, it results in a decision without oral argument in over half of the circuit's cases.[32] In the next section we will examine the procedures used in a full hearing.

Three-Judge Panels. Those cases given the full treatment are normally considered by panels of three judges rather than by all the judges in the circuit. This means that several cases can be heard at the same time by different three-judge panels, often sitting in different cities throughout the circuit. The panel assignments are made by the chief judge or by some other method decided upon by the individual circuit. In the Eleventh Circuit, for example, a committee of judges that does not include the chief judge uses a computer-generated random matrix to set the composition of every panel a year in advance.[33] Since all the circuits now contain more than three judges, the panels change frequently so that the same three judges do not sit together permanently.

As one might guess, there has been some criticism of panel assignments, especially those made by a chief judge. An excellent example is offered by the Fifth Circuit in the early 1960s. Judge Ben F. Cameron claimed that Chief Judge Elbert F. Tuttle stacked the panels hearing civil rights cases so that they would be decided favorably to black claimants.[34] Whether panels are stacked or not, one fact remains clear: a decision reached by a majority of a three-judge panel does not necessarily reflect the views of a majority of all the judges in the circuit.

En Banc Proceedings. Occasionally, different three-judge panels within the same circuit may reach conflicting decisions in similar cases. To resolve such conflicts and to promote circuit unanimity, federal statutes provide for an *en banc* procedure, in which all the circuit's judges sit together on a panel and decide a case. The en banc procedure may also be used when the case involves an issue of extraordinary importance, as in the famous *Tinker* decision.[35] That case raised the question of whether high school students wearing black armbands in the classroom to protest the Vietnam war should be protected by the First Amendment. When the Court of Appeals for the Eighth Circuit heard that case in 1967, the en banc procedure was used.

The en banc procedure may be requested by the litigants or by the judges of the court. The circuits themselves have discretion to decide if and how the procedure will be used. Clearly, its use is the exception rather than the rule.

Oral Argument.   Cases that have survived the screening process and have not been settled by the litigants are scheduled for oral argument. Attorneys for each side are given a short amount of time (in some cases no more than ten minutes) to discuss the points made in their written briefs and to answer questions from the judges.

The Decision.   Following the oral argument the judges may confer briefly and, if they are in agreement, announce their decision immediately. Otherwise, a decision will be announced only after the judges confer at greater length. Following the conference some decisions will be announced with a brief order or per curiam opinion of the court. A small portion of decisions will be accompanied by a longer, signed opinion and perhaps even dissenting and concurring opinions. Recent years have seen a general decrease in the number of published opinions, although circuits vary in their practices.

U.S. District Courts

The U.S. district courts represent the basic point of input for the federal judicial system. While some cases are later taken to a court of appeals or perhaps even to the Supreme Court, most cases never move beyond the U.S. trial courts. In terms of sheer numbers of cases handled, the district courts are the workhorses of the federal judiciary. As we shall see, however, their importance extends beyond simply disposing of a large number of cases.

The First District Courts

Congress made the decision to create a national network of federal trial courts when it passed the Judiciary Act of 1789. Section 2 of the act established 13 district courts by (1) making each of the eleven states then in the union a district, and (2) making the parts of Massachusetts and

Virginia that were to become Maine and Kentucky into separate districts. That organizational scheme established the practice, which still exists, of honoring state boundary lines in drawing districts. Thus, from the very beginning "the federal judiciary was state-contained, with the administrative and political structure of the states becoming the organizational structure of the federal courts." [36]

The First District Judges

Each federal district court was to be presided over by a single judge who resided in the district. As soon as this became known, President Washington began receiving letters from individuals desiring appointment to the various judgeships. Many asked members of Congress or Vice President Adams to recommend them to President Washington. Personal applications were not necessarily successful and were not the only way in which names came to the president's attention. Harry Innes, for example, was not an applicant for the Kentucky judgeship but received it after being recommended by a member of Congress from his state.[37]

Not everyone nominated was willing to serve as a district judge, however, and three of the 13 whose names were originally submitted to the Senate for confirmation declined the appointment—perhaps because the nominating process "did not permit consultation either with the individuals concerned or representatives of the 'neighborhood' who might know if the office would be accepted." [38] The rejections were somewhat embarrassing, and we are told that Washington resorted to careful preliminary screening of future appointments and relied more and more on his secretary of state for recommendations.

In our discussion of early Supreme Court nominations we noted that many prospective nominees preferred state level appointments. The same held true for district court appointments. Some declined judgeships in order to pursue other positions. Still others simply held both a district judgeship and a state office simultaneously.[39] Eventually, states began to pass laws prohibiting state officeholders from accepting federal positions.

As new states came into the Union, additional district courts were created. The additions, along with resignations, gave Washington an opportunity to offer judgeships to 33 people, 28 of whom accepted. A student of the early courts offers a profile of the 28 judges Washington appointed. Their average age at appointment was 46. All but three were born in the United States, and 16 had received college educations. All were members of the bar and all but seven had state or local legal experience as judges, prosecutors, or attorneys general.[40] As we shall see in Chapter 4, presidents have continued to appoint lawyers with public service backgrounds to the federal bench.

Present Organization of the District Courts

The practice of respecting state boundaries in establishing district court jurisdictions began in 1789 and has been periodically reaffirmed by statutes ever since. As the country grew, new district courts were created. Eventually, Congress began to divide some states into more than one district. California, New York, and Texas have the most, with four each. Figure 1-1 *(p. 18)* shows the number of districts and their boundaries in each state. Other than consistently honoring state lines, the organization of district constituencies appears to follow no rational plan. Size and population vary widely from district to district. Over the years, a court was added for the District of Columbia, and several territories have been served by district courts. There are presently 95 U.S. district courts serving the 50 states, the District of Columbia, Guam, Puerto Rico, the Virgin Islands, and the Northern Mariana Islands.

Congress often provides further organizational detail by creating divisions within a district. In doing this, the national legislature precisely lists the counties included in a particular division as well as the cities in which court will be held.

As indicated, the original district courts were each assigned one judge. With the growth in population and litigation, Congress has periodically had to add judges to most of the districts. In 1978, for example, it passed the Omnibus Judgeship Act, which created 177 new federal district judgeships and 35 new court of appeals judgeships—the largest number of judgeships ever created by a single act of Congress. The net effect of the legislation was to increase the number of federal district judges from 398 to 515. Today, most districts have more than one judge; the Southern District of New York, which includes Manhattan and the Bronx, currently has 27 judges and is thus the largest. Since each federal district court is normally presided over by a single judge, several trials may be in session at various cities within the district at any given time. The judges fulfill several functions, which we examine below.

The District Courts as Trial Courts

Congress established the district courts as the trial courts of the federal judicial system and gave them original jurisdiction over virtually all cases. They are the only federal courts in which attorneys examine and cross-examine witnesses. The factual record is thus established at this level; subsequent appeals of the trial court decision will focus on correcting errors rather than on reconstructing the facts. The task of determining the facts in a case often falls to a jury, a group of citizens from the community who serve as impartial arbiters of the facts and apply the law to the facts.

The Constitution guarantees the right to a jury trial in criminal cases in the Sixth Amendment and the same right in civil cases in the Seventh Amendment. The right can be waived, however, in which case the judge becomes the arbiter of both questions of fact and of matters of law. Two types of juries are associated with federal district courts. The *grand jury* is a group of men and women convened to determine whether there is probable cause to believe that a person has committed the federal crime of which he or she has been accused. Grand jurors meet periodically to hear charges brought by the U.S. attorney. *Petit jurors* are chosen at random from the community to hear evidence and determine whether a defendant in a civil trial has liability, or whether a defendant in a criminal trial is guilty or not guilty. Federal rules call for 12 jurors in criminal cases but permit fewer in civil cases. The federal district courts generally use six-person juries in civil cases.

Norm Enforcement by the District Courts

Some students of the judiciary make a distinction between norm enforcement and policy making by the courts.[41] Trial courts are viewed as engaging primarily in norm enforcement, while appellate courts are seen as having greater opportunity to make policy.

Norm enforcement is closely tied to the administration of justice, since all nations develop standards considered essential to a just and orderly society. Societal norms are embodied in statutes, administrative regulations, prior court decisons, and community traditions. Criminal statutes, for example, incorporate concepts of acceptable and unacceptable behavior into law. A judge deciding a case involving an alleged violation of that law is basically practicing norm enforcement. Because cases of this type rarely allow the judge to escape the strict restraints of legal and procedural requirements, he or she has little chance to make new law or develop new policy. In civil cases, too, judges are often confined to norm enforcement; opportunities for policy making are infrequent. Rather, such litigation generally involves a private dispute whose outcome is of interest only to the parties in the suit.

Policy Making by the District Courts

The district courts also play a policy-making role. One leading judicial scholar explains how this function differs from norm enforcement:

> When they make policy, the courts do not exercise more discretion than when they enforce community norms. The difference lies in the intended impact of the decision. Policy decisions are intended to be

guideposts for future actions; norm-enforcement decisions are aimed at the particular case at hand.[42]

The discretion that a federal trial judge exercises should not be overlooked, however. As Americans have become more litigation-conscious, disputes that were once resolved informally are now more likely to be decided in a court of law. The courts find themselves increasingly involved in domains once considered private. What does this mean for the federal district courts? According to a recent study, "These new areas of judicial involvement tend to be relatively free of clear, precise appellate court and legislative guidelines; and as a consequence the opportunity for trial court jurists to write on a clean slate, that is, to make policy, is formidable." [43] In other words, when the guidelines are not well established, district judges have a great deal of discretion to set policy. Some district judges, in fact, have gained considerable notoriety because of their policy-making activities. Two good examples are Judge Frank M. Johnson of the Middle District of Alabama and Judge William Wayne Justice of the Eastern District of Texas.

In the early 1970s Judge Johnson sent shockwaves throughout Alabama when he ruled that conditions in one of that state's mental hospitals prevented patients from receiving adequate treatment and thus deprived them of due process guaranteed by the Constitution.[44] Johnson mandated more than 50 specific changes that he felt were necessary to bring the state's mental facilities up to minimum constitutional standards. His guidelines required changes in state budgetary and personnel policies as well. In short, Judge Johnson translated constitutional standards into policies affecting every mental patient in a state facility and, indirectly, every taxpayer in Alabama.

Judge William Wayne Justice has become familiar to public officials in Texas. It was said that "while he will never win a popularity contest among Texas lawmakers, no one can dispute the fact that his bold and aggressive rulings are changing the face of Texas politics." Justice is perhaps best known in the state for rulings in three particular areas: public education, criminal justice, and legislative redistricting. For example, he has ruled that bilingual educational programs must be extended through the twelfth grade. In another case he required the state to provide one-prisoner cells or at least 60 square feet of space for each inmate.[45] Like Johnson's rulings in Alabama, Justice's decisions in Texas have had an impact upon the state budget and, ultimately, on all taxpayers.

Texas legislators have not been reluctant to express their dissatisfaction with Judge Justice's policy-making activities. For example, following a court-ordered reform of the state's juvenile justice system in 1977, the Texas House of Representatives retaliated by amending an appropriations bill to require construction of a new juvenile halfway house next door to Justice's home in Tyler.[46]

Three-Judge District Courts

In 1903, Congress passed legislation providing for the use of special three-judge district courts in certain types of cases. Such courts are created on an ad hoc basis, with the panels being disbanded when a case has been decided. Each panel must include at least one judge from the federal district court and at least one judge from the court of appeals. Normally, two district judges and one appellate judge comprise the panel. Appeals of decisions of three-judge district courts go directly to the Supreme Court.

The earliest types of cases to be heard by three-judge district courts involved suits filed by the attorney general under the Sherman Antitrust Act or the Interstate Commerce Act. Congress later provided that these special courts could decide suits brought by private citizens challenging the constitutionality of state or federal statutes and seeking injunctions to prevent enforcement of the challenged statutes.

An example of the use of a three-judge district court is provided by the abortion case of *Roe v. Wade*.[47] Jane Roe (a pseudonym), a single, pregnant woman, challenged the constitutionality of the Texas antiabortion statute and sought an injunction to prohibit further enforcement of the law. The case was initially heard by a three-judge court consisting of district judges Sarah T. Hughes and W. N. Taylor and Fifth Circuit Court of Appeals judge Irving L. Goldberg. The three-judge district court held the Texas abortion statute invalid but declined to issue an injunction against its enforcement on the ground that a federal intrusion into the state's affairs was not warranted. Roe then appealed the denial of the injunction directly to the Supreme Court.

Over the years congressional statutes, such as the Civil Rights Act of 1964, the Voting Rights Act of 1965, and the Presidential Election Campaign Fund Act of 1974, have specified the use of three-judge district courts. However, increases in the number of cases decided by such courts led to complaints about caseload problems, since appeals from the three-judge panels go directly to the Supreme Court. To relieve some of the caseload pressure, Congress passed legislation in 1976 restricting the use of three-judge district courts.

Constitutional Courts and Legislative Courts

The Judiciary Act of 1789 established the three levels of the federal court system in existence today. Periodically, however, Congress has exercised its power, found in Article III and Article I of the Constitution, to create other federal courts. Courts established under Article III are known as *constitutional courts*, while those created under Article I are called *legislative courts*. The former handle the bulk of litigation in our system and, for this reason, will remain our focus throughout the remainder of the book. The Supreme Court, courts of appeals, and federal district courts are, of course, constitutional courts. The U.S. Court of Military Appeals provides one example of a legislative court. It was created in 1950 under authority found in Article I, Section 8, clause 9 of the Constitution, "to constitute Tribunals inferior to the Supreme Court," and Article I, Section 8, clause 14, "to make Rules for the Government and Regulation of the land and naval Forces." Other important legislative courts currently in existence include (1) the Court of Appeals for the Federal Circuit (created in 1982), (2) the United States Claims Court (created in 1982), (3) the Court of International Trade (formerly the Customs Court, its name was changed in 1980), and (4) the United States Tax Court (formerly an administrative agency called the Tax Court of the United States until its name was changed by a 1969 statute).

The two types of courts may be further distinguished by their functions. Legislative courts, unlike their constitutional counterparts, often possess administrative and quasi-legislative as well as judicial duties. Another difference is that legislative courts are often created for the express purpose of helping to administer a specific congressional statute. Constitutional courts, on the other hand, are tribunals established to handle litigation.

Finally, the constitutional and legislative courts vary in their degree of independence from the other two branches of government. Article III (constitutional court) judges serve during a period of good behavior, or what amounts to life tenure. Since Article I (legislative court) judges have no constitutional guarantee to "good behavior" tenure, Congress may set specific terms of office for them. Judges of Article III courts are also constitutionally protected against salary reductions while in office. Those who serve as judges of legislative courts have no such protection. In sum, the constitutional courts have a greater degree of independence from the other two branches of government than the legislative courts. How important is such independence? Recent events surrounding the fate of federal bankruptcy courts reveal independence to be a major consideration, as we shall see.

On November 6, 1978, President Jimmy Carter signed into law the Bankruptcy Reform Act. That legislation (1) required that bankruptcy cases be filed in bankruptcy courts rather than in district courts; (2) extended the terms of current bankruptcy judges through March 1984; (3)

provided that after March 3, 1984, bankruptcy judges were to be appointed by the president, with Senate confirmation, for 14-year terms; (4) simplified existing bankruptcy law; and (5) expanded the jurisdiction of bankruptcy judges. A system of bankruptcy courts was seemingly in place.

Trouble began, however, less than three years later. In a brief order issued on April 23, 1981, and a supplemental memorandum issued on July 24, 1981, U.S. District Judge Miles W. Lord of Minnesota held that the Bankruptcy Reform Act's delegation of trial authority to bankruptcy judges was unconstitutional.[48] Judge Lord argued that Congress had exceeded its constitutional power when it authorized bankruptcy judges to exercise the jurisdiction and duties of district judges without at the same time vesting them with the tenure and salary protections given Article III judges. The independence question was at the heart of Judge Lord's decision.

The case was appealed to the Supreme Court, which, in a June 1982 decision, agreed that portions of the Bankruptcy Reform Act were unconstitutional. The Court held that certain powers granted by the act to bankruptcy judges could be exercised only by Article III judges, who are insulated from political pressures by life tenure and protection from pay cuts.[49] The Supreme Court asked Congress to pass remedial legislation aimed at handling the bankruptcy problem. After several failures on Congress's part, the federal district courts put into operation a contingency plan recommended by the Judicial Conference of the United States in September 1982.[50] Among other things, the Judicial Conference's emergency rule removed contested matters from bankruptcy judges to district court judges.

After several unsuccessful attempts Congress passed a law in July 1984 to correct the problem. The new legislation provides for the creation of bankruptcy courts as units of the district courts. Bankruptcy judges are now appointed for 14-year terms by the court of appeals for the circuit in which the district is located. Most bankruptcy cases can be handled entirely by the bankruptcy judge. However, in certain types of cases, such as those involving personal injury or wrongful death, the bankruptcy judge may only submit proposed findings of fact and the district judge then enters the final order or judgment.

The Federal Courts in the American Political System

The role of the federal courts in the American political system generally, and in the policy-making process specifically, has long been debated by students of the judiciary. There is widespread agreement that all three levels of federal courts engage in policy making to some extent. How the courts handle this function has been subject to a good deal of controversy, however. We will now examine the federal judiciary's policy-making role within the context of the larger American political system, which includes Congress, the executive, and other political institutions, such as elections.

In a 1957 article focusing on the Supreme Court's power of judicial review, one political scientist concluded that "the policy views dominant on the Court are never for long out of line with the policy views dominant among the lawmaking majorities of the United States." In other words, according to this author the Supreme Court justices generally hold policy views that are similar to those espoused by a majority of the Congress. Obviously, the Court does not always agree completely with the policies developed by Congress. He argued, however, that the Supreme Court's weaker position in relation to Congress and the president means that "it would be most unrealistic to suppose that the Court would, for more than a few years at most, stand against any major alternatives sought by a lawmaking majority." Only during a period of political upheaval or transition from one electoral coalition to another might we expect to find the Court in a position to block a particular policy. In short, this approach sees the Court not so much a protector of fundamental minority rights as a legitimator of the policies of the majority.[51]

This view of the Supreme Court and its role in the American political system has been widely debated by judicial scholars.[52] A 1973 study, for example, focused on the historical periods of party realignment and found that there was intense conflict between the High Court and the lawmaking majority after each realigning election. Perhaps even more important is Adamany's conclusion that the historical evidence simply does not support the earlier assertion that the Supreme Court serves to legitimize the policies of the new coalition.[53] Two years later, however, another political scientist, also analyzing Supreme Court activity during periods of electoral realignment, concluded that earlier studies "have been correct in emphasizing the Court's function as a legitimating agency."[54]

Yet another scholar entered the debate by pointing out two serious limitations of Dahl's 1957 study: (1) that its time frame did not include the entire Warren Court period and (2) that it did not include judicial review over actions of the states. Extending the analysis to cover the 1958-1974 period and including state cases presented a different picture of the Supreme Court's policy-making role. Casper noted several areas in which the Court was influential in developing policy; he pointed out that "the

Court can and does get its way a good deal more frequently than [the 1957] analysis implies." [55]

The debate over the Supreme Court's role in the American political system has been a lively one. Depending upon the scope of the study and the particular method of analysis, scholars have reached different conclusions. Whatever their conclusions, however, there can be no doubt that the Supreme Court is involved in the policy-making process. The following statement aptly summarizes current thinking in the debate: "The Court may be a legitimator . . . but it is also a significant wielder of power." [56]

The lower federal courts, as we have noted, also operate within the context of the larger political system and thus are participants in the policy-making process. Not only has increasing litigation opened up new areas of district court decision making but, like the appeals courts, the bottom rung of the federal judiciary is the tribunal of last resort in the vast majority of cases it hears. In the late 1960s, for example, one judicial scholar stated:

> Trial Judges, because of the multitude of cases they hear which remain unheard or unchanged by appellate courts, as well as because of their fact- and issue-shaping powers, appear to play an independent and formidable part in the policy impact of the federal court system upon the larger political system. [57]

Although the district courts have been active policy makers in several issue areas, perhaps the civil rights arena stands out above all others. Following the Supreme Court's school desegregation decision in 1954, federal district judges, especially in the South, were faced with the problem of applying to local communities the general ruling that racially defined dual school systems were in violation of the Constitution. It has been pointed out, too, that the district judges have a good deal of discretion in developing desegregation policies to fit specific local needs. [58] As the judges develop policy in this area, they often make decisions that are not only unpopular but go against the tide of prevailing local opinion, as these extreme examples indicate:

> [Some] Southern judges suffered . . . social indignities after decisions favorable to civil rights, among them Judge Skelly Wright of the Louisiana eastern district and Judge Frank Johnson of the middle district of Alabama. Graves of their relatives were desecrated, crosses burned on home lawns, dynamite blasts set off near relatives' homes, and professional ostracism was inflicted by local bar groups. [59]

While incurring various atrocities, a federal district judge may at the same time invite further litigation and thus increase his or her opportunities as a policy maker. For example, one study found that

Judge Skelly Wright's record in favor of civil liberties cases, particularly race relations cases, undoubtedly encouraged litigation in his court. Litigants unable to secure favorable decisions elsewhere in Louisiana regarded the federal district court in New Orleans as a haven to which they might turn for favorable judgments on civil liberties problems.

As evidence that Judge Wright did indeed have ample opportunity to be involved in the policy-making process, the study noted that in the 1956-1961 period he handled nearly twice as many labor and civil liberties cases as any other judge in the Fifth Circuit.[60]

Examinations of civil rights policy making by lower federal judges have indicated that a surprisingly large number of liberal decisions have come from judges sitting in southern cities.[61] Although noting that their civil rights and liberties category is broader than the ones used in the 1960s studies, the authors of a more recent analysis say that

> southern cities are well represented among the most liberal metropolitan areas. Four of the six most liberal cities are clearly from the Deep South: New Orleans, Houston, Atlanta, and Miami. None of the cities in the least liberal civil rights and liberties category is a traditional southern community.[62]

Summary

This chapter offers a brief historical review of the development of the federal judiciary. From preconstitutional times to the current uncertainty surrounding the bankruptcy courts there has been a perennial concern for an independent federal court system.

Our focus throughout this chapter has been on three basic court systems created by the Judiciary Act of 1789. We have noted, however, that Congress has periodically created both constitutional and legislative courts. Still, the bulk of litigation is handled by U.S. district courts, courts of appeals, and the Supreme Court.

The organization and function of each of the three courts has been spelled out in detail, to provide a thorough understanding of its importance to the federal judicial system. We have stressed the fact that although the courts are dependent on one another, each retains a measure of independence. Finally, we have briefly examined the role of the federal courts in the American political system as a whole.

Notes

1. Charles Evans Hughes, *The Supreme Court of the United States* (New York: Columbia University Press, 1966), 1.
2. Ibid., 2.
3. Charles Warren, *The Supreme Court in United States History*, vol. 1 (Boston: Little, Brown, 1924), 4.
4. Fred Rodell, *Nine Men* (New York: Random House, 1955), 47.
5. See Warren, *The Supreme Court in United States History*, vol. 1, 44.
6. John P. Frank, *Marble Palace* (New York: Knopf, 1968), 9.
7. Warren, *The Supreme Court in United States History*, vol. 1, 51.
8. *Chisholm v. Georgia*, 2 Dallas 419 (1793).
9. Frank, *Marble Palace*, 79.
10. See Sheldon Goldman, *Constitutional Law and Supreme Court Decision-Making* (New York: Harper & Row, 1982), 41.
11. *Marbury v. Madison*, 1 Cranch 137 (1803).
12. See Lawrence Baum, *The Supreme Court*, 2d ed. (Washington, D.C.: CQ Press, 1985), 19.
13. *Gibbons v. Ogden*, 9 Wheaton 1 (1824).
14. *McCulloch v. Maryland*, 4 Wheaton 316 (1819).
15. Goldman, *Constitutional Law and Supreme Court Decision-Making*, 249.
16. See *National Labor Relations Board v. Jones and Laughlin Steel Corp.*, 301 U.S. 1 (1937); *Steward Machine Co. v. Davis*, 301 U.S. 548 (1937); and *West Coast Hotel Co. v. Parrish*, 300 U.S. 379 (1937).
17. *Brown v. Board of Education*, 347 U.S. 483 (1954).
18. See *Gideon v. Wainwright*, 372 U.S. 335 (1963); *Mapp v. Ohio*, 367 U.S. 643 (1961); *Miranda v. Arizona*, 384 U.S. 436 (1966); *Baker v. Carr*, 369 U.S. 186 (1962); and *Engel v. Vitale*, 370 U.S. 421 (1962) respectively.
19. Robert H. Birkby, *The Court and Public Policy* (Washington, D.C.: CQ Press, 1983), 1.
20. *Plessy v. Ferguson*, 163 U.S. 537 (1896).
21. See Baum, *The Supreme Court*, 115.
22. *Stanley v. Georgia*, 394 U.S. 557 (1969).
23. Stephen T. Early, Jr., *Constitutional Courts of the United States* (Totowa, N.J.: Littlefield, Adams, 1977), 100.
24. See Warren, *The Supreme Court in United States History*, vol. 1, 85, 86.
25. Richard J. Richardson and Kenneth N. Vines, *The Politics of Federal Courts* (Boston: Little, Brown, 1970), 27.
26. J. Woodford Howard, Jr., *Courts of Appeals in the Federal Judicial System: A Study of the Second, Fifth, and District of Columbia Circuits* (Princeton, N.J.: Princeton University Press, 1981), 75-76.
27. See Richard J. Richardson and Kenneth N. Vines, "Review, Dissent and the Appellate Process: A Political Interpretation," *Journal of Politics*, 29 (August 1967): 597-616.
28. See Howard, *Courts of Appeals in the Federal Judicial System*, 42.

29. *Office of Communications of the United Church of Christ v. F.C.C.*, 359 F. 2d 994 (D.C. Cir. 1966).
30. *Hawkins v. Town of Shaw, Mississippi*, 437 F. 2d 1286 (5th Cir. 1971).
31. Howard, *Courts of Appeals in the Federal Judicial System*, 79.
32. See *The Third Branch* 15 (December 1983): 5.
33. See *The Third Branch* 15 (July 1983): 5.
34. See Early, *Constitutional Courts of the United States*, 112-113, for the specifics of Judge Cameron's charges.
35. *Tinker v. Des Moines Independent Community School District*, 393 U.S. 503 (1969).
36. Richardson and Vines, *The Politics of Federal Courts*, 21.
37. See Dwight F. Henderson, *Courts for a New Nation* (Washington, D.C.: Public Affairs Press, 1971), 27.
38. Ibid., 28.
39. Ibid., 29-30.
40. Ibid., 30-31.
41. See Herbert Jacob, *Justice in America*, 4th ed. (Boston: Little, Brown, 1984), chap. 2.
42. Ibid., 37.
43. Robert A. Carp and C. K. Rowland, *Policymaking and Politics in the Federal District Courts* (Knoxville: University of Tennessee Press, 1983), 3.
44. See *Wyatt v. Stickney*, 325 F. Supp. 781 (1971) and 344 F. Supp. 373 (1972).
45. Donald G. Martin, ed., *Texas Government Newsletter* 9 (April 27, 1981): 2.
46. Ibid. The amendment was later removed by the Texas Senate.
47. The decision of the three-judge district court may be found in *Roe v. Wade*, 314 F. Supp. 1217 (1970) and the Supreme Court decision in *Roe v. Wade*, 410 U.S. 113 (1973).
48. See *Northern Pipeline Construction Co. v. Marathon Pipe Line Company*, 6 B.R. 928 (1981) and 12 B.R. 946 (1981).
49. *Northern Pipeline Construction Co. v. Marathon Pipe Line Company*, 458 U.S. 50 (1982).
50. See *The Third Branch* 15 (January 1983): 1 and 8, for a chronology of events in this matter.
51. Robert A. Dahl, "Decision-Making in a Democracy: The Supreme Court as a National Policy-Maker," *Journal of Public Law* 6 (Fall 1957): 285, 294.
52. See, for example, David Adamany, "Legitimacy, Realigning Elections, and the Supreme Court," *Wisconsin Law Review* (September 1973): 790-846; Richard Funston, "The Supreme Court and Critical Elections," *American Political Science Review* 69 (September 1975): 795-811; Bradley C. Canon and S. Sidney Ulmer, "The Supreme Court and Critical Elections: A Dissent," *American Political Science Review* 70 (December 1976): 1215-1218; Jonathan D. Casper, "The Supreme Court and National Policy Making," *American Political Science Review* 70 (March 1976): 50-63; and Roger Handberg and Harold F. Hill, Jr., "Court Curbing, Court Reversals,

and Judicial Review: The Supreme Court Versus Congress," *Law and Society Review* 14 (Winter 1980): 309-322.

53. See Adamany, "Legitimacy, Realigning Elections, and the Supreme Court."

54. Funston, "The Supreme Court and Critical Elections," 808-809. It should be noted that the Funston study was criticized, primarily on methodological grounds, in Canon and Ulmer, "The Supreme Court and Critical Elections."

55. See Casper, "The Supreme Court and National Policy Making," 59.

56. Handberg and Hill, "Court Curbing, Court Reversals, and Judicial Review," 321.

57. Kenneth M. Dolbeare, "The Federal District Courts and Urban Public Policy: An Exploratory Study (1960-1967)," in *Frontiers of Judicial Research,* edited by Joel B. Grossman and Joseph Tanenhaus (New York: Wiley, 1969), 395.

58. See, for example, Jack W. Peltason, *Fifty-Eight Lonely Men* (New York: Harcourt, Brace and World, 1961), and Micheal W. Giles and Thomas G. Walker, "Judicial Policy-Making and Southern School Segregation," *Journal of Politics* 37 (May 1975): 917-936.

59. Richardson and Vines, *The Politics of Federal Courts,* 98-99.

60. Ibid., 101.

61. See Richardson and Vines, *The Politics of Federal Courts.* Also see Dolbeare, "The Federal District Courts and Urban Public Policy"; Kenneth N. Vines, "Federal District Judges and Race Relations Cases in the South," *Journal of Politics* 26 (May 1964): 337-357; and Kenneth N. Vines, "The Role of Circuit Courts of Appeals in the Federal Judicial Process: A Case Study," *Midwest Journal of Political Science* 7 (November 1963): 305-319.

62. Carp and Rowland, *Policymaking and Politics in the Federal District Courts,* 141.

Jurisdiction, Workload, and Policy-Making Boundaries

2

In setting out the jurisdictions of the federal courts, Congress and the Constitution mandate the types of cases each court can hear. Our examination of the courts' legal boundaries includes a discussion of a related topic—a court's workload, or the number of cases a court hears and the types of dispositions available to it. In Chapter 1 we began our survey with the Supreme Court and proceeded to the appeals and district courts; we followed the order in which the courts were established. In this chapter we shall reverse the order, since the flow of litigation is in the opposite direction—from the bottom layer, the trial courts, upward through the appellate levels.

Because Congress's role in setting jurisdiction is an ongoing one, we will consider how the national legislature can influence the courts' behavior by redefining the types of cases they can hear. The chapter will close with a discussion of judicial self-restraint; we will examine ten specific principles, derived from legal tradition and constitutional and statutory law, that govern the Supreme Court's decisions about whether to review a case.

U.S. District Courts

In the United States Code Congress has set forth the jurisdiction of the federal district courts. These tribunals have *original jurisdiction* in federal criminal and civil cases—that is, by law, the cases must be first heard in these courts, no matter who the parties are or how significant the issues. In the next two sections we will examine the criminal and civil caseloads.

Criminal Cases

For the 12-month period ended June 30, 1983, some 35,872 criminal cases were commenced in the federal district courts, up 9.8 percent from the 1981-1982 period. These were cases for which the local U.S. attorneys had reason to believe that a violation of the U.S. Penal Code had occurred.

After first obtaining an indictment from a federal grand jury, the U.S. attorney files charges against the accused in the district court in which he or she serves. Criminal activity as defined by Congress covers a wide range of behavior, including interstate theft of an automobile, failure to register with Selective Service, illegal importation of narcotics, assassination of a president, conspiracy to deprive persons of their civil rights, or even the killing of a migratory bird out of season. For the past decade or so the most numerous types of criminal code violations have been embezzlement and fraud, larceny and theft, drunk driving and other traffic offenses, drug-related offenses, and forgery and counterfeiting. Some federal crimes, such as robbery, are comparatively uniform in occurrence in each of the 94 U.S. judicial districts, whereas others are endemic to certain geographic areas. For example, those districts next to the U.S. borders get an inordinate number of immigration cases, and districts in the southern states have had more than their share of criminal violations of the civil rights laws.

After charges are filed against an accused for violation of a federal crime, a trial is conducted by a U.S. district judge. In court the defendant enjoys all the privileges and immunities granted in the Bill of Rights (such as "the right to a speedy and public trial") or by congressional legislation or Supreme Court rulings (for instance, a 12-person jury must render a unanimous verdict). As noted in Chapter 1, defendants may waive the right to a trial by a jury of their peers. A defendant who is found not guilty of the crime is set free and may never be tried again for the same offense (the Fifth Amendment's protection against double jeopardy). If the accused is found guilty, the district judge determines the appropriate sentence within a range set by Congress. The length of a sentence is not appealable so long as it is within the range prescribed by Congress. A verdict of not guilty may not be appealed by the government, but convicted defendants may appeal if they believe that the judge or jury made an improper legal determination.

In the fiscal year ending June 30, 1983, some 68.8 percent of all criminal cases were resolved with guilty pleas; 11.7 percent ended in convictions; and 1.6 percent resulted in pleas of *nolo contendere,* in which defendants admit the charges against them but refuse to plead guilty, thereby saving themselves a shred of dignity. Dismissals were ordered by

Table 2-1 Cases Commenced in the U.S. District Courts: 1963, 1973, and 1983

	1963	1973	1983	Percent Change 1963-1973	Percent Change 1973-1983
Criminal	31,746	42,434	35,872	33.6	−15.4
U.S. civil	19,755	22,949	91,449	16.1	298.4
Private civil	39,621	58,393	119,618	47.3	104.8
Prisoner petitions					
Federal	1,630	4,535	4,354	178.2	−3.9
State	2,624	12,683	26,421	383.3	108.3
Total criminal	31,746	42,434	35,872	33.6	−15.4
Total civil	63,630	98,560	241,842	54.8	145.3
Total	95,376	140,994	277,714	47.8	96.9
Number of authorized judgeships	289	400	515	38.4	28.7

Note: The 1963 statistics exclude the District of Columbia, the Canal Zone, Guam, and the Virgin Islands.

Source: *Annual Reports of the Director of the Administrative Office of the U.S. Courts* (1963, 1973, and 1983).

the trial judges in 15.2 percent of the cases, and the accused were acquitted 2.7 percent of the time.[1]

Civil Cases

The lion's share of the district court caseload is of a civil nature—that is, suits between private parties or between the U.S. government, acting in its nonprosecutorial capacity, and a private party. In 1983 a whopping 241,842 civil cases were commenced in the district courts, representing over 87 percent of its total caseload. As Table 2-1 reveals, the size of the civil docket has increased dramatically—not only in comparison with criminal cases but in absolute terms. The increase in civil filings increased over 54 percent in the years between 1963 and 1973, and then jumped an overwhelming 145.3 percent between 1973 and 1983. By comparison criminal filings actually declined by over 15 percent in the most recent 10-year period.

Civil cases that originate in the U.S. district courts may be placed in one of several categories. The first covers litigation involving the interpretation or application of the Constitution, acts of Congress, or U.S. treaties in which at least $10,000 is at stake. Examples of cases in this category would include the following: a petitioner claims that one of his federally protected civil rights has been violated, a litigant alleges that she is being harmed by a congressional statute that is unconstitutional, or a plaintiff argues that he is suffering injury from a treaty that is improperly affecting him. The key point is that a *federal* question must be involved in order for the U.S. trial courts to have jurisdiction. It is not enough to say that the federal courts should hear a case "because there is an important issue involved" or "because an awful lot of money is at stake." Unless one is able to invoke the Constitution or a federal law or treaty, the case must be litigated elsewhere (probably in the state courts).

The jurisdictional amount of $10,000 is waived if the case falls into one of several categories which by law must be adjudicated by the federal courts regardless of the dollar amount in controversy. For example, an alleged violation of a civil rights law, such as the Voting Rights Act of 1965, must be heard by the federal rather than the state judiciary. Other types of cases in this category are patent and copyright claims, passport and naturalization proceedings, admiralty and maritime disputes, violations of the U.S. postal laws, and appeals from decisions of the Interstate Commerce Commission.

Another broad category of cases over which the U.S. trial courts exercise general original jurisdiction are known as diversity of citizenship disputes—that is, the parties are from different states, or the dispute is between an American citizen and a foreign country or citizen. Thus if a citizen of New York were injured in an automobile accident in Chicago by a driver from Illinois, the New Yorker could sue in federal court, since the parties to the suit were of "diverse citizenship." The requirement that at least $10,000 be at stake in diversity cases does not appear to be much of a barrier to the gates of the federal judiciary: even if actual injuries come to less than $10,000, one can always ask for "psychological damages" to push the amount in controversy above the jurisdictional threshold.

Federal district courts also have jurisdiction over petitions from convicted prisoners who contend that their incarceration (or perhaps their denial of parole) is in violation of their federally protected rights. In the vast majority of these cases prisoners ask for what is termed a *writ of habeas corpus*—that is, an order issued by a judge to determine whether a person has been lawfully imprisoned or detained. The judge would demand that the prison authorities either justify the detention or release the petitioner.

Prisoners convicted in a state court must take care to argue that a *federally protected* right was violated—for example, the right to be represented by counsel at trial. Otherwise the federal courts would have no jurisdiction. Federal prisoners have a somewhat wider range for their appeals, since all their rights and options are within the penumbra of the U.S. Constitution. Petitions from state and federal prison inmates constituted about 13 percent of the total civil caseload in 1983—2 percent from federal prisoners and 11 percent from those hosted by state institutions.

Finally, the district courts have the authority to hear any other cases that Congress may validly prescribe by law. For example, while the Constitution grants to the U.S. Supreme Court original jurisdiction to hear "Cases affecting Ambassadors, other public Ministers and Consuls," Congress has also authorized the district courts to have concurrent original jurisdiction over cases involving such parties.

U.S. Courts of Appeals

The U.S. appellate courts have no original jurisdiction whatsoever: every case or controversy that comes to one of these intermediate-level panels has been first argued in some other forum. As indicated in Chapter 1, these tribunals, like the district courts, are the creations of Congress and their structure and functions have varied considerably over time. As Table 2-2 reveals, in 1963 only 5,437 cases found their way into one of the regional circuit courts, whereas by 1973 this figure had jumped to 15,629 cases—an increase of over 187 percent. During the past decade the number of filings has continued to mount but at a somewhat slower rate. In 1984, 29,630 cases were commenced in one of the twelve U.S. appellate courts. As with the district courts, the increase in civil cases has outstripped those of a criminal nature. During the past decade the number of criminal cases was up less than 8 percent, whereas the number of civil cases climbed by over 122 percent.

Basically there are two general categories of cases over which Congress has granted the circuit courts appellate jurisdiction. The first of these are ordinary civil and criminal appeals from the federal trial courts, including the U.S. territorial courts, the U.S. Tax Court, and some District of Columbia courts. In criminal cases the appellant is the defendant because the government is not free to appeal a verdict of "not guilty." (However, if the question in a criminal case is one of defining the legal rights of the defendant, then the government may appeal an adverse trial court ruling.) For civil cases it is usually the party that lost in the trial court that is the appellant, although it is not unheard of for the winning party to appeal if it is not satisfied with the lower-court judgment. The U.S. government, acting in its private capacity, is a party to about 18

Table 2-2 Cases Commenced in the U.S. Courts of Appeals: 1963, 1973, and 1983

	1963	1973	1983	Percent Change 1963-1973	Percent Change 1973-1983
Criminal	965	4,453	4,790	361.4	7.5
U.S. civil	1,054	1,703	4,562	61.5	167.8
Private civil	2,030	4,344	10,360	64.7	138.5
Prisoner petitions					
Federal	N/A	1,001	1,258		25.6
State	N/A	1,828	4,069		122.5
Bankruptcy	144	338	688	134.7	103.5
Administrative					
appeals	1,141	1,616	3,069	41.6	89.9
D.C. Court					
of Appeals	3	—	N/A		
Original proceedings	99	346	834	249.4	141.0
Other	1				
Total criminal	965	4,453	4,790	361.4	7.5
Total civil	4,472	11,176	24,840	149.9	122.2
Total	5,437	15,629	29,630	187.4	89.6
Number of authorized					
judgeships	78	97	132	24.3	36.0

Source: *Annual Reports of the Director of the Administrative Office of the U.S. Courts* (1963, 1973, and 1983).

percent of the civil appeals, while 42 percent are between totally private parties. Prisoners' petitions also constitute a significant portion of the appeals from adverse rulings of trial jurists. In 1983, 21 percent of the civil appeals from the lower federal courts were centered on prisoners' petitions.

The second broad category of appellate jurisdiction centers on appeals from certain federal administrative agencies and departments and also from the important independent regulatory commissions, such as the Securities and Exchange Commission and the National Labor Relations Board. In 1983 about one case in eight of the civil docket consisted of administrative appeals. Because so many of the administrative and regulatory bodies have their home base in Washington, the appeals court for that circuit gets an inordinate number of such cases.

U.S. Supreme Court

The United States Supreme Court is the only federal court mentioned by name in the Constitution, which spells out the general contours of the High Court's jurisdiction. Although we usually think of the Supreme Court as an appellate tribunal, it does have some general *original* jurisdiction. Probably the most important area of such jurisdiction is a suit between two or more states. For example, every so often the states of Texas and Louisiana spar with one another in the Supreme Court over the proper boundary between their separate jurisdictions. By law the Sabine River divides the two states, but with great regularity this effluent changes its snaking course, thus requiring the Supreme Court (with considerable help from the U.S. Army Corps of Engineers) to determine where Louisiana ends and the Lone Star State begins.

In addition the High Court shares original jurisdiction (with the U.S. district courts) in certain cases brought by or against foreign ambassadors or consuls, in cases between the United States and a state, and in cases commenced by a state against citizens of another state or against aliens. In situations such as these, where jurisdiction is shared, the courts are said to have *concurrent jurisdiction.*

Cases over which the Supreme Court has original jurisdiction are often important, but they do not represent a sizable portion of the overall caseload. In 1983 the High Court's docket consisted of 5,079 cases, but only 17 of these (a mere one third of one percent) were heard on original jurisdiction.

The U.S. Constitution declares that the Supreme Court "shall have appellate Jurisdiction . . . under such Regulations as the Congress shall make." Over the years Congress has passed much legislation setting forth the "Regulations" under which cases may appear before the nation's most august judicial body. In essence there are two main avenues through which appeals may reach the Supreme Court. First, there may be appeals from all lower federal constitutional and territorial courts and also from most, but not all, federal legislative courts. Second, the Supreme Court may hear appeals from the highest court in a state—so long as there is a "substantial federal question" involved.

With some of these cases the appeal is "as of right," which means that Congress has enacted legislation granting appellants an absolute right to take certain types of cases before the Court. For example, if a court of appeals finds that a state law is invalid because it conflicts with the U.S. Constitution or a federal law or treaty, the losing party may appeal as of right to the Supreme Court. However, even here the justices are not absolutely forced to hear the case on the merits; the Court must be convinced that a truly important issue is involved. More than one appeal as of right has been dismissed by the justices "for want of a substantial federal question." That is, even in appeals "as of right," the Court has an escape route. A decision on the merits can be avoided if the justices are not convinced that the case involves such compelling, nationally significant issues that the nation's highest tribunal must spend its limited time and resources on it.

Since the passage of the Judges Bill in 1925, Congress has given the Court a great deal of discretion as to the cases it chooses to hear on appeal. Most of the High Court's docket consists of cases in which it has agreed to issue a writ of certiorari—a totally discretionary action. Such a writ (which must be supported by at least four justices) is an order from the Supreme Court to a lower court demanding that it send up a complete record of a case so that the Supreme Court can review it. Historically the Supreme Court has agreed to grant the petition for a writ of certiorari in only a tiny portion of cases—usually less than 10 percent of the time.

Besides appeals as of right and writs of certiorari, there is another method by which the Supreme Court exercises its appellate jurisdiction— by *certification*. This procedure occurs when one of the appeals courts asks the Supreme Court for instructions regarding a question of law. The justices may then choose to give the appellate judges binding instructions, or they may ask that the entire record be forwarded to the Supreme Court for review and final judgment.

All in all, roughly half the litigation that arrives on the Supreme Court's doorstep are "paid cases"—that is, cases for which the appellant was able to pay the cost of the filing fee and of the multiple copies of required documents. The other half are in the form of paupers' petitions filed by indigent persons for whom the filing fee and the multiple-copy requirements are waived. Over three-quarters of the paupers' petitions are filed by inmates in federal and state prisons.

The overall caseload of the Supreme Court is high by historical standards, although since about 1973 the workload appears to have leveled off (see Table 2-3). In 1963, 2,294 cases filled the Court's docket; this number jumped by over 121 percent, to 5,079 cases, in 1973. However, the caseload in 1983 was exactly the same as it was ten years earlier.

One student of the trend in Supreme Court caseloads has speculated about the causes of the leveling off in workload after 1973. He concludes that

> there is no way to determine if this marks a fundamental (long-term) change in caseload pattern or not. However, it does stand out as a variation and there may be some significance to it in the long term. What may have caused this fluctuation is certainly not apparent.

Perhaps economic and social conditions changed in such a way that filings were dampened. People may have found alternative arenas in which to settle some kinds of disputes, which the Court did not appear amenable to hearing. . . . It may also be that potential litigants perceived that the Court would not be persuadable to their particular policy demands. Thus, the Court was not a viable policymaking body for these groups and interests. Certainly the Burger Court has been relatively conservative on some matters that would have received a liberal treatment by the Warren Court. Thus, these interests may have been "forced" to seek alternative remedies. It is possible that many of the social and civil liberties demands that were raised in the 1950s and 1960s have been resolved favorably and fewer such demands are being made on the Court now that the essential foundation of rights and liberties has been established. This explanation does not seem intuitively correct as many interests would normally seek to build on the foundation begun in the Warren Court, expand on these initial victories to reach new rights for new segments of the population, and thus have to litigate a large variety of claims—perhaps more specific than during the Warren years.[2]

Perhaps the key point to remember about the workload of the Supreme Court is that for all practical purposes the tribunal has time to consider on the merits only a few hundred cases per year and to write full opinions in only about 150. These figures have remained fairly constant for well over 50 years. What this means is that most appeals to the Supreme Court will never be considered by the high tribunal; in fact, the number of signed opinions constitutes less than 3 percent of all cases presented to the Court. Many angry litigants may exclaim, "I'll take my case all the way to the Supreme Court." Maybe so, but the odds are against it.

Jurisdiction and Congressional Politics

In any discussion of the jurisdiction of the three levels of the federal judiciary, there is one political reality that cannot be overemphasized: to all intents and purposes, it is the Congress of the United States that really determines what sorts of issues and cases the courts will hear. And equally important, what the omnipotent Congress giveth, it may also taketh away. It is true that some judges and judicial scholars argue that Article III of the Constitution confers upon the judiciary a certain *inherent* jurisdiction on some matters, independent of the legislative will. Nevertheless it is still abundantly clear that the jurisdictional boundaries of the U.S. courts are a product of congressional judgments—determinations often flavored with the bittersweet spice of politics.

Table 2-3   Cases Commenced in the U.S. Supreme Court: 1963, 1973, and 1983

	1963	1973	1983	Percent Change 1963-1973	Percent Change 1973-1983
Appellate docket	1,017	2,480	2,170	143.8	−12.5
Miscellaneous docket	1,276	2,585	2,352	102.5	−9.0
Original docket	1	14	17	1,300.0	21.4
Total	2,294	5,079	5,079	121.4	0.0
Number of authorized judgeships	9	9	9		

Source: *Annual Reports of the Director of the Administrative Office of the U.S. Courts* (1963 and 1983); *Statistical Abstracts of the United States 1982-1983*, 103rd ed., 187.

As we shall see in subsequent chapters, Congress may advance a particular cause by giving courts the authority to hear cases in a public-policy realm that theretofore had been forbidden territory for the judiciary. For example, when Congress passed the Civil Rights Act of 1968, it gave judges the authority to penalize individuals who interfere with "any person because of his race, color, religion or national origin and because he is or has been . . . traveling in . . . interstate commerce" (18 U.S.C.A., Sec. 245). Prior to 1968 the courts had no jurisdiction over incidents that stemmed from interference by one person with another's right to travel. Likewise Congress may consider withdrawing certain subject matters from judicial purview. For instance, in the more conservative mood in which the United States has bathed itself since the 1970s, Congress has passed legislation that has sought to remove the authority of judges to order busing as a means of achieving school integration.

Perhaps the most vivid illustration of congressional power over federal court jurisdiction occurred just after the Civil War, and the awesome nature of this legislative prerogative haunts the judiciary to this day. On February 5, 1867, Congress empowered the federal courts to grant habeas corpus to individuals imprisoned in violation of their constitutional rights. The Supreme Court was authorized to hear appeals of such cases. William McCardle was incarcerated by the military government of Mississippi for being in alleged violation of the Reconstruction laws. McCardle was alleged to have published "incendiary and libelous" articles that attacked his "unlawful restraint by military force."

He sought relief in the circuit court but it was denied. He then appealed to the Supreme Court, which agreed to take the case.

After the arguments had been made before the High Court (but prior to a decision), Congress got into the act. Its antisouthern majority feared that the Court would use the *McCardle* case as a vehicle to strike down all or part of the Reconstruction Acts—something Congress had no intention of permitting. And so, over President Andrew Johnson's veto, the following statute was enacted: "That so much of the act approved February 5, 1867 [as] authorized an appeal from the judgment of the Circuit Court to the Supreme Court of the United States, or the exercise of any such jurisdiction by said Supreme Court, on appeals which have been, or may hereafter be taken, [is] hereby repealed." Thus, while the Court was in the very process of deciding the case, Congress removed the subject matter from the federal docket. And was all this strictly legal and constitutional? Yes, indeed. Stunned by Congress's action but obedient to the clear strictures of the Constitution, the Court limply ruled that McCardle's appeal must now "be dismissed for want of jurisdiction." [3]

In other words, while discussing what courts do or may do, we must not lose sight of the commanding reality that the jurisdiction of U.S. courts is established by "the United States of America in Congress assembled."

Judicial Self-Restraint

To this point we have examined what courts have been authorized to do under the U.S. legal and judicial system; we have stressed that Congress is primarily responsible for such authorizations. We will now look at the other side of the coin—at the activities that judges are forbidden, or at least discouraged, from doing. These "forbidden activities" deal not so much with technical matters of jurisdiction but with the broader term that courts call *justiciability*—that is, the question of whether judges in our system *ought* to hear or refrain from hearing certain types of disputes. It is only by exploring both sides of the demarcation line between prescribed and proscribed activity that we can acquire insight into the role and function of the federal judiciary. In the following sections we shall look at ten separate aspects of judicial self-restraint, ten principles that serve to check and contain the power of American federal judges.[4] These maxims originate in a variety of sources—the Constitution, acts of Congress, the common law tradition—and whenever possible we shall indicate their roots and the nature of their evolution. Some apply more to the Supreme Court than to the appeals and trial courts, as we shall note.

A Definite Controversy Must Exist

The U.S. Constitution states that "the judicial Power shall extend to all *Cases*, in Law and Equity, arising under this Constitution, the Laws of the United States, and Treaties made . . . under their Authority" (Article III, Section 2). [Emphasis added.] The key word here is *cases*. Since 1789 the federal courts have chosen to interpret the term in its most literal sense—that is, that there must be an actual controversy between legitimate adversaries who have met all the technical, legal standards to institute a suit. The dispute must involve the protection of a meaningful, nontrivial right or the prevention or redress of a wrong that directly affects the parties to the suit. There are two corollaries to this general principle that breathe a little life into its rather abstract-sounding admonitions.

The first is that the federal courts do not render advisory opinions— that is, rulings about hypothetical situations. A dispute must be real and current before a court will agree to accept it for adjudication. Let us look at an example in which the Court refused to involve itself in a dispute because the facts and would-be parties were not considered "real." In 1902 Congress passed a law allocating certain pieces of land to the Cherokee Indians. Because such disbursements often stimulate a good deal of questions about property rights, Congress sought to head off any possible disputes over land by authorizing certain land recipients to bring suits against the U.S. government in the court of claims, with appeal to the Supreme Court. They were permitted to do so "on their own behalf and on behalf of all other Cherokee citizens" who received land "to determine the validity of any acts of Congress passed since the said act." Stripped of the legalese, the law thus said: "If you have any hypothetical questions about how the law might affect anyone, just sue the United States, and the courts will answer these questions for you." The Supreme Court politely but pointedly said, "We don't do that sort of thing; we settle only real, actual cases or controversies." The act of Congress was found to be nothing more

> than an attempt to provide for judicial determination, final in this court, of the constitutional validity of an act of Congress. [It] is true the United States is made a defendant to this action, but *it has no interest adverse to the claimants.* The object is not to assert a property right as against the government, or to demand compensation for alleged wrongs because of action on its part. . . . In a legal sense the judgement [amounts] to no more than an expression of opinion upon the validity of the [1902 act]. If such actions as are here attempted [are] sustained, the result will be that this court, instead of keeping within the limits of judicial power, and deciding cases or controversies arising between opposing parties, [will] be required to give opinions in the nature of

advice concerning legislative action—a function never conferred upon it by the Constitution. [Emphasis added.][5]

A second corollary of the general principle is that the parties to the suit must have proper *standing*. This notion deals with the matter of *who* may bring litigation to court. While there are many aspects to the term *standing*, the most prominent component is that the person bringing suit must have suffered (or be immediately about to suffer) a direct and significant injury. As a general rule, a litigant cannot bring a claim on behalf of others (except for parents of minor children, or in special types of suits called *class actions*). In addition, the alleged injury must be personalized and immediate—not part of some generalized complaint. Again, a real-life example brings this down to earth.

In 1974 a case reached the Supreme Court in which a group of anti-Vietnam war protesters sued the secretaries of defense, the Army, the Navy, and the Air Force. They asked that members of Congress be enjoined from serving in the Armed Forces Reserve. Their claim was based on the Constitutional stricture that "no Person holding any Office under the United States shall be a Member of either House during his continuance in Office" (Article I, Section 6). The members of Congress who were officers in the reserve were clearly in violation of the Constitution; no one ever seemed to question this fact. But where was the injury that would enable these particular litigants to make a court case out of the violation? The antiwar group contended that members of Congress who held a reservist position under control of the executive branch might be subject to undue influence by the president. Also, reserve membership was said to place upon members of Congress possible inconsistent obligations that might cause them to violate their duty faithfully to perform either or both of their two functions. As citizens, the protesters were concerned, and they asked the Court to grant them standing to sue. "No," replied the Court in a six-to-three ruling. Despite the fact that an apparent violation of both the letter and spirit of the Constitution was in progress, no one was directly or personally injured enough so as to create sufficient standing to sue. As the decision noted,

the Court [has] held that whatever else the "case or controversy" requirement embodied, its essence is a requirement of "injury in fact." This personal stake is what the Court has consistently held enables a complainant authoritatively to present to a court a complete perspective upon the adverse consequences flowing from the specific set of facts undergirding his grievance. . . . [All] citizens, of course, share equally an interest in the independence of each branch of government. In some fashion, every provision of the Constitution was meant to serve the interests of all. [But the] proposition that all constitutional provisions are enforceable by any citizen simply because citizens are ultimate beneficiaries of those provisions has no boundaries.[6]

Thus we have one great principle of judicial self-restraint, of what federal judges may not do. They may not decide an issue unless there is an actual case or controversy. From this it follows that they do not consider abstract, hypothetical questions, nor do they take a case unless the would-be litigants can demonstrate direct and substantial personal injury. This principle is an important one because it means that judges are not free to wander about the countryside like medieval knights slaying all the evil dragons they encounter. They may rule only on concrete issues brought by truly injured parties directly affected by the facts of a case.

A Plea Must Be Specific

Another constraint upon the federal judiciary is that judges will hear no case on the merits unless the petitioner is first able to cite a specific part of the Constitution as the basis of the plea. For example, the First Amendment forbids government from making any laws "prohibiting the free exercise" of religion. Recently Robert Dale Callahan from Santa Rosa, California, won a lawsuit against state and federal authorities who insisted that a Social Security number be issued to Callahan's daughter. Social Security identification is required for those wishing to receive welfare benefits, which Callahan had requested for his child. The father, a man of fundamentalist religious beliefs, argued that any universal numbers used to designate human beings are "the mark of the beast" as described in the Bible's Book of Revelations. In other words, Callahan argued, the government regulation imposed an unreasonable burden on the free exercise of his religion. The government of course responded that an exemption for Callahan's daughter would "impede the goal of government efficiency." [7] Despite what we may think about the substantive wisdom of the court's ruling in favor of Callahan, there is little doubt that the specific criteria for securing judicial review had been met: the Constitution specifically forbids the government from prohibiting the free exercise of one's religion; the litigant in question held "serious religious belief" that the government regulation struck at the very heart of the values and practices of his faith.

On the other hand, if one went into court and contended that a particular law or official action "violated the spirit of the Bills of Rights" or "offended the values of the Founding Fathers," a judge would dismiss the proceeding on the spot. For if judges were free to give concrete, substantive meaning to vague generalities such as these, there would be little check on what they could do. Who is to say what is the "spirit of the

Bill of Rights" or the collective motivation of those who hammered out the Constitution? Judges who were free to roam too far from the specific clauses and strictures of the constitutional document itself would soon become judicial despots.

Despite what we have just said, we must also concede that in the real world this principle is not so simple and clear-cut as it sounds, because the Constitution contains many clauses that are open to a wide variety of interpretations. For example, the Constitution forbids Congress from creating any law "respecting an establishment of religion," but few can agree exactly what the term *establishment* means. The Eighth Amendment prohibits "excessive bail" for criminal defendants, but what is *excessive?* The states are forbidden, in the Fourteenth Amendment, Section 1, from abridging "the privileges and immunities of citizens of the United States," but who is to say what these privileges and immunities are? The Constitution gives hardly a clue. Our point is that although petitioners must cite a particular constitutional clause as the basis for their plea—as opposed to some totally ambiguous concept—there are nevertheless enough vague clauses in the Constitution itself to give federal judges plenty of room to maneuver and make policy.

Beneficiaries May Not Sue

A third aspect of judicial self-restraint is that a case will be rejected out of hand if it is apparent that the petitioner has been the beneficiary of a law or an official action that he or she has subsequently chosen to challenge. Judges do not look kindly on those who want to have their cake and eat it, too. Let us suppose that Farmer Brown had long been a member of the Soil Bank Program (designed to cut back on grain surpluses); under the program he agreed to take part of his land out of production, and periodically was paid a subsidy by the federal government. After years as a participant he learns that his lazy, ne'er-do-well neighbors, the Joneses, are also drawing regular payments for letting their farmland lie fallow. The idea that his neighbors are getting something for nothing starts to offend Farmer Brown, and he begins to harbor grave doubts about the constitutionality of the whole program. Armed with a host of reasons why Congress had acted illegally, Brown challenges the legality of the Soil Bank Act in the local federal district court. As soon as it is brought to the judge's attention that Farmer Brown had himself been a member of the program and had gained financially from it, the suit is dismissed: one may not benefit from a particular governmental endeavor or official action and subsequently attack it in court.

The Supreme Court Rules on Legal—Not Factual—Questions

In the real world it is often very difficult to tell whether a particular legal dispute concerns who did what to whom (the facts of the case) or how one is to weigh and assess a series of events (the legal interpretation of the facts). Nevertheless a working proposition of Supreme Court practice is that it will not hear cases if the grounds for appeal are that the trial judge or jury wrongly amassed and identified the basic factual elements of the case. It is not that trial judges and juries always do a perfect job of making factual determinations. Rather, there is the belief that they are closer, sensorially and temporally, to the actual parties and physical evidence of the case. The odds are, so the theory goes, that they will do a much better job of making factual assessments than would an appellate body reading only a stale transcript of the case some months or years after the trial. On the other hand, legal matters—that is, which law(s) one is to apply to the facts of the case, or how one is to assess the facts in light of the prevailing law—are appropriate for appellate review. On such issues collegial, or multijudge, appellate bodies presumably have a legitimate and better capacity "to say what the law is," as Chief Justice John Marshall put it. Let us look at an illustration.

If X were convicted of a crime and the sole grounds for his appeal were that the judge and jury had mistakenly found him guilty (that is, incorrectly sifted and identified the facts), the Supreme Court would dismiss the case out of hand. However, let us assume that X provided evidence that he had asked for and been refused counsel during his FBI interrogation and that his confession was therefore illegal. At trial the district judge ruled that the Sixth Amendment (providing for "the Assistance of Counsel") did not apply to X's interrogation by the FBI. The defendant argued to the contrary. Such a contention would be appealable to the Supreme Court because the issue is one of legal—not factual—interpretation.

The fact that the High Court is restricted to interpreting the law and not to identifying and assembling facts is one additional check on the scope of the Court's decision making.

The Supreme Court Is Not Bound by Precedents

If the High Court is free to overturn or circumvent past and supposedly controlling precedents when it decides a case, this might appear to be an argument for judicial activism—not restraint. In fact, however, this practice must be placed in the restraint column. If the Supreme Court were totally bound by the dictates of its prior rulings, it would have very little flexibility. It would not be free to "pull in its horns" when discretion advised a cautious approach to a problem; it would not have liberty to withdraw from a confrontation in which it might not be in the nation's or the Court's interest to engage. By occasionally allowing itself the freedom to overrule a past decision or to turn a blind eye toward a precedent that would seem to be controlling, the Supreme Court carves out for itself a corner of safety to which it can retreat if need be. When wisdom dictates that the Court bend with the wind in time of storm or at least to confront a new situation with an open mind, this principle of self-restraint is readily plucked from the judicial kit bag.

Other Remedies Must Be Exhausted

There is another principle of self-restraint that often frustrates the anxious litigant but is essential to the orderly administration of justice: the federal courts will not accept a case until all other remedies, legal and administrative, have been exhausted. While this caveat is often associated with the U.S. Supreme Court, it is in fact a working principle for virtually all American judicial tribunals—namely, that one must work up the ladder with one's legal petitions. In its simplest form this doctrine means that federal cases must first be heard by the U.S. trial courts, then reviewed by one of the appellate tribunals, and finally heard by the U.S. Supreme Court. This orderly procedure of events must and will occur despite the "importance" of the case or of the petitioners who filed it. For instance, in 1952 President Truman seized the American steel mills in order to prevent a pending strike which he believed would imperil the war effort in the Korean conflict; both labor and management were suddenly told they were now working for Uncle Sam. The mill owners were furious and immediately brought suit, charging that the president had abused the powers of his office. A national legal-political crisis erupted. One might think that the Supreme Court would immediately grasp a case of this magnitude. Not so. In the traditional and orderly fashion of American federal justice, the controversy first went to the local district court in Washington, D.C., just as if it were the most run-of-the mill dispute. After the district court had ruled, the case was appealed to the circuit court, and then—and only then—did the nation's highest tribunal receive the chance to sink its teeth into this hearty piece of judicial meat.

Exhaustion of remedies refers to possible administrative relief as well as to adherence to the three-tiered judicial hierarchy. Such relief might be in the form of an appeal to an administrative officer, a hearing before a board or committee, or formal consideration of a matter by a legislative body. Let us consider a hypothetical illustration. Professor D. W. Brady is denied tenure at a staunchly conservative state university. He is told that tenure was not granted because of his poor teaching record and lack of scholarly publications. He, however, contends it is in retaliation for his having founded the nearby Sunshine Socialist Society, a nudist colony for gay atheists. While he has the option of a hearing before the university's Grievance Committee, he declines it saying, "It would do no good; it would just be a waste of time." Rather, he takes his case immediately to the local federal district court, claiming that his Fourteenth Amendment rights have been violated. When the case is brought before the trial court, the judge will say in effect to Professor Brady: "Before I will even look at this matter, you must first take your case before the official, duly established administrative Grievance Committee at your university. It doesn't matter whether you believe that you will win or lose your petition before the committee. You must establish your record there and avail yourself of all the administrative appeals and remedies that your institution has provided. If you are then still dissatisfied with the outcome, you may at that time invoke the power of the federal district courts."

Thus, judicial restraint means that judges do not jump immediately into every controversy that appears to be important or that strikes their fancy. The restrained and orderly administration of justice requires that before any court may hear a case all administrative and inferior legal remedies must first be exhausted.

Courts Do Not Decide 'Political Questions'

U.S. judges are often called upon to determine the winner of a contested election, to rule on the legality of a newly drawn electoral district, or to involve themselves in voting rights cases. How then can one say that "political questions" are out of bounds for the American judiciary? The answer lies in the narrow, singular use of the word *political*. To U.S. judges the executive and the legislative branches of government are political in that they are elected by the people for the purpose of making public policy. The judiciary, in contrast, was not designed by the Founding Fathers to be an instrument manifesting the popular will and is therefore not political. According to this line of reasoning, then, a political question is one that ought properly to be resolved by one of the other two branches of government (even though it may appear before the courts wrapped in judicial clothing). When judges determine that something is a political question and therefore not appropriate for judicial review, what they are saying in effect is this: "You litigants may have couched your plea in judicial terminology, but under our form of government, issues such as this ought properly to be decided at the ballot box, in the legislative halls, or in the chambers of the executive."

For example, when the state of Oregon gave its citizens the right to vote on popular statewide referendums and initiatives around the turn of the century, the Pacific States Telephone and Telegraph Company objected.[8] (The company feared that voters would bypass the more business-oriented legislature and pass laws restricting its rates and profits.) The company claimed that by permitting citizens directly to enact legislation, the state has "been reduced to a democracy," whereas Article IV, Section 4, of the Constitution guarantees to each state "a Republican Form of Government"—a term that supposedly means that laws are to be made only by the elected representatives of the people—not by the citizens directly. Pacific Telephone demanded that the Court take action. Opting for discretion rather than valor, the High Court refused to rule on the merits of the case, declaring the issue to be a "political question." The Court reasoned that since Article IV primarily prescribes the duties of Congress, then it follows that the Founders wanted Congress—not the courts—to oversee the forms of government in the several states. In other words the Court was being asked to invade the decision-making domain of one of the other (political) branches of government. And this it refused to do.

In recent decades perhaps the most important political/nonpolitical dispute has been over the matter of reapportionment of legislative districts. Prior to 1962 a majority on the Supreme Court refused to rule on the constitutionality of legislative districts with unequal populations, saying that such matters were "nonjusticiable" and that the Court dared not enter what Justice Frankfurter called "the political thicket." According to traditional Supreme Court thinking, the Founding Fathers wanted legislatures to redistrict themselves—perhaps with some gentle prodding from the electorate. However, with the Supreme Court's decision in *Baker v. Carr,* the majority began to do an about-face.[9] During the past two decades the Court has held in scores of cases that the equal-protection clause of the Fourteenth Amendment requires legislative districts to be of equal population size and furthermore that the courts would see to it that this mandate is carried out.

Although the line between a taboo political question and a proper justiciable issue is not always a clear one, this doctrine provides the courts with still another opportunity and impetus to exercise restraint.

The Burden of Proof Is on the Petitioner

Another weighty principle of self-restraint is the general agreement among the nation's jurists that an individual who would challenge the constitutionality of a statute bears the burden of proof. This is just a different way of saying that laws and official deeds are all presumed to be legal unless and until proven otherwise by a preponderance of evidence. The question of who has the burden of proof is of keen interest to lawyers because in effect it means: which side has the biggest job to perform in the courtroom? and which party must assume the lion's share of the burden of convincing the court—or lose the case entirely? Thus, if one were attacking a particular statute, one would have to do more than demonstrate that it was "questionable" or "of doubtful constitutionality"; one must persuade the court that the evidence against the law was clear-cut and overwhelming—not often an easy task. In giving the benefit of the doubt to a statute or an executive act, judges have yet another area in which to exercise restraint.

Laws Are Overturned on the Narrowest Grounds Only

Sometimes it becomes clear to a judge during a trial that the strictures of the Constitution have indeed been offended by a legislative or executive act. Even here, however, there is ample opportunity to proceed with caution. There are two common ways in which judges may act in a restrained manner even when they must reach for the blue pencil.

First, a judge may have the option of invalidating an official action on what is called statutory rather than constitutional grounds. Statutory invalidation means that a judge overturns an official's action because the official acted beyond the authority delegated to him or her by the law. Such a ruling has the function of saving the law itself while still nullifying the official's misdeed.

Let us look at a hypothetical example. Suppose that Congress continues to authorize postal officials to seize all obscene nude photographs that are shipped through the mails. A photographer attempts to mail pictures taken at his "art studio," but the pictures are seized by postal officials. The photographer protests that the statute violates his First Amendment rights and the case is eventually taken to the federal courts. Assuming that the judges are generally sympathetic to the position of the photographer, they have two basic options. They may declare the statute to be in violation of the Constitution and thus null and void, or they may select another stance that permits them to have the cake of judicial restraint and eat it, too. They may decide that the law itself passes constitutional muster, but that the postal official in question mistakenly decided that the nude photos were obscene. Thus the statute is preserved and a direct confrontation between the courts and Congress is averted, but the court is able to give the petitioner virtually all of what he wants. This is an example of deciding a case on statutory rather than constitutional grounds.

There is a second method whereby restraint may be exercised under this general principle: judges may, if possible, invalidate only that portion of a law they find constitutionally defective rather than overturn the entire statute. For instance, in 1963 Congress passed the Higher Education Facilities Act, which provided construction grants for college buildings. Part of the law declared that for a 20-year period no part of the newly built structures could be used for "sectarian instruction, religious worship, or the programs of a divinity school." Since church-related universities as well as public institutions benefited from the act, the entire law was challenged in court as being in violation of the establishment of religion clause of the First Amendment. The Supreme Court determined that the basic thrust of the law did not violate the Constitution, but it did find the "20-year clause" to be objectionable. After all, the Court reasoned, most buildings last a good deal longer than two decades, and a building constructed at public expense could thus house religious activities during the vast majority of its lifetime. Rather than strike down the entire act, however, the court majority merely inserted the word *never* for the phrase *20 years*.[10] Thus the baby was not thrown out with the constitutional bath water and judicial restraint was maintained.

No Rulings Are Made on the 'Wisdom' of Legislation

This final aspect of judicial self-restraint is probably the least understood by the public, the most often violated by the courts, and yet potentially the greatest harness on judicial activism in existence. What this admonition means, if followed strictly, is that the only basis for declaring a law or an official action unconstitutional is that it literally violates the Constitution on its face. Statutes do not offend the Constitution merely because they are unfair, are fiscally wasteful, or constitute bad public policy. Official actions can be struck down only if they step across the boundaries clearly set forth by the Founding Fathers. If taken truly to heart, this means that judges and justices are not free to invoke their own personal notions of right and wrong or of good and bad public policy when they examine the constitutionality of legislation.

A keen expression of this phenomenon of judicial self-restraint is found in Justice Potter Stewart's dissenting opinion in the case of *Griswold v. Connecticut.* The Court majority had struck down the state's law which forbid the use of contraceptive devices or the dissemination of birth control information. Stewart said, in effect, that the law was bad, but that its weaknesses didn't make it unconstitutional:

> Since 1897 Connecticut has had on its books a law which forbids the use of contraceptives by anyone. I think this is an uncommonly silly law. As a practical matter, the law is obviously unenforceable, except in the oblique context of the present case. . . . But we are not asked in this case to say whether we think this law is unwise, or even asinine. We

are asked to hold that it violates the United States Constitution. And that I cannot do.[11]

Another spinoff of this principle is that a law may be passed that all agree is good and wise but that is nevertheless unconstitutional; conversely, a statute may legalize the commission of an official deed that all know to be bad and dangerous but that still does not offend the Constitution. Permitting the police to dispose of "known criminals" without benefit of trial would probably save taxpayers a good deal of money and also reduce the crime rate, but it would be a clear, prima facie violation of the Constitution. On the other hand, a congressional tax on every act of human procreation might be constitutionally permissible but would be a very unwise piece of legislation—not to mention difficult to enforce. Thus when speaking of laws or official acts, the adjectives *goodness* and *constitutionality* are no more synonymous than are *badness* and *unconstitutionality.*

While few legal scholars would disagree with what we have just said, virtually all would point out that the principle of not ruling on the "wisdom" of a law is difficult to follow in the real world and is often honored in the breach. This is so because the Constitution, a rather brief document, is silent on many areas of public life and contains a number of phrases and admonitions that are open to a variety of interpretations—a theme that we shall touch upon continuously throughout this text. For instance, the Constitution says that Congress may regulate interstate commerce. But what exactly is commerce, and how extensive does it have to be before it is of an "interstate" character? As human beings, judges have differed in the way they have responded to this question. The Constitution guarantees a person accused of a crime the right to a defense attorney. But does this right continue if one appeals a guilty verdict and, if so, for how many appeals? Strict constructionists and loose constructionists have responded differently to these queries.

Still in all, despite the inevitable intrusion of judges' personal values into their interpretation of many portions of the Constitution, virtually every jurist subscribes to the general principle that laws can be invalidated only if they offend the Constitution—not the personal fancies of the judges.

Summary

The focus of this chapter has been on what the federal courts are supposed to do and on what they must refrain from doing. They adjudicate cases that come within their lawful original or appellate jurisdiction. Federal district courts hear U.S. criminal cases and civil suits that deal with federal questions, diversity of citizenship matters, prisoners' petitions, and any other issues authorized by Congress. The appellate courts, having no original jurisdiction whatever, take appeals from the district courts and from numerous administrative and regulatory agencies. The U.S. Supreme Court has original jurisdiction over suits between two or more states and in cases where ambassadors or public ministers are parties to a suit. Its appellate jurisdiction, regulated entirely by Congress, permits it to hear appeals from the circuit courts and from state courts of last resort. Such appeals can be "as of right," in the form of highly discretionary writs of certiorari, or by certification from one of the appeals courts.

Under our legal system federal courts are not to adjudicate questions unless there is a real case or controversy at stake, and all pleas must be based on a *specific* portion of the Constitution. Judges are also to dismiss suits in which a petitioner is challenging a law from which he or she has benefited. The Supreme Court may rule only on matters of law—not on factual questions. Not being bound entirely by its precedents, the Supreme Court is free to exercise flexibility and restraint if it wishes to do so. All courts insist that litigants exhaust every legal and administrative remedy before a case will be decided. All federal courts in America are to eschew "political questions" and insist that the burden of proof rests on those who contend that a law or official action is unconstitutional. If judges must nullify an act of Congress or of the president, they are to do so on the narrowest grounds possible. Finally, courts ought not rule on the wisdom or desirability of a law but are to strike down legislation only if it clearly violates the letter of the Constitution.

Notes

1. *The Third Branch* 16 (September 1984): 3.
2. William P. McLauchlan, *Federal Court Caseloads* (New York: Praeger, 1984), 69.
3. *Ex Parte McCardle*, 74 U.S. (7 Wall.) 506 (1869).
4. For our discussion of the many aspects of judicial self-restraint we acknowledge our debt to Henry J. Abraham, on whose classic analysis of the subject we greatly relied. See *The Judicial Process*, 4th ed. (New York: Oxford University Press, 1980), chap. 9.
5. *Muskrat v. United States*, 219 U.S. 346 (1911).
6. *Schlesinger v. Reservists Committee to Stop the War*, 418 U.S. 208 (1974).

7. William Overend, "Man Who Believes Social Security Numbers Devilish Wins Legal Appeal," *Houston Chronicle,* July 7, 1984, 1:5.
8. *Pacific States Telephone & Telegraph v. Oregon,* 223 U.S. 118 (1912).
9. *Baker v. Carr,* 369 U.S. 186 (1962).
10. *Tilton v. Richardson,* 403 U.S. 672 (1971).
11. *Griswold v. Connecticut,* 381 U.S. 479 (1965).

Administrative and Staff Support in the Federal Judiciary

3

The two previous chapters have discussed the organization and jurisdiction of the federal courts. A closely related topic is judicial administration, or the concern for day-to-day operation of the courts, which includes a wide range of activities—some would say anything having to do with the judicial process. At the least, "judicial administration involves two broad areas: the management of court organization and personnel and the processing of litigation." [1] Because those charged with managing the courts and overseeing the flow of litigation are obviously interested in improving the methods by which their tasks may be accomplished, reform has historically been closely associated with court management.

In this chapter we focus on the daily operation of U.S. federal courts, a task that requires a myriad of personnel. While judges are the most visible actors in the federal judicial system, a large supporting cast is also at work. Their efforts help free judges to perform their most important job—to decide cases. Some members of the support team, such as law clerks, may work specifically for one judge. Others—for example, U.S. magistrates—are assigned to a particular court. Still others may be employees of an agency, such as the Administrative Office of the United States Courts, that serves the entire federal judicial system. The chapter will look at the judicial reform movement first and then examine the administrative and policy-making agencies of the court system. It will conclude with a discussion of major judicial support staffs, including key participants from the Justice Department—the solicitor general, U.S. attorneys, and assistant U.S. attorneys.

A Brief History of the
Judicial Administration Movement

The Judiciary Act of 1789:
Decentralization and Individualism

To understand the problems associated with the development of an effective administrative system for the federal courts we must once again consider the nature of the judicial system created by the first Congress. A leading student of federal judicial administration has said:

> From the Act of 1789 and subsequent measures pertaining to the structure of the federal judiciary emerged three important characteristics: independence, decentralization, and individualism. These characteristics were particularly apparent in judicial administration.[2]

Let us look for a moment at the characteristic of independence. Article III of the Constitution established the judiciary as one of the three separate branches of the federal government. In Chapter 1 we noted that judges of the constitutional courts serve during a period of good behavior (in reality, life tenure) and cannot have their salaries reduced while they hold office. The independence from Congress and the president that the Constitution guarantees has helped promote the administrative autonomy of individual judges.

The Judiciary Act of 1789 created a three-tier federal court system. The two lower levels were set up in a manner that instilled a high degree of decentralization. The geographical jurisdiction of the three original circuit courts coincided with the boundaries of several states, while the district courts were contained within the single states. In the circuit courts which consisted of two members of the Supreme Court and one district judge residing within the circuit, the district judge assumed the major responsibility for developing the agenda of these courts. Further, the role of the Senate in the appointment process (described in Chapter 4) has meant that lower court judges are likely to be recruited from the area in which they will eventually serve. Once on the bench they may continue to be influenced to some extent by local customs and traditions.[3]

Independence and decentralization both contribute to individualism among judges. Because judges have the constitutional protection of life tenure, they do not face the political and electoral pressures that confront members of Congress and the president. (They may be removed from office through the impeachment process, but this is not generally a significant threat.) As a result, judges often are freer than legislators and the executive to express their individual views. Geographical separateness also promotes autonomy.

At first glance, the Judiciary Act of 1789 appears to have established a hierarchy in which the Supreme Court, at the top, directly supervises the lower federal judges. However, a close analysis of the legislation reveals that no court was given significant supervisory powers over judges. Instead, Congress "created a hierarchical system of courts, not of judges." [4] Thus even within the judicial structure itself judges had a good deal of independence; higher-court justices were not their lower-court brothers' keepers.

The impact of the Judiciary Act of 1789 was most evident in single-judge federal district courts. Until the Court of Appeals Act of 1891, such courts disposed of a major share of all litigation in the federal courts. The situation has been described in the following terms:

> Isolated and sometimes underworked district judges thus stood at the crossroads of the federal judicial system. In an era of limited federal jurisdiction, mastery of the law lay well within their grasp. They became lions on their relatively remote thrones. However they might find or make the law, delay or accelerate the flow of cases, reward or punish friends and foes with patronage and favorable bench rulings, concerned none but themselves. Only appellate court reversals on points of law and impeachment for crimes and misdemeanors limited their conduct. [5]

The independence of district judges fostered an administrative autonomy that existed well into the twentieth century. Throughout the 1880s Congress created new federal district courts to accommodate a growing population and the entry of new states into the Union. When a new court was created, it became an autonomous administrative unit. Most of the new district courts were presided over by a single judge who was the master of his or her court and possessed complete discretion over patronage. Reinforcing the early administrative autonomy was the fact that district judges could not hold court in districts other than their own. Their districts were established within state boundaries and the judges were confined to them. It was not until the mid-1800s that Congress passed legislation allowing limited assignment of a district judge to another district within his or her circuit or to a contiguous circuit for the express purpose of assisting a sick or disabled judge.

Thus the nature of the judiciary itself was the primary obstacle to the formation of an administrative system in the nineteenth century. However, events taking place outside the courtroom provided the chief impetus for reform in the twentieth century.

The Move Toward Reform

Throughout the 1800s the judicial heritage of independence, decentralization, and individualism reigned supreme. By the end of the nineteenth century, however, America had changed. Industrialization helped transform the United States from a small, rural society to a large, urban, technologically complex one. The changes created new legal relationships: between landlords and tenants, merchants and consumers, and employers and workers. The uncertainties over these new legal relationships more and more frequently found their way into court in the form of lawsuits. Attorneys and judges were often forced to become specialists in specific subject areas. Thus, social and economic development in the early twentieth century "helped produce a greater sense of professionalism and heightened specialization within the legal community." [6]

The early 1900s also saw a major reform effort known as the Progressive movement, which addressed a variety of societal problems brought about by urbanization and industrialization. Judicial reform was one aspect of the Progressive movement and "attention to judicial administration throughout this century has been influenced heavily by this early Progressive legacy." [7]

The Progressive movement attracted many famous Americans; among them was Roscoe Pound, a leading judicial-reform advocate and dean of the Harvard Law School. Pound, recognized as one of the founders of the judicial administration movement, was critical of court organization and procedures for handling civil cases. Cumbersome procedures and defective judicial administration were only part of the problem, however. A growing number of federal regulations created new litigation for the already-congested federal courts. As a result, case backlogs developed and judicial reformers became increasingly alarmed at what they called "delayed justice." Reformers such as Pound and William Howard Taft stepped up their demands for efficiency, integration, unification, and coordination in the federal judicial system. These "slogans of the judicial-reform movement . . . were part of a broader campaign for the adoption of 'businesslike' methods in government." [8] More specifically, judicial reformers have focused on two major objectives: changes in the organization of courts and the development of auxiliary agencies within the judicial branch.

Taft, the former U.S. president who became chief justice in 1921, worked tirelessly for these objectives. He was successful in obtaining congressional creation of an auxiliary agency: the Conference of Senior Circuit Judges (later to become the Judicial Conference of the United

States). Taft was also instrumental in the passage of the Judges Bill of 1925, which established the basic scheme of appellate review under which our federal courts now operate.

Perhaps following the precedent established by Taft, more recent chief justices have also accepted a responsibility to help meet the administrative needs of the federal courts. Earl Warren, for example, was involved in the creation of the Federal Judicial Center in 1967. Prior to his retirement, Warren said that the "most important job of the courts today is not to decide what the substantive law is, but to work out ways to move the cases along and relieve court congestion." [9] The current chief justice, Warren Burger, has a keen interest in judicial administration, frequently addressing both the legal profession and the general public on a wide variety of topics such as court congestion, the creation of new courts, legal training, and prison reform. Given these developments, it is understandable that one judicial scholar would say, "The most important change in the judicial branch of the federal government during the past half century has been the creation of a number of administrative structures linked to, but not part of, the federal courts." [10]

In the next section we will discuss in detail some of the major administrative structures that serve the federal judiciary. Following that, our focus will shift to the personnel support for the judges and courts.

Major Administrative Support Structures

Judicial Conference of the United States

The central administrative policy-making organization of the federal judicial system is the Judicial Conference of the United States. The conference—composed of the chief justice of the Supreme Court as the presiding member, the chief judges of each of the judicial circuits, and one district judge from each circuit—meets semiannually for two-day sessions. A variety of topics are dealt with, such as establishing policy on the transfer of judges within circuits, recommending new judgeships, increasing judicial salaries, and developing budgets for court operations. Recommendations generally take the form of proposed legislation that is ultimately transmitted to Congress. The conference's "most important function is the promulgation and revision of the various rules of federal civil and criminal procedure. . . ." [11] At its fall 1984 meeting, for example, the Judicial Conference approved two important changes in the Federal Rules of Criminal Procedure. One rule change gives state employees who are cooperating in the enforcement of federal laws access to federal grand jury materials. Another modification authorizes federal courts to permit disclosure to state officials of information concerning possible violation of state laws.[12]

Quite obviously, a group of judges meeting twice a year for two days cannot hope to accomplish a great deal. Therefore, a network of about 25 committees has been established to perform the substantive work of the conference. Groups such as the Judicial Conference Committee on the Budget and the Judicial Conference Committee on Court Administration, to name just two, meet for several days throughout the year. Working on its particular specialty, each committee submits a report on its findings or recommendations to the full conference.

The chief justice appoints the members of each committee from among judges and lawyers throughout the twelve circuits. In spite of the long hours and unpaid labor involved, positions on the committees are coveted. A committee appointment is seen as a status symbol through which judges gain esteem among their peers.[13]

Thus judges themselves play the major role in developing policy for the federal judiciary. Because the Judicial Conference of the United States involves district and circuit judges in the process of national judicial administration, however, the system has not moved significantly toward the type of centralized administration favored by many judicial reformers.

Administrative Office of the U.S. Courts

The day-to-day affairs of the federal courts are managed by the Administrative Office of the U.S. Courts, an agency established by Congress in 1939 as a consequence of President Franklin D. Roosevelt's attacks upon the Supreme Court two years earlier. The federal courts generally lost prestige and political support during the great depression of the 1930s. The problem was aggravated by the fact that the conservative Supreme Court declared unconstitutional much of Roosevelt's New Deal legislation. Following his reelection in 1936, Roosevelt put forth his famous plan to "pack" the Court with additional justices who, presumably, would rule in favor of congressional legislation. He also accused the High Court of administrative inefficiency, a criticism that carried over to the entire federal judiciary.

As a solution to the problem of administrative inefficiency, FDR proposed new legislation to transfer judicial administration from the Department of Justice (an agency of the executive branch) to the courts themselves. The Roosevelt proposal called for the creation of a national court administrator who would be appointed by the chief justice and would have absolute authority to manage the judicial system.

Given the judiciary's heritage of independence, decentralization, and individualism, it is understandable that most judges objected to the plan for national control of judicial administration. Still, the judges were dissatisfied with the old system of court management and what they perceived as the Justice Department's failure to represent their interests in Congress.[14] A movement developed among federal judges and national court reformers to clean their own house, and a compromise plan for judicial administration was offered. The Administrative Office Act of 1939 was "the judiciary's substitute for the Court bill introduced by President Roosevelt in 1937." The legislation created the Administrative Office as an agency of the Judicial Conference, although its director is appointed by the Supreme Court and holds office at its pleasure. The Administrative Office's director, who answers to the Judicial Conference, is not at all like the powerful court administrator envisioned in the Roosevelt proposal. Neither the director nor the Administrative Office itself served the function of policy making; that duty still belongs to the Judicial Conference. Instead, the Administrative Office has been described as "the judiciary's housekeeping agency." [15]

The initial organization of the Administrative Office lends some insight into the functions that Congress expected the new agency to fulfill. First, it was expected to carry out the administrative duties then being performed by the Department of Justice. Second, it was expected to collect and report judicial statistics. Consequently, two divisions were created: the Division of Business Administration and the Division of Procedural Studies and Statistics. The former became the business or managerial agency of the federal judiciary, serving a number of staff functions for both the courts and the Judicial Conference. Several sections were established within this division to perform such specialized duties as (1) allotting authorized funds and supervising their expenditure, (2) providing estimates for judicial appropriations, (3) auditing the accounts of court personnel, (4) distributing supplies, (5) negotiating with other government agencies for court accommodations in federal buildings, and (6) maintaining judicial personnel records.

The Division of Procedural Studies and Statistics took on the job of collecting data on cases in federal courts. Initially, the division amassed data only on civil and bankruptcy cases, while the U.S. attorneys gathered data on criminal cases. Beginning in 1941, however, the Administrative Office assumed responsibility for collecting data on criminal cases as well.[16] This division was able to provide "case flow" statistics showing the relationship between the number and types of cases commenced and terminated. It also began to keep records on such matters as length of trials, causes of delay, selection and use of jurors, methods and effect of pretrial proceedings, and comparative times spent by judges in disposing of cases. These statistics, along with personal inspections, were used to prepare a picture of judicial business conditions in each district.

In the more than 40 years of its existence the Administrative Office has revised the initial organization to reflect its expanded duties for the federal judiciary. Figure 3-1 shows the current organization of the Administrative Office. As the figure indicates, there has been a considerable increase in the number of divisions. It should also be noted that some restructuring of the two original divisions has taken place.

The Administrative Office also serves a staff function for the Judicial Conference. In addition to providing statistical information to the conference's many committees, it acts as a reception center and clearinghouse for information and proposals directed to the Judicial Conference.

Closely related to the staff function is the Administrative Office's role as liaison for both the federal judicial system and the Judicial Conference. The Administrative Office serves as advocate for the judiciary in its dealings with Congress, the executive branch, individual judges, professional groups, and the general public. Especially important in this regard is the fact that the Administrative Office acts as the Judicial Conference's official representative in Congress, presenting the judiciary's budget proposals, requests for additional judgeships, suggestions for changes in court rules, and other key measures. Although the literature indicates that some early supporters of the Administrative Office envisioned it as the nucleus of a lobbying effort, it "generally has not been particularly powerful in obtaining money for the courts or congressional support for court proposals." [17]

One final service performed by the Administrative Office deserves brief mention. It has, from time to time, arranged seminars and institutes to help orient new judges. This function, however, is now primarily carried out by the agency to be discussed next.

The Federal Judicial Center

In 1967 Congress created the Federal Judicial Center as the research and development arm of the federal judiciary. The legislation made it clear that the new agency was not a part of the Administrative Office. Instead, it was established as a distinct institution within the judicial branch of the government. It was vested with an independent status so that it might more effectively, and objectively, carry out its responsibilities. Those duties fall generally into three categories: (1) conducting research on the federal courts, (2) making recommendations to improve the administration and management of the federal courts, and (3) developing educational and training programs for personnel of the judicial branch.

Figure 3-1 Administrative Office of the U.S. Courts

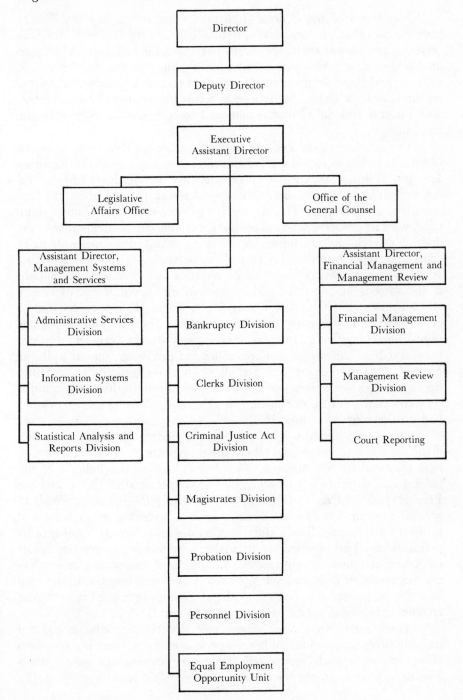

Source: Administrative Office of the U.S. Courts, December 1980.

The board of the Federal Judicial Center constitutes an advisory body for the center. It consists of the chief justice of the United States, who serves as permanent chair; the director of the Administrative Office, who also serves as a permanent member; two judges of the U.S. courts of appeals; and three judges of the U.S. district courts. The judges who serve on the board are elected for four-year terms by the Judicial Conference. The Federal Judicial Center is managed by a director appointed by the chief justice.

The activities of the Federal Judicial Center are wide-ranging, as we noted above. Let us consider its research role for a moment. The Research Division is given the primary responsibility for study of the federal courts.[18] The staff includes sociologists, social psychologists, political scientists, and lawyers. The Research Division resembles a small think tank, with its group of scholars bringing different areas of expertise to the division's work. Recent topics for study have included investigations of court-annexed arbitration, reviews of the psychological literature dealing with a jury's competency to evaluate complex fact situations, evaluations of the various management styles found in metropolitan district courts, and an analysis of the roles of magistrates in the district courts.

In addition to using its own staff, the Federal Judicial Center negotiates with private firms, law schools, and other government agencies for research on various judicial operations and problems. For example, the Mitre Corporation engaged in a study of court congestion for the center. Specific judges were given cases that differed in complexity; the technique was analyzed with an eye toward determining what effects the practice had on the court's calendar.[19]

The studies conducted by, and for, the Federal Judicial Center are made available to judges and other judicial personnel. Announcements of new publications are made in *The Third Branch,* the bulletin of the federal courts published monthly by the Administrative Office and the Federal Judicial Center. In addition, *The Third Branch* recommends to judicial personnel books and articles from a wide variety of legal and professional journals. The Center also publishes an annual catalog of its publications. The objective is to make available to judges and court employees the most current research findings and suggestions for improving the administration and management of the federal courts. In the final analysis, however, the Federal Judicial Center can only suggest and recommend—it has no direct supervisory power.

As we noted, the Center plays a role in developing educational and training programs for judicial branch personnel. First, there is a conscious effort to help newly appointed judges by sponsoring New Judges Seminars, held whenever the number of new judges is sufficient to justify them. Generally, a new judge may attend the seminar any time between the first month and the first year of his or her tenure. The focus and subject matter of the seminars vary from year to year.

How helpful are the New Judges Seminars? A study of 28 federal district judges who attended one of the seminars says that 23 reported that they had benefited from the experience.[20] The same study concludes that there appear to be two key elements that make the seminars helpful: the specific contents of the lectures and papers presented, and the opportunity to meet, talk, and exchange notes with other judges. The New Judges Seminars may also have a specific impact on the novice judges' work. One researcher found, for example, that judges who attended seminars on civil litigation were more productive in handling civil cases than colleagues who had not attended the seminars.[21]

The center also assists new judicial personnel by publishing manuals for judges, clerks, and magistrates. *The Judge's Bench Book,* for example, was introduced by the center in 1969. It contains information on various federal court procedures and may serve as a checklist for a judge unfamiliar with a certain procedure. Training programs are not aimed solely at new judicial personnel, however. The Division of Continuing Education and Training organizes or sponsors a large number of seminars and workshops annually; during fiscal year 1982, for instance, the division was responsible for 192 seminars and workshops.[22]

A closer look at the Federal Judicial Center's activities in fiscal 1982 gives us valuable insight into the breadth of its educational and training effort. In keeping with its goals of providing every district judge an opportunity to attend at least one center-developed course each fiscal year, 28 seminars, workshops, and institutes were offered, including two sentencing institutes (also attended by some chief probation officers), three conferences for metropolitan district chief judges, and 11 mini-seminars, or video orientation programs for groups of newly appointed district judges.

District judges are not the only ones to benefit from the center's programs, however. In fiscal 1982 the Division of Continuing Education and Training presented five workshops and seminars for bankruptcy judges; five orientations and advanced seminars for U.S. magistrates; and 20 programs for U.S. probation officers, including a teleconference on white-collar crime that was held simultaneously in 20 different cities via satellite-beamed closed-circuit television. The division also serves the needs of clerks of court. In fiscal 1982 there were 13 programs for these officials. Federal public defenders were the recipients of three programs, while two programs were designed for federal public defender investigators. Finally, a wide variety of in-court training programs are also provided. In fiscal 1982 the Division of Continuing Education and Training offered 88 such sessions.

One of the Federal Judicial Center's major goals in offering its continuing education programs is to keep court personnel abreast of recent developments. Let us look at a timely example. During the last several years many workers in certain industries have contracted asbestosis and have sought to recover damages by suing their employers in federal district court. In response to this wave of cases, the Federal Judicial Center sponsored an Asbestos Case Management Conference.[23] Judges, clerks, and magistrates from federal district courts with large numbers of asbestos-related cases met in Baltimore in June 1984 to share their experiences.

The Judicial Conference of the United States, the Administrative Office of the U.S. Courts, and the Federal Judicial Center all serve the entire federal court system. We will now look at two agencies that operate on a regional, rather than national, scope.

Circuit Judicial Conferences

Each circuit has its own Judicial Conference, as is required by statute, that meets at least once a year. Conferences are attended by all district and appellate judges in the circuit, the Supreme Court justice assigned to the circuit, and a number of special guests such as lawyers, law school professors, law clerks, and court administrators. Although the specific program varies from circuit to circuit, a general pattern can be described. The agenda usually includes (1) papers and panels presented by judges, lawyers, law professors, and administrative personnel, (2) panels and conferences that allow for interchange between district and appellate judges, and (3) structured and unstructured social contact between the conference's participants. Although all the activities of the Circuit Judicial Conferences are to a certain extent social gatherings, they provide a forum for the exchange of ideas. Furthermore, they establish communication links between judges within the circuit, between the circuit and lawyers who practice in that region, and between the circuit and the Judicial Conference of the United States.

Circuit Judicial Councils

Each circuit also has a Judicial Council, consisting of judges of that circuit's court of appeals and a varying number of district judges. Federal legislation requires that each judicial council have at least two district judges as members; councils with more than six court of appeals judges as members must have at least three district judges on the council. Table 3-1

Table 3-1 Membership of the Circuit Judicial Councils

Circuit	Circuit Judges	District Judges
D.C.	11	6
First	4	3
Second	11	6
Third	10	5
Fourth[a]	5	4
Fifth	14	9
Sixth	11	5
Seventh	8	4
Eighth	9	5
Ninth[a]	5	4
Tenth[a]	6	4
Eleventh	12	3

[a] These circuits do not have all appellate judges in the circuit as members of the council.

Source: *The Third Branch* 16 (October 1984): 7.

shows the current membership of the Circuit Judicial Council of each of the eleven circuits. The Administrative Office Act of 1939 authorizes the councils to order the judges within the circuit to comply with policies established by it, by the Judicial Conference of the United States, and by Congress.

Much of the council's work is an effort to see that the district courts operate as effectively as possible. In this regard the council monitors district court caseloads, judge assignments, and the conduct of district judges. Traditionally, the major weapons at the disposal of the council have been persuasion, peer group pressure, and publicity directed at those judges who are reluctant to comply with circuit policy. Although formal council orders may be issued to district judges in an effort to gain compliance with council policy, such orders usually concern the more mundane aspects of judicial administration. For example, orders directing that a judge receive no new cases until his or her docket has been cleared are occasionally issued.[24]

Not everything the Circuit Judicial Council does is routine, however. In fact, some council actions have a far-reaching effect. One good example concerns the Fifth Circuit Judicial Council in 1980. For many years the Fifth Circuit, which then contained the states of Alabama, Florida, Georgia, Louisiana, Mississippi, and Texas as well as the Canal Zone, had been plagued by heavy caseloads and a developing backlog. Innovative techniques in docket management and decision making, increases in authorized judgeships, and the aid of visiting judges served only to postpone what was seen as an inevitable disaster. However, the Omnibus Judges Act of 1978 authorized circuits with more than 15 judges to divide themselves administratively and to set their own rules for the number of judges in *en banc* proceedings. Two years later the Fifth Circuit Judicial Council proposed that Congress create a Fifth Circuit composed of Louisiana, Mississippi, and Texas and a new Eleventh Circuit including Alabama, Florida, and Georgia. Meanwhile, the court would operate as two administrative units, but with the judges serving circuitwide.[25] As we noted in Chapter 1, Congress did divide the old fifth circuit according to the recommendation, effective on October 1, 1981.

Recently, the Committee on Juries of the Second Circuit Judicial Council invited trial judges in the circuit to adopt one or more experimental jury procedures. The district judges were asked to choose from seven procedures and use them for at least six trials in both civil and criminal cases. The experimental procedures included allowing attorneys, in addition to the judge, to question prospective jurors; allowing judges to ask detailed questions of potential jurors in their chambers after asking general questions of all jurors; allowing jurors to submit questions (screened by the judge) to witnesses; and allowing jurors to take notes. The committee issued a report that evaluated responses to the experimental jury procedures. While the Second Circuit Judicial Council did not recommend that any of the procedures be made mandatory, it encouraged their discretionary use.[26]

It should be noted that the traits of independence, decentralization, and individualism that are characteristic of the federal judiciary in general are clearly reflected in the organization and actual operation of the Circuit Judicial Councils. As a part of the middle tier of the judicial administrative system, the councils fit nicely into the scheme of local or decentralized control of the courts. Moreover, the appeals court judges on the Circuit Judicial Councils generally see themselves as professional colleagues of the district judges rather than as supervisors directing their work. This relationship accounts in large part for the use of persuasion and compromise instead of direct orders to bring about administrative changes.

Personnel Support

United States Magistrates

In an effort to help federal district judges deal with increased workloads, Congress passed the Federal Magistrates Act in 1968. The legislation created the office of U.S. magistrate to replace the former U.S. commissioners, who had performed limited duties for the federal trial courts for a number of years. The result was the creation of "a new first echelon of judicial officers in the federal judicial system." [27] The scope and authority of the U.S. Magistrates has been clarified and expanded twice since 1968, by the Federal Magistrates Acts of 1976 and 1979.

As the duties of magistrates have expanded, so too has the number of fulltime magistrates assigned to the district courts. Between 1970, when a pilot program was begun in five districts, and September 1982, the number of full-time magistrates increased from 61 to 228, while the number of part-time magistrates declined from 449 to 238.[28]

New magistrates' positions are authorized by the Judicial Conference (subject to funding by Congress) after it considers recommendations from the Administrative Office of U.S. Courts, the district courts, the circuit councils, and the Magistrates Committee of the Judicial Conference. Table 3-2 shows the number of positions recommended by each group during the 1970-1982 meetings of the Judicial Conference, as well as the total number of authorized magistrates each year. As you can see, the district courts and circuit councils have consistently recommended more positions over the years than have been approved by the Judicial Conference. It is also apparent from Table 3-2 that the Judicial Conference has generally followed very closely the recommendations of the Magistrates Committee.

The judges of the district court appoint full-time magistrates for eight-year terms of office. However, they can be removed before the expiration of their term for "good cause." A full-time magistrate is required to be a lawyer and a member of the state bar. If a qualified person cannot be found, the judges may appoint a person competent to perform the duties as a part-time magistrate for a term of four years.

The magistrates system constitutes a structure that responds to each district court's specific needs and circumstances. Within guidelines set by the Federal Magistrates Acts of 1968, 1976, and 1979, the judges in each district court establish the duties and responsibilities of their magistrates. The 1968 legislation generally described the magistrates' duties as including all the powers and duties formerly exercised by U.S. commissioners, the trial and disposition of minor criminal offenses, and "additional duties" to assist the district judges.[29] Although some districts established local rules authorizing magistrates to perform "additional duties," controversies developed among courts as to what kinds of duties might be delegated to the magistrates.

As a consequence of this uncertainty, both the 1976 and 1979 acts clarified and expanded the scope of the magistrates' authority. The 1976

Table 3-2 Recommended and Authorized Full-Time Magistrates: 1970-1982

	Number of Recommended Positions					
Date	Administrative Office	District court	Circuit council	Magistrates Committee	Judicial Conference	Number of authorized positions
Spring 1970	0	26	25	8	10	61
Fall 1970	16	28	25	19	21	82
Spring 1971	1	3	1	1	1	83
Fall 1971	5	6	5	5	5	88
Spring 1972	2	7	3	2	2	90
Fall 1972	12	13	10	12	13	103
Spring 1973	1	5	1	0	0	103
Fall 1973	8	9	8	8	9	112
Spring 1974	0	0	0	0	0	112
Fall 1974	19	21	18	18	18	130
Spring 1975	3	4	3	3	3	133
Fall 1975	12	12	12	10	10	143
Spring 1976	7	9	7	7	7	150
Fall 1976	9	9	9	8	9	159
Spring 1977	5	6	7	5	5	164
Fall 1977	4	4	4	2	2	166
Spring 1978	10	13	12	10	10	176
Fall 1978	13	12	14	11	11	187
Spring 1979	11	12	12	9	9	196
Fall 1979	5	6	6	5	5	201
Spring 1980	5	6	6	3	3	204
Fall 1980	10	19	12	7	6	210
Spring 1981	8	9	9	7	7	217
Fall 1981	5	5	5	2	2	219
Spring 1982	9	13	11	3	4	223
Fall 1982	8	11	10	5	5	228
Total	188	268	235	170	177	

Source: Carroll Seron, *The Roles of Magistrates in Federal District Courts* (Washington, D.C.: Federal Judicial Center, 1983), 11.

act says that a magistrate may be designated to hear and determine certain kinds of pretrial matters brought before the court, to conduct hearings, and to submit proposed findings and recommendations on motions. The court can then accept, reject, or modify the recommendations in whole or in part. The 1979 legislation permits a magistrate, with the consent of the involved parties, to conduct all proceedings in a jury or nonjury civil matter and to enter a judgment in the case, and to conduct a trial of persons accused of misdemeanors (less serious offenses than felonies) committed within the district, provided the defendants consent.

In other words, Congress has given federal district judges the authority to expand the scope of magistrates' participation in the judicial process. However, because each district has its own particular needs, a magistrate's specific duties may vary from one district to another. The decision to delegate responsibilities to the magistrate is still made by the judges; therefore, a magistrate's participation in the processing of cases may be considerably narrower than that permitted by statute. The author of a recent in-depth study of U.S. magistrates sums it up this way:

> Some judges may, as a matter of common practice, request a magistrate's assistance in hearing all discovery motions, request a magistrate's assistance in scheduling . . . "initial" pretrial conferences, or request a magistrate's assistance in settlement conferences. In contrast, other judges may request a magistrate's assistance on a selective (i.e., case-by-case) basis for each of these types of matters.[30]

Perhaps the most important power magistrates now possess is the authority to conduct trials in civil cases, with the consent of the parties involved. Since they have held this power only since 1979, at least two important questions have been raised: First, how likely are the parties to agree to having the case heard by a magistrate? Table 3-3, based on a 1983 study conducted by the Federal Judicial Center, indicates that there is little reluctance to allowing a magistrate to handle the case.

Second, what types of cases are magistrates receiving for trial? Table 3-4 reveals that prisoner petitions top the list, although the magistrates hear a variety of cases.

Table 3-3 Frequency of Parties' Consent to Magistrates in Civil Suits

Frequency	Participating magistrates (n = 123)	
	Number	Percentage
Almost always	74	60%
Frequently	22	18
Occasionally	23	19
Rarely	4	3

Source: Carroll Seron, *The Roles of Magistrates in Federal District Courts* (Washington, D.C.: Federal Judicial Center, 1983), p. 65.

There is no doubt that the approximately 500 full-time and part-time magistrates are now vital cogs in the federal judicial system. As Table 3-4 shows, the magistrates, in addition to handling many preliminary matters for the district judges, disposed of over 2,000 cases themselves in 1982.[31]

Law Clerks

In this section we examine the work of another individual who is vital to the operation of our federal courts: the law clerk. The first use of law clerks by an American judge is generally traced to Horace Gray of Massachusetts. In the summer of 1875, while serving as chief justice of the Massachusetts Supreme Court, he employed, at his own expense, a highly ranked new graduate of the Harvard Law School.[32] Each year, he would employ a new clerk from Harvard. When Gray was appointed to the U.S. Supreme Court in 1882, he brought a law clerk with him to the nation's highest court.

One of Gray's law clerks at the Supreme Court, Samuel Williston, left a record of his clerkship that provides some details about the tasks of the first law clerks.[33] Williston served Justice Gray as both a sounding board and an editor. He was expected to review all the new cases and to formulate a recommended disposition that he would discuss with Justice Gray before the Supreme Court's conference. Williston was frequently asked to draft opinions in cases assigned to Justice Gray, and to read the opinions circulated by the other justices and discuss them with his justice. Justice Gray and Samuel Williston became close friends during the clerkship, as indicated by the fact that Gray, then 60 years old, became engaged and sought the clerk's advice on an engagement ring. Gray also altered Williston's schedule and doubled his pay so that the young clerk, who was also engaged, could save more money for the marriage.

In spite of Gray's happy experiences with the young Harvard Law School graduates, his method was not quickly adopted by his colleagues, even after Congress assumed the cost in 1886. By 1888, all nine justices were employing assistants, but the typical pattern was to obtain a law clerk through friends or relatives or from the bar and law schools of the District of Columbia and to retain that assistant as long as possible.

Justice Gray's successor on the High Court was Oliver Wendell Holmes, like Gray a former chief justice of the Massachusetts Supreme Court. Holmes also adopted the practice of hiring annual honor graduates of Harvard Law School as his clerks. At first, Holmes's clerks were selected by Professor John Chipman Gray. Upon Gray's death in 1915, Holmes asked a young Harvard Law School professor named Felix Frankfurter (later a famous Supreme Court justice himself) to serve as

Table 3-4   Civil Cases Assigned upon Consent to Trial to 141 Magistrates in Statistical Year 1982

Nature of suit	Number	Percentage
Prisoner petition	677	28%
Tort	526	21
Contract	365	15
Nonprisoner civil rights	254	10
Other	253	10
Social Security	170	7
Labor	101	4
Real property	73	3
Forfeiture	15	0.6
Property rights	14	0.6
Total	2,448	

Source: Carroll Seron, *The Roles of Magistrates in Federal District Courts* (Washington, D.C.: Federal Judicial Center, 1983), 68.

procurer of law clerks. When he joined the Court in 1916, Louis Brandeis made the same request of Frankfurter. Professor Frankfurter, whose protégés were known as the "happy hot dogs," thus supplied clerks for Holmes, Brandeis, and Holmes's successor Benjamin Cardozo.

When William Howard Taft became chief justice, he secured a new law clerk annually from the dean of the Yale Law School. Harlan Fisk Stone, the former dean of the Columbia Law School, joined the Court in 1925 and made it his practice to hire a Columbia graduate each year. Over a period of time, then, the justices gradually shifted their views so that the short-term law professor protégé became the typical Supreme Court law clerk.

During the 1919-1939 period the use of law clerks flourished at the lower-court level. Congress authorized a law clerk for each circuit judge in 1930 and one for selected district judges in 1936. Recent decades have seen a steady growth in the use of law clerks by all federal courts. Supreme Court justices, for example, now have three or four clerks; each circuit judge has two, or in some cases three; and each district judge has one or two. The number of clerks varies because there is some discretion in salaries that may be paid.

What sorts of tasks do law clerks perform? Obviously the duties vary according to the type of court and the judge for whom the clerk works. Nevertheless, several tasks common to law clerks at any level may be identified.

Their earliest involvement in the litigation process comes when they review petitions and motions. Law clerks working for the Supreme Court spend a great deal of their time on the appeals and certiorari petitions filed with the Court. They digest information contained in the many petitions and lower-court records, and summarize the material for the justices. Since 1972, several justices have participated in a "certpool," whereby a single clerk is designated to prepare a memorandum for the mutual use of the participating justices.

As we saw in Chapter 1, the U.S. courts of appeals do not have the same discretion to accept or reject a case that the Supreme Court has. Nevertheless, the courts of appeals now use certain screening devices to differentiate between cases that can be handled quickly and those that require more time and effort. Law clerks are an integral part of this screening process.

Traditionally, the law clerk is selected by a particular judge and works exclusively for that individual. About 1960, however, some courts of appeals began to utilize a new concept: the staff law clerk.[34] The staff clerk, who works for the entire court, began to be used primarily because of the rapid increase in the number of *pro se* matters (generally speaking, those involving indigents) coming before the courts of appeals. In some circuits the staff law clerks deal only with pro se matters, while in others they review nearly all cases on the court's docket. As a result of the review process, a case may be dealt with in a truncated procedure—that is, without oral argument or full briefing.

Law clerks working for federal district judges spend a good deal of their time examining the various motions filed in civil and criminal cases. They review each motion, noting the issues and the positions of the parties involved, research important points raised in the motions, and prepare written memoranda for the judge. Although a large part of the law clerk's work is devoted to the earliest stages of the litigation process, the work does not end there. The information provided by law clerks continues to be important to the judges who must actually decide the cases. In the courts of appeals, for example, intensive analysis of the record by judges prior to oral argument or decision is not always possible. They seldom have time to do more than scan pertinent portions of the record called to their attention by law clerks. As one judicial scholar aptly put it, "To prepare for oral argument, all but a handful of circuit judges rely upon bench memoranda prepared by their law clerks, plus their own notes from reading briefs." [35]

Many judges expect their law clerks to serve as sounding boards for their views about how a particular case should be decided. Such exchanges between judge and clerk contribute to the sharpening of thought processes and to the quality of judicial decisions. As one recent study put it, the judge "considers it the job of his law clerks to prevent him from making mistakes."[36]

The law clerk often differs ideologically from his or her judge—a situation that allows the judge to get a very different perspective on a case. The following account of Supreme Court justice Lewis Powell and one of his law clerks, Joel Klein, provides a good example of what we are talking about:

> Powell quickly grasped that Klein's brash, outspoken style would be a perfect counterpoint to his own genteel Southern background. He prided himself on hiring liberal clerks. He would tell his clerks that the conservative side of the issues came to him naturally. Their job was to present the other side, to challenge him. He would rather encounter a compelling argument for another position in the privacy of his own chambers, than to meet it unexpectedly at conference or in a dissent.[37]

Once a decision has been reached, the law clerk will frequently participate in writing the order or opinion that accompanies the decision. A district judge, for example, said, "I even allow my law clerks to write memorandum opinions. I first tell him what I want and then he writes it up. Sometimes I sign it without changing a word."[38]

A similar practice occurs at the Supreme Court, where the writing of the Court's opinion may be a long drawn-out process. One High Court observer describes the procedure as follows:

> Once [Justice] Powell is assigned an opinion, either he or his clerk roughs out a draft opinion. Who does the first draft depends on what the workload is in the office at the time. The opinion then goes back and forth between the Justice and his clerk like a shuttlecock, being worked and reworked, drafted and redrafted until both are satisfied. Then the opinion is given to a second clerk, who goes over it like an editor, looking for mistakes, poor reasoning, unclear writing. Then the opinion is sent to the print shop the Court maintains inside the building. Then the third Powell clerk reads the opinion, acting as an editor-proofreader.[39]

We should note that there has been some debate about the influence of law clerks. Without doubt they have an effect on decisions such as whether certiorari should be granted and whether cases should receive a full hearing or be disposed of through a truncated procedure. However, law clerks have strong incentives to provide accurate summaries for their judges rather than trying to deceive them. Also, judges are sensitive to the problem of potential loss of control should they delegate too much responsibility to their clerks. Justice William Rehnquist, himself a former law clerk for Justice Robert Jackson, provides a good example. In a 1957 magazine article he expressed concern that the ideological biases of law clerks could affect their work on petitions for Supreme Court hearings.[40] Although he argued in the article that law clerks generally play minor roles in the decision process, he was careful when he first became a member of the Supreme Court to write all first drafts of opinions himself. It has been noted, however, that Rehnquist grew to trust his clerks and now realizes that they are helpful with first drafts.[41]

The issue of trust between justice and clerk has yet another dimension—secrecy about the Court's thinking prior to announcement of a final decision. Traditionally, the High Court does not provide information about conference discussions and votes or about ideas expressed in the various drafts of opinions. Still, the law clerks are in a position to know the views of their own justice and perhaps others as well. The Court is simply dependent upon the clerks to refrain from leaking information prematurely. Occasionally a book such as *The Brethren* will provide a "behind-the-scenes" look at the Court, but traditionally the law clerks have not betrayed their trust.

Court Administrators

The clerk of the court has traditionally maintained the judge's calendar, handled courtroom arrangements, kept records of case proceedings, and prepared orders and judgments resulting from court actions. In reality, the clerks have now become more like administrators, as this description of the U.S. district clerk for the Southern District of Texas suggests:

> Jesse E. Clark is a clerk who doesn't type, file or "wear a green eyeshade," as he puts it. . . . Actually, Clark compares his job to that of a hospital administrator who keeps the facility running smoothly while the doctors, or in Clark's case, the judges, perform the major work.

As a court administrator, Clark has a $3 million annual budget and 96 deputy clerks to assist him.[42]

The professional court administrator is also active at the two upper levels of the federal judiciary. Since 1971 each court of appeals has been authorized to hire a circuit executive to provide managerial expertise and assistance for the chief judge. The Supreme Court now has an administrative assistant to the chief justice.

Probation Officers

These members of the judicial supporting cast are important at the district court level. Probation officers serve within the jurisdiction and under the direction of the district judges. The probation officer's main function lies in advising a judge on the sentencing of criminal defendants. The Administrative Office of the U.S. Courts fixes the salaries of probation officers and provides for their necessary expenses through its Probation Division (see Figure 3-1, page 69); the Federal Judicial Center runs training programs for the probation officers.

Other Support Personnel

Many other people, of course, perform vital tasks for the federal court system, including marshals, bailiffs, secretaries, and deputy clerks. Scattered throughout the federal courts, they enable the judicial system to function as efficiently as it does.

U.S. marshals are responsible for providing security in courtrooms, delivering legal orders to litigants and witnesses, guarding and transporting prisoners, making arrests, and protecting witnesses. The bailiff, a familiar figure in the courtroom, announces the judge's arrival, keeps order in the court, and administers oaths to witnesses. Deputy clerks and secretaries maintain records on the thousands of cases filed annually and generally help the courts keep up with the numerous items that must be typed, copied, and recorded daily.

Major Participants from the Department of Justice

Although the Justice Department is an agency of the executive branch of the government, it has a natural association with the judicial branch. Many of the cases heard in the federal courts involve the national government in one capacity or another. Sometimes the government is sued, while in other instances the government initiates the lawsuit. In either case, an attorney must represent the government. Most of the litigation involving the federal government is handled by the Justice Department, although a number of other government agencies have attorneys on their payrolls.

The Justice Department has several key divisions. The Office of Solicitor General is extremely important in cases argued before the Supreme Court, while at the trial level the offices of U.S. attorneys play the most significant roles. There are also six legal divisions within the Justice Department: Antitrust, Civil, Civil Rights, Criminal, Land and Natural Resources, and Tax, each with a staff of specialized lawyers and headed by an assistant attorney general. The six legal divisions supervise the handling of litigation by the U.S. attorneys, take cases to the courts of appeals, and aid the solicitor general's office in cases argued before the Supreme Court. Because of the special significance of the work of the solicitor general and the U.S. attorneys, we will examine each in detail.

Solicitor General. The primary function of the solicitor general is to decide, on behalf of the United States, which cases will and will not be presented to the Supreme Court for review. Whenever an executive branch department or agency loses a case in one of the courts of appeals and wishes a Supreme Court review, that department or agency will formally request the Justice Department to seek certiorari. The solicitor general will then determine whether to appeal the lower-court decision.

Naturally, there are many factors to be taken into account when making such a decision. A former solicitor general, Wade H. McCree, Jr., explained what he thought was the most important consideration:

> I have to be aware of the fact that when I am asked to seek certiorari there is a limit to the number of cases that the Supreme Court can hear. I have to ask myself, "Is this one of the 250 most important cases that the Supreme Court will be asked to hear this year?"

McCree went on to say that in the previous year the Supreme Court had received 3,715 petitions for certiorari, only 68 of which were submitted by the Justice Department. Furthermore, he noted that 72 percent of the Justice Department's petitions for certiorari were granted, whereas only 6 percent of the total 3,715 petitions were granted.[43]

In addition to deciding whether to seek Supreme Court review of a particular lower-court decision, the solicitor general personally argues most of the government's cases heard by the High Court. However, there are some kinds of cases that the solicitor general may feel are more appropriate to be argued by a person who holds a particular office in government. Another former solicitor general, Rex E. Lee, pointed out that the "tradition has been that the hardest cases—the most important cases— usually are argued by the Solicitor General." [44]

U.S. Attorneys. The office of U.S. attorney came into being in 1789 with passage of the Judiciary Act. Today, each federal judicial district has a U.S. attorney and one or more assistant U.S. attorneys. The number of assistants varies from district to district, with large urban areas, such as the Southern District of New York (New York City), having perhaps as many as a hundred.

U.S. attorneys are appointed by the president with Senate confirmation. Nominees must reside in the district to which they are appointed and must be attorneys. They serve a formal term of four years but can be reappointed indefinitely or removed at the president's discretion.[45] In fact, it has become customary over the years for U.S. attorneys to resign their position when the opposition party wins the presidency.

The appointment of a U.S. attorney is often a political reward.[46] Overwhelmingly, only lawyers who belong to the president's party are considered. Since each nominee must be confirmed by the Senate, the senator or senators of the president's party in the state where the vacancy exists become important actors in the appointment process. The assistant U.S. attorneys are formally appointed by the attorney general, although in actual practice they are chosen by the U.S. attorney, who then forwards the selection to the attorney general for ratification. Assistant U.S. attorneys may be fired by the attorney general.

The basic tasks handled by U.S. attorneys and their assistants are to prosecute defendants in the federal district courts and to defend the United States when it is sued in a federal trial court. Primarily, then, they function as prosecutors for the federal government, with considerable discretion in deciding which criminal cases to prosecute. In civil cases the U.S. attorneys have the authority to determine which cases to try to settle out of court and which ones to take to trial. As you can see, the U.S. attorney is in a position to have a significant impact on the federal district court's docket.

The other major federal participants in prosecution or litigation— federal district judges—are in a position to exert both direct and indirect influence over U.S. attorneys and their assistants.[47] Judges may decide which types of cases U.S. attorneys will prosecute and how they will actually argue their cases in court. One judicial scholar says that U.S. attorneys and assistant attorneys "inevitably shape their behavior to conform to the predilections of the judge hearing the case." [48]

Since U.S. attorneys and judges within a district must work together on an ongoing basis, their relationship is extremely important. In some districts the relationship may be close and informal, while in other districts the atmosphere may be more businesslike. Although many factors play a role, one leading study notes that a close rapport between the judge and the U.S. attorney is most likely in a small district because of the close physical proximity of their offices. At the other extreme, "large districts must institutionalize procedures for scheduling cases and arranging the docket, cutting the occasions for informal contact."[49] It should be noted that U.S. attorneys engage in more litigation in the federal district courts than anyone else. Therefore, they and their staffs of assistants are vital participants in the policies fashioned in the federal trial courts.

Summary

This chapter has focused on the agencies and individuals that help the federal courts process cases. Our emphasis has been not so much on judges as on those who assist them. We began with a brief history of the judicial administration movement—a movement closely associated with government reform in general and court reform in particular. Judicial changes have not come easily, however, because of the constitutional heritage of judicial independence, decentralization, and individualism. Still, ever-growing caseloads have forced judges to look for help in handling their dockets by relying increasingly on law clerks, magistrates, and professional court administrators. Agencies such as the Administrative Office of U.S. Courts now aid the judges in dealing with administrative duties and in devising more efficient court procedures. The Federal Judicial Center offers training programs for a wide range of judicial personnel.

In spite of all these changes, however, the judges themselves still retain control over major decisions affecting the federal courts. The Judicial Conference of the United States remains the policy maker for the federal judiciary, and circuit conferences and circuit councils help to decentralize decision making. In short, while the federal court system may look like a hierarchy, there is still a good deal of local control and independence and some variation in how the courts of appeals and district courts handle their cases.

Notes

1. Henry R. Glick, *Courts, Politics, and Justice* (New York: McGraw-Hill, 1983), 48.
2. Peter G. Fish, *The Politics of Federal Judicial Administration* (Princeton, N.J.: Princeton University Press, 1973), 7.
3. This point is perhaps best documented in the case of southern federal judges called upon to enforce the Supreme Court's school desegregation decisions. See Jack W. Peltason, *Fifty-Eight Lonely Men* (New York: Harcourt, Brace and World, 1961).
4. Felix Frankfurter and James M. Landis, *The Business of the Supreme Court* (New York: Macmillan, 1928), 218.
5. Fish, *The Politics of Federal Judicial Administration*, 13.
6. Russell R. Wheeler and Howard R. Whitcomb, eds., *Judicial Administration: Text and Readings* (Englewood Cliffs, N.J.: Prentice-Hall, 1977), 27.

7. Ibid., 28.
8. Ibid.
9. Fred P. Graham, "Warren, Justice 15 Years, to Seek Speed in Courts," *New York Times,* September 30, 1968, 1.
10. Carl Baar, "Federal Judicial Administration: Political Strategies and Organizational Change," in *Judicial Administration: Text and Readings,* ed. Wheeler and Whitcomb, 97.
11. Sheldon Goldman and Thomas P. Jahnige, *The Federal Courts as a Political System,* 2nd ed. (New York: Harper & Row, 1976), 99.
12. See *The Third Branch* 16 (November 1984): 2.
13. See Fish, *The Politics of Federal Judicial Administration,* 273.
14. See ibid., 121-123.
15. Ibid., 124, 166.
16. The discussion of the initial organization of the Administrative Office is drawn from Fish, *The Politics of Federal Judicial Administration,* 172-176.
17. Glick, *Courts, Politics, and Justice,* 51.
18. Our discussion of the research role is drawn from "The Federal Judicial Center," *Law and Society Newsletter* (March 1984): 5.
19. Ernest C. Friesen, Jr., Edward C. Gallas, and Nesta M. Gallas, *Managing the Courts* (Indianapolis: Bobbs-Merrill, 1971), 200.
20. See Robert A. Carp and Russell R. Wheeler, "Sink or Swim: The Socialization of a Federal District Judge," *Journal of Public Law* 21 (1972): 382.
21. See Beverly Blair Cook, "The Socialization of New Federal Judges: Impact on District Court Business," *Washington University Law Quarterly* (1971): 269-270.
22. See *The Third Branch* 15 (January 1983): 6. All the information and figures on the activities in fiscal year 1982 are drawn from this source.
23. See *The Third Branch* 16 (August 1984): 2.
24. See Fish, *The Politics of Federal Judicial Administration,* 418-419.
25. See J. Woodford Howard, Jr., *Courts of Appeals in the Federal Judicial System: A Study of the Second, Fifth, and District of Columbia Circuits* (Princeton, N.J.: Princeton University Press, 1981), 273.
26. See *The Third Branch* 16 (October 1984): 3.
27. Steven Puro, "United States Magistrates: A New Federal Judicial Officer," *Justice System Journal* 2 (Winter 1976): 141.
28. See Carroll Seron, *The Roles of Magistrates in Federal District Courts* (Washington, D.C.: Federal Judicial Center, 1983), 8.
29. See 28 U.S.C. 636.
30. Seron, *The Roles of Magistrates in Federal District Courts,* 8.
31. Ibid., 67.
32. Our discussion of the historical evolution of law clerks is drawn from John Bilyeu Oakley and Robert S. Thompson, *Law Clerks and the Judicial Process* (Berkeley: University of California Press, 1980), 10-22.
33. See Samuel Williston, *Life and Law* (Boston: Little, Brown, 1940), and Samuel Williston, "Horace Gray," in *Great American Lawyers,* edited by

W. Lewis (Philadelphia: J. C. Winston, 1907-1909; South Hackensack, N.J.: Rothman Reprints, 1971).

34. See Steven Flanders and Jerry Goldman, "Screening Practices and the Use of Para-Judicial Personnel in a U.S. Court of Appeals," in *Judicial Administration: Text and Readings,* ed. Wheeler and Whitcomb, 244.

35. Howard, *Courts of Appeals in the Federal Judicial System,* 198.

36. Oakley and Thompson, *Law Clerks and the Judicial Process,* 103.

37. Bob Woodward and Scott Armstrong, *The Brethren* (New York: Simon and Schuster, 1979), 354-355.

38. Quoted in Carp and Wheeler, "Sink or Swim," 379.

39. Nina Totenberg, "Behind the Marble, Beneath the Robes," *New York Times Magazine,* March 16, 1975, 66.

40. William H. Rehnquist, "Who Writes Decisions of the Supreme Court?" *U.S. News & World Report,* December 13, 1957, 74-75.

41. See Woodward and Armstrong, *The Brethren,* 269.

42. Nancy Stancili, "Clerk for U.S. District Court Works Hard to Keep Things Going Smoothly," *Houston Chronicle,* January 15, 1984, 3:6.

43. "Interview with Solicitor General Wade H. McCree, Jr.," *The Third Branch* 12 (August 1980): 3.

44. For a fuller discussion of this matter see "Interview with Solicitor General Rex E. Lee," *The Third Branch* 14 (May 1982): 5.

45. For a good case study of the firing of a U.S. attorney, see Howard Ball, *Courts and Politics: The Federal Judicial System* (Englewood Cliffs, N.J.: Prentice-Hall, 1980), 202-206.

46. For an in-depth analysis of the appointment process for U.S. attorneys, see James Eisenstein, *Counsel for the United States: U.S. Attorneys in the Political and Legal Systems* (Baltimore: Johns Hopkins University Press, 1978), chap. 3.

47. A detailed study of the relationship between U.S. attorneys and federal district judges may be found in *Counsel for the United States,* chap. 7.

48. Ibid., 133.

49. Ibid., 147.

The Federal Judges

4

Previous chapters have explored the history, organization, and workload of the federal judiciary and have identified those staff and support agencies that make the wheels of American justice spin with at least a modicum of efficiency. It is now time to focus upon the main actors in the federal court system—the men and women who serve as judges and justices. As we take an analytical look at the black-robed decision makers to whom most Americans still look with such reverence, we will keep several questions in mind: What characteristics do these people have that distinguish them from the rest of the citizenry? What are the qualifications—both formal and informal—for appointment to the federal bench? How are the judges selected and who are the participants in the process? Is there a policy link between the citizenry, the appointment process, and the subsequent decisions of the jurists? How are they socialized into their judicial roles—that is, how do judges learn to be judges? Finally, we shall say a few words about how and when judges stop being judges—the retirement, discipline, and removal of federal jurists.

Background Characteristics

In America we still cling eagerly to the log cabin-to-White House myth of attaining high public office—that is, to the notion that someone born in the humblest of circumstances (such as Abe Lincoln) may one day grow up to be president of the United States, or at least a U.S. judge. As with most myths, there is a kernel of truth to it. In principle virtually anyone can become a prominent public official, and there are in fact a few

89

well-known examples of people from poor backgrounds who climbed to the top of the heap of power and respectability. For instance, there are Justice Thurgood Marshall, the great-grandson of a slave and the son of a Pullman car steward, and Chief Justice Warren Burger, whose father earned his daily bread as a traveling salesman and as a railroad car inspector. Despite these occasional exceptions, the pattern is usually quite different. For a long time uncontested data have clearly shown that America's federal judges, like other public officials and the captains of commerce and industry, come from a very narrow stratum of American society. As we shall momentarily see, while potential judges need not necessarily be the sons and daughters of *millionaires,* it is at least helpful if they come from a special segment of the nation's middle- and upper-middle classes.

District Judges

Before we can offer some generalizations about who U.S. trial judges are and where they come from, we need some facts and figures. Background data for all federal district judges for the past 200 years have never been collected, but for judges who have served in recent decades we know a good deal. Table 4-1 profiles some key factors for trial jurists appointed by Presidents Johnson, Nixon, Ford, Carter, and Reagan.

In terms of their primary occupation before assuming the federal bench, a plurality had been judges at the state or local levels. Around 28 percent of Nixon's judges had had extensive judicial experience, and as many as 45 percent of Carter's judicial team had previously worn the black robe. The next largest bloc had served in moderate-size law firms—that is, a firm with five to 24 partners or associates. Few had been professors of law.

Their educational background reveals something of their elite nature. All obviously graduated from college; about half attended either the costly Ivy League or private universities to receive their college and their law degrees. Most adult Americans have never gone to college, and of those who have, only a tiny portion could meet the admission requirements—not to mention the expense—of most private or Ivy League schools.

At least a third of the district judges had had some experience on the bench, and in the case of Carter's appointees, more than 54 percent had some taste of judicial duties. No fewer than a third had been former prosecutors; as many as half of Ford's judicial team had served in that capacity.

Judges differ in yet another way from the population as a whole. Among trial judges—and all U.S. judges for that matter—there is a strong tendency toward "occupational heredity"—that is, for judges to come from families with a tradition of judicial and public service.[1] A story about one of President Reagan's recent trial court appointees, Howell Cobb of Beaumont, Texas, is typical of this phenomenon. The nominee's hometown paper said of him in part:

> The appointee is the fourth generation of a family of lawyers and judges. His great-grandfather, a Confederate officer, served as secretary of the Treasury under President James Buchanan and was governor of Georgia and speaker of the U.S. House of Representatives. Cobb's grandfather was a justice on the Georgia Supreme Court, and his father was a circuit judge in Georgia. Cobb's son, a lawyer in El Paso, also follows tradition. "Most trial lawyers aspire to a seat on the bench," Cobb said.[2]

The percentage of ethnic and racial minorities on the trial bench has always been small, not only in absolute numbers but also in comparison with figures for the overall population. Only Jimmy Carter, who made affirmative action a cornerstone of his presidency, stands out as having appointed a significant number of non-Anglos to the federal bench—over 21 percent.[3]

Although the United States is about 51 percent female, it is clear that judging is still a man's business. Until Carter's presidency fewer than 2 percent of the lower judiciary were female, and even Carter was able to include only 14.4 percent women among his nominees to the trial bench. Being female is clearly not an asset if one covets a judicial robe.

The American Bar Association (ABA) ratings reveal that few make it to the federal bench who are not rated as "qualified" by this self-appointed evaluator of judicial fitness. More surprising, perhaps, is that precious few are dubbed as "exceptionally well qualified" by the ABA. The difference in quality between the Republican and Democratic appointees is trivial.

Appeals Court Judges

Because the statistics and percentages of the appellate court appointees of the five presidents from Johnson through Reagan are quite similar to those for the trial judges, we shall offer some commentary only on those figures that suggest a difference between the two sets of judges (see Table 4-2).

Appeals judges are twice as likely to have had previous judicial experience as their counterparts on the trial court bench. Also, Presidents Carter and Reagan were more apt to look to the ranks of law school pro-

Table 4-1 Background Characteristics of the District Court Appointees of Presidents Johnson, Nixon, Ford, Carter, and Reagan

	Johnson	Nixon	Ford	Carter	Reagan (97th Congress)
Occupation					
Politics/government	21.3%	10.6%	21.2%	4.4%	7.4%
Judiciary	31.1	28.5	34.6	44.6	36.8
Large law firm					
100+					
partners/associates	0.8	0.6	1.9	2.0	4.4
50-99	1.6	0.6	3.9	6.0	1.5
25-49	—	10.1	3.9	6.0	5.9
Moderate-size firm					
10-24					
partners/associates	12.3	8.9	7.7	9.4	17.6
5-9	6.6	19.0	17.3	10.4	10.3
Small firm					
2-4 partners/associates	11.5	14.5	7.7	11.4	7.4
Solo practitioner	11.5	4.5	1.9	2.5	4.4
Professor of law	3.3	2.8	—	3.0	4.4
Other	—	—	—	0.5	—
Undergraduate education					
Public-supported	38.5	41.3	48.1	57.4	32.4
Private (not Ivy)	31.1	38.5	34.6	32.7	51.5
Ivy League	16.4	19.5	17.3	9.9	16.2
None indicated	13.9	0.6	—	—	—
Law school education					
Public-supported	40.2	41.9	44.2	50.5	44.1
Private (not Ivy)	36.9	36.9	38.5	32.2	47.1
Ivy League	21.3	21.2	17.3	17.3	8.8
Experience					
Judicial	34.3	35.1	42.3	54.5	44.1
Prosecutorial	45.8	41.9	50.0	38.6	42.7
Neither one	33.6	36.3	30.8	28.2	30.9

fessors for their appeals court appointments than they were for their nominations to the district courts.

If the trend toward seeking out private school and Ivy League graduates was strong for trial judge appointments, it is even more pronounced for those selected for seats on the appeals courts. Com-

Table 4-1   (Continued)

	Johnson	Nixon	Ford	Carter	Reagan (97th Congress)
Party					
Democratic	94.3	7.2	21.2	94.1	2.9
Republican	5.7	92.8	78.8	4.5	97.1
Independent	—	—	—	—	—
Past party activism	49.2	48.6	50.0	60.4	64.7
Religious origin or affiliation					
Protestant	58.2	73.2	73.1	60.4	63.2
Catholic	31.1	18.4	17.3	27.2	30.9
Jewish	10.7	8.4	9.6	12.4	5.9
Ethnicity or race					
White	93.4	95.5	88.5	78.7	95.6
Black	4.1	3.4	5.8	13.9	—
Hispanic	2.5	1.1	1.9	6.9	2.9
Asian	—	—	3.9	0.5	1.5
Sex					
Male	98.4	99.4	98.1	85.6	95.6
Female	1.6	0.6	1.9	14.4	4.4
ABA ratings					
Exceptionally well qualified	7.4	4.8	—	4.0	1.5
Well qualified	40.9	40.4	46.1	47.0	47.1
Qualified	49.2	54.8	53.8	47.5	51.5
Not qualified	2.5	—	—	1.5	—
Total number of appointments	122 ·	179	52	202	68

Source: Data from Sheldon Goldman, "Reagan's Judicial Appointments at Mid-Term: Shaping the Bench in His Own Image," *Judicature* 66 (March 1983): 338-339.

pared with the population at large or even U.S. district judges, appellate court jurists appear to be true members of America's social and economic elite.

In terms of presidents making opposite-party selections, there is little difference between trial and appellate court appointments. How-

Table 4-2 Background Characteristics of the Appeals Court Appointees of Presidents Johnson, Nixon, Ford, Carter, and Reagan

	Johnson	Nixon	Ford	Carter	Reagan (97th Congress)
Occupation					
Politics/government	10.0%	4.4%	8.3%	5.4%	— %
Judiciary	57.5	53.3	75.0	46.4	68.4
Large law firm					
100+ partners/associates	—	—	—	1.8	—
50-99	2.5	2.2	8.3	5.4	5.3
25-49	2.5	2.2	—	3.6	5.3
Moderate-size firm					
10-24 partners/associates	7.5	11.1	—	14.3	—
5-9	10.0	11.1	8.3	1.8	5.3
Small firm					
2-4 partners/associates	2.5	6.7	—	3.6	—
Solo practitioner	5.0	—	—	1.8	—
Professor of law	2.5	2.2	—	14.3	15.8
Other	—	6.7	—	1.8	—
Undergraduate education					
Public-supported	32.5	40.0	50.0	30.4	31.6
Private (not Ivy)	40.0	35.6	41.7	50.0	36.8
Ivy League	17.5	20.0	8.3	19.6	31.6
None indicated	10.0	4.4	—	—	—
Law school education					
Public-supported	40.0	37.8	50.0	39.3	36.8
Private (not Ivy)	32.5	26.7	25.0	19.6	36.8
Ivy League	27.5	35.6	25.0	41.1	26.3
Experience					
Judicial	65.0	57.8	75.0	53.6	73.7
Prosecutorial	47.5	46.7	25.0	32.1	21.1
Neither one	20.0	17.8	25.0	37.5	21.1

ever, there is a slight tendency for appeals judges to be more active in their respective parties than their colleagues on the trial bench.

As with district judges, most appellate court appointees have been disproportionately white and male. Only the Carter team stands out: over 21 percent of his appeals court judges were nonwhite, and

Table 4-2   (Continued)

	Johnson	Nixon	Ford	Carter	Reagan (97th Congress)
Party					
Democratic	95.0	6.7	8.3	89.3	—
Republican	5.0	93.3	91.7	5.4	100.0
Independent	—	—	—	5.4	—
Past party activism	57.5	60.0	58.3	73.2	57.9
Religious origin or affiliation					
Protestant	60.0	75.6	58.3	60.7	57.9
Catholic	25.0	15.6	33.3	23.2	31.6
Jewish	15.0	8.9	8.3	16.1	10.5
Ethnicity or race					
White	95.0	97.8	100.0	78.6	94.7
Black	5.0	—	—	16.1	5.3
Hispanic	—	—	—	3.6	—
Asian	—	2.2	—	1.8	—
Sex					
Male	97.5	100.0	100.0	80.4	100.0
Female	2.5	—	—	19.6	—
ABA ratings					
Exceptionally well qualified	27.5	15.6	16.7	16.1	26.3
Well qualified	47.5	57.8	41.7	58.9	42.1
Qualified	20.0	26.7	33.3	25.0	31.6
Not qualified	2.5	—	8.3	—	—
No report requested	2.5	—	—	—	—
Total number of appointments	40	45	12	56	19

Source: Data from Sheldon Goldman, "Reagan's Judicial Appointments at Mid-Term: Shaping the Bench in His Own Image," *Judicature* 66 (March 1983): 344-345.

over 19 percent were women. Those bearing the "exceptionally well qualified" stamp of the American Bar Association are in much greater number in the appeals court camp than in the ranks of the trial court judges.

Supreme Court Justices

Since 1789, 101 men and one woman have sat on the bench of America's highest judicial tribunal. If we have suggested that judges of the trial and appeals courts have been culled primarily from America's cultural elite, then members of the U.S. Supreme Court are truly the crème de la crème. Let's take a look at the Court's collective portrait.

While perhaps 10 percent of the justices were of essentially humble origin, the remainder "were not only from families in comfortable economic circumstances, but were chosen overwhelmingly from the socially prestigious and politically influential gentry class in the late 18th and early 19th century, or the professionalized upper class thereafter." [4] A majority of the justices came from politically active families, and about a third were related to jurists and closely connected with families with a tradition of judicial service. Thus the justices were raised in far from commonplace American families.

Until the 1960s the High Court had been all white and all male, but in 1967 President Johnson appointed Thurgood Marshall as the first black member of the Court, and in 1981 the sex barrier was broken when President Reagan named Sandra Day O'Connor to the Court. In terms of religious background, the membership of the Court has been overwhelmingly Protestant although during this century there has been a "Catholic seat" and a "Jewish seat" on the Court. Most Protestants have been affiliated with the more prestigious denominations (such as the Episcopalian, Presbyterian, and Unitarian churches). Thus in terms of ethnicity, gender, and religious preference, the Court is by no means a cross section of American society.

As for the nonpolitical occupations of the justices, all 102 had legal training and all had practiced law at some stage in their careers. An inordinate number had served as corporation attorneys before their appointments. Only 20 percent had state or federal judicial experience *immediately* prior to their appointments, although over half had served on the bench at some time before their nomination to the Supreme Court. As with their colleagues in the lower federal judiciary, the justices were much more likely to have been politically active than the average American, and virtually all shared many of the ideological and political orientations of their appointing president.

An Appraisal of the Statistics

Several conclusions are readily apparent from the summary data we have just presented. First, it is clear that federal judges in the United States are an elite within an elite. They come from upper- or upper-middle-class families that are politically active and that have a tradition of public and, often, judicial service. Is the narrow judicial selection process the result of pure chance? Has there been a sinister conspiracy for the past two centuries to keep women, blacks, Roman Catholics, the poor, and so on out of the U.S. judiciary, or are the causes more subtle and complex? We think the evidence points to the latter explanation. Let us look at a few variables indicative of the selection route to the federal bench—race, family background, and sex.

Legislation has never been passed that forbade non-Anglos from wearing the black robe. But there have been laws, traditions, and unwritten codes that have kept them from entering the better law schools, from working in the more prestigious law firms and corporations, and from making the kind of social and political connections that may lead to nomination to judicial office. Likewise no statutes have excluded the children of the poor from potential seats on the bench. But few youngsters from impoverished homes can afford expensive, good-quality colleges and law schools that would give them the training and the contacts they would need. Traditionally, too, many more young men than young women have been encouraged to apply to law school. For all discriminated-against groups, then, the process of exclusion has not been part of a conscious, organized conspiracy; rather, it has been the inevitable consequence of more subtle social and economic forces in our society.

Another observation about the background profile of our federal judges is worthy of mention. Because they tend to come from the same kinds of families, to go to the same universities and law schools, and to belong to churches, clubs, and societies that uphold similar values, federal judges generally are much more alike than they are different. There may be Democrats and Republicans, former defense attorneys and former prosecutors on the bench, but to a significant degree virtually all play the game by the same rules. What one scholar has said about the recruitment process to the appeals courts is true for federal judgeships in general:

> Broadly speaking [the recruitment process] tends to reward supporters of the presidential party; weed out incompetents, mavericks, and ideological extremists; and ensure substantial professional and political experience among those who wield federal appellate power. Forged thereby are continuous links between judges and their political and professional surroundings. Restricted thereby are the types of persons inducted into Courts of Appeals. The multiple filters through which recruits must pass put a premium on moderate, middle-class, and political lawyers, successful people advantaged in life.[5]

The fact that the recruitment process produces a corps of jurists who agree on how the judicial game is to be played is the primary reason why the loosely organized judicial hierarchy, outlined in Chapter 1, does not come flying apart. It is a key explanation for the predictability of most judicial decisions, a subject that we shall explore in the next two chapters. The judicial machinery runs as smoothly and consistently as it does not because of outside watchdogs or elaborate enforcement mechanisms but because the principal participants largely share the same values and orientations and are working to further similar goals.

③ Formal and Informal Qualifications

Formal Qualifications

Students often torture one another with horror stories of the hurdles to be overcome in order to achieve success in a particular profession. Medical students are awed by the years of training that await them; would-be professors hear of the horrors of the publish-or-perish environment. It would be logical, then, to assume that the formal requirements for becoming a federal judge—and surely a Supreme Court justice—must be formidable indeed. Not so. There are in fact no constitutional or statutory qualifications for serving on the Supreme Court or the lower federal courts. The Constitution merely indicates that "the judicial Power of the United States, shall be vested in one supreme Court" as well as in any lower federal courts that Congress may establish (Article III, Section 1) and that the president "by and with the Advice and Consent of the Senate, shall appoint . . . Judges of the supreme Court" (Article II, Section 2). Congress has applied the same selection procedure to the appeals and the trial courts. There are no exams to pass, no minimum age requirement, no stipulation that judges be native-born citizens or legal residents, nor is there even a requirement that judges have a law degree. Despite the absence of any formal qualifications for a federal judgeship, there are nevertheless some rather well-defined informal requirements, which we shall look at in the next section.

Informal Requirements

It is possible to identify at least four vital although informal factors that determine who sits on the federal bench in America: professional competence, political qualifications, self-selection, and the element of pure luck.

Professional Competence. While candidates for U.S. judicial posts do not have to be attorneys—let alone prominent ones—it has been the custom to appoint lawyers who have distinguished themselves professionally—or at least not to appoint those obviously without merit. *Merit* may mean no more than an association with a prestigious law firm, publication of a few law review articles, or respect among fellow attorneys; a potential judge need not necessarily be an outstanding judicial scholar. Nevertheless one of the unwritten codes is that a judicial appointment is different from run-of-the-mill patronage. Thus while the political rules may allow a president to reward an old ally with a seat on the bench, even here tradition has created an expectation that the would-be judge have some reputation for professional competence, the more so as the judgeship in question goes from the trial to the appeals to the Supreme Court level.

A modern-day example of the unwritten rule that potential judges be more than just warm bodies with a law degree is found in President Nixon's nomination of G. Harrold Carswell to the Supreme Court in 1970. After investigations by the press and the Senate Judiciary Committee revealed that Carswell's record was unimpressive at best, his nomination began to stall on the floor of the Senate. To his aid came the well-meaning senator Roman Hruska of Nebraska, who stated in part: "Even if Carswell were mediocre, there are a lot of mediocre judges and people and lawyers. They are entitled to a little representation, aren't they, and a little chance? We can't have all Brandeises, and Frankfurters, and Cardozos and stuff like that there." [6] With such support Carswell must have wondered why he needed any detractors. In any case the acknowledgment by a friendly senator that the Supreme Court nominee was "mediocre" probably did more than anything else to prompt the Senate to reject Carswell. Although tradition may allow judgeships to be political payoffs and may not require eminence in the nominee, candidates for federal judicial posts are expected to meet a reasonable level of professional competence.

Political Qualifications. When at least 90 percent of all federal judicial nominees are of the same political party as the appointing president, it must strike even the most casual observer that there are certain political requirements for a seat on the bench. The fact that well over half of all federal judges were "politically active" before their appointments—in comparison with a 10 percent figure for the overall population—is further evidence of this phenomenon. What are the political criteria? In some cases a judgeship may be a reward for major service to the party in power or to the president or a senator. For example, when federal judge Peirson Hall (of the Central District of California) was asked how important politics was to his appointment, he gave this candid reply:

I worked hard for Franklin Roosevelt in the days when California had no Democratic Party to speak of. In 1939 I began running for the Senate, and the party convinced me it would be best if there wasn't a contest for the Democratic nomination. So I withdrew and campaigned for Martin Downey. They gave me this judgeship as sort of a consolation prize—and one, I might add, that I have enjoyed.[7]

While examples like this are not uncommon, it would be a mistake to think of federal judgeships merely as political plums handed out to the party faithful. As often as not, a seat on the bench goes to a reasonably active or visible member of the party in power but not necessarily to someone who has made party service the central focus of a lifetime. Political activity that might lead to a judgeship includes service as chair of a state or local party organization, an unsuccessful race for public office, or financial backing for partisan causes.

The reason why most nominees for judicial office must have some record of political activity is two-fold. First, to some degree judgeships are still considered part of the political patronage system; those who have served the party are more likely to be rewarded with a federal post than those who have not paid their dues. Second, even if a judgeship is not given as a direct political payoff, some political activity on the part of a would-be judge is often necessary, because otherwise the candidate would simply not be visible to the president or senator(s) or local party leaders who send forth the names of candidates. If the judicial power brokers have never heard of a particular lawyer because that attorney has no political profile, his or her name will not come to mind when a vacancy occurs on the bench.

Self-Selection. In seeking the presidency or in running for Congress, it doesn't pay to be shy. One needs to declare one's candidacy, meet a formal filing deadline, and spend considerable time and money to advertise one's qualifications. While Americans profess to admire modesty and humility in their leaders, *successful* candidates for elected office do well not to overindulge these virtues. With the judiciary, however, the informal rules of the game are a bit different. Many would consider it undignified and "lacking in judicial temperament" for someone to announce publicly a desire for a federal judgeship—much less to campaign openly for such an appointment.

There is evidence, though, that some would-be jurists orchestrate discreet campaigns on their own behalf or at least pass the word that they are available for judicial service. While few will admit to seeking an appointment actively, credible anecdotes suggest that attorneys often position themselves in such a way that their names will come up when the powers-that-be have a vacant seat to fill. At judicial swearing-in ceremonies it is often said that "the judgeship sought the man (or woman) rather than vice versa," and surely this does happen. But sometimes the judgeship does its seeking with a little nudge from the would-be jurist.

The Element of Luck. If all that were involved in the picking of a Supreme Court justice or a lower-court judge were professional and political criteria, the appointment process would be much easier to explain and predict. If, for instance, one wanted to know who was going to be appointed to a vacancy on the Sixth Circuit bench, one would need only to identify the person in the Sixth Circuit to whom the party was most indebted and who had a reputation for legal competence. The problem is that there would be hundreds of capable attorneys in the Sixth Circuit to whom the prevailing party owed much. Why should one of them be selected and several hundred others not? Until judicial scholarship becomes more of a science and less of an art, we cannot make accurate predictions about who will wear the black robe; there are just too many variables and too many participants in the selection process. Let us look at the example of President Truman's appointment of Carroll O. Switzer to fill a vacant district judgeship in 1949.

The story began in 1948 when Truman was seeking a full term as president. The campaign had not gone well from the start. Even the party faithful could barely muster a faint cheer when Truman proclaimed to sparse crowds, "We're gonna win this election and we're gonna make those Republicans like it. You just wait 'n' see." Almost everyone predicted Truman would lose, and lose badly. Then one morning his campaign train stopped in the little town of Dexter, Iowa. An unexpectedly large number of farmers had put aside their milking chores and the fall corn harvest to see the feisty little man from Missouri "give those Republicans hell." Truman picked up a real sense of enthusiasm among the cheering crowd, and for the first time in the campaign he smelled victory.

On the campaign platform with Truman that morning was Carroll Switzer, a bright young Des Moines attorney who was the (unsuccessful) Democratic candidate for Iowa governor that year. No evidence exists that Truman met Switzer before or after that one propitious day. But when a vacancy occurred on the U.S. bench a year later, Truman's mind jumped like a spring to the name of his lucky horseshoe, Carroll Switzer. A long-time administrative assistant to an Iowa senator related the story as follows:

> I am sure that this day at Dexter was the first time President Truman and his staff were sure he could win—later proved right. I am sure that he recalled that day favorably when an appointment . . . came up in the

Iowa judgeship. . . . Every time the Iowa judgeship came up, Truman would hear of no one but Switzer. Truman would say "That guy Switzer backed me when everyone else was running away, and, by God, I'm going to see that he gets a judgeship." [8]

That morning in Dexter was Switzer's lucky day. While he had the professional and political credentials for a judicial post, no one could have foreseen that he would happen to appear with Truman the day the national winds of political fortune began to blow in the president's favor. Had it been any other day, Switzer might never have been more than just a bright attorney from Des Moines.

This account illustrates the point that there is a good measure of happenstance involved in virtually all judicial appointments. Being a member of the right party at the right time or being visible to the power brokers at a lucky moment often has as much to do with becoming a judge as the length and sparkle of one's professional résumé.

The Selection Process and Its Participants

The skeletal framework of judicial selection is the same for all federal judges, although the roles of the participants vary depending on what level of the U.S. judiciary we are considering. All nominations are made by the president after due consulation with the White House staff, the attorney general's office, certain senators, and other politicos; it has been customary for the FBI to perform a routine security check. After the nomination is announced, various interest groups that believe they have a stake in the appointment may lobby for or against the candidate. Also, the candidate's qualifications will be evaluated by a committee of the American Bar Association. The candidate's name is then sent to the Senate Judiciary Committee, which conducts an investigation of the nominee's fitness for the post. If the committee's vote is favorable, the nomination is sent to the floor of the Senate, where it is either approved or rejected by a simple majority vote. In the next sections we will take a close look at the role of the various participants in the selection process.

The President

Technically the chief executive nominates all judicial candidates, but history has shown that the president manifests greater personal involvement in appointments to the Supreme Court than to the lower courts. This is so for two major reasons. First, Supreme Court appointments are seen by the president—and by the public at large—as generally more important and politically significant than openings on the lesser tribunals.

Presidents often use their few opportunities for High Court appointments to make a political statement or to set the tone of their administration. For example, during the period of national stress prior to U.S. entry into World War II, Democratic president Franklin D. Roosevelt elevated Republican Harlan Stone to chief justice as a gesture of national unity; in 1969 President Nixon used his appointment of the conservative Warren Burger to make good on his campaign pledge to restore "law and order"; and President Reagan hoped to dispel his reputation for being unsympathetic toward the women's movement by being the first to name a woman to the High Court. Because appointments to the lower judiciary are less newsworthy, they are less likely to command the personal involvement of the president, who will probably rely much more heavily on the judgment of the White House staff or the Justice Department in selecting and screening candidates for appeals and trial court benches.

A second reason why presidents are less likely to devote much attention to lower-court appointments is that tradition has allowed for individual senators and local party bosses to influence and often dominate such activity. In fact, the practice known as *senatorial courtesy* is a major restriction on the president's capacity to make district judge appointments. The conditions for this unwritten rule of the game are these: senators of the president's political party who object to a candidate that the president wishes to appoint to a district judgeship in their home state have a virtual veto over the nomination. They exercise this veto through use of the "blue slip"—the printed form that a senator from the nominee's state is supposed to return to the Senate Judiciary Committee to express his or her views about a particular candidate.[9] So significant a restriction is this on the chief executive's appointing prerogatives that it caused one former assistant attorney general to quip, "The Constitution is backwards. Article II, Section 2 should read: 'The senators shall nominate, and by and with the consent of the President, shall appoint.' "[10] Senatorial courtesy does not apply to appellate court appointments, although it is customary for presidents to defer to senators of their party from states that make up the appellate court circuit. Thus in lower-court appointments presidents have less incentive to devote effort to a game in which they are not the star player.

The president also has authority "to fill up all Vacancies that may happen during the Recess of the Senate, by granting Commissions which shall expire at the End of their next Session" (Article II, Section 2). One reason why a chief executive may wish to make a *recess appointment* is to fill a judicial vacancy in a court that has a large backlog of business. The other reason is more political. A president may find it easier to secure confirmation for a "sitting" judge than for a candidate named while the

Senate is in session—that is, the Senate might be less likely to reject a *fait accompli*. For example, when President Kennedy selected Judge Irving Ben Cooper to fill an opening on the federal bench in New York State, the nomination stirred up great opposition in the Senate Judiciary Committee. Although Cooper enjoyed a good public image, he was not well liked by lawyers and other judges.[11] Most observers felt that the fact that Cooper was then serving an interim appointment was extremely useful, if not essential, to his subsequent confirmation. If the Senate had rejected Cooper, a new jurist would have had to be nominated, causing further delay in the appointment of a badly needed new jurist to the court.

During the presidency of Jimmy Carter a new wrinkle was added (but quickly abandoned by Reagan) to the appointment of appellate court judges. By executive order Carter created a U.S. Circuit Judge Nominating Commission.[12] The commission was split into thirteen panels, one for each circuit and two for each of the largest two circuits. The panels were instructed to review candidates for appellate vacancies and to make recommendations based on merit—not on political factors. Carter promised to appoint judges only from the panels' lists of best-qualified candidates. The Omnibus Judgeship Act of 1978 furthered this trend by giving the president the authority to recommend—but not to require—that similar panels be established to assist senators in their suggestions for trial bench appointments in their respective states. The effect of these commission panels is still the subject of controversy. They did indeed come up with candidates that reflected a broader spectrum of American society. (Tables 4-1 and 4-2 indicate the unprecedented number of women and blacks appointed by Carter.) It is doubtful, however, that the commissions took politics out of the selection process: 89.3 percent of Carter's appeals court judges and 94.1 percent of his trial judges somehow managed to be Democrats—most with a liberal bent. In any case on May 4, 1981, President Reagan signed an executive order quietly burying the nominating commission.

The Department of Justice

Assisting the president and the White House staff in the judicial selection process are the two key presidential appointees in the Justice Department—the attorney general of the United States and the deputy attorney general. Their primary job is to seek out candidates for federal judicial posts that conform to general criteria set by the president. For example, if a vacancy were to occur on the Seventh Circuit appellate bench, the attorney general (or a staff member) might phone the U.S. attorneys in the states of Illinois, Wisconsin, and Indiana and ask, "Are there some attorneys in your district who would make good judges and who are members of our political party or who at least share the president's basic philosophy?" Once several names are obtained, the staff of the Justice Department will subject each candidate to further scrutiny. They may order an FBI investigation of the candidate's character and background; they will usually read copies of all articles or speeches the candidate has written or they will evaluate a sitting judge's written opinions; they might check with local party leaders to determine that the candidate is a party faithful and is in tune with the president's major public policy positions.

In the case of district judge appointments, where names are often submitted by home-state senators, the Justice Department's function is more of screener than of initiator. But regardless of who comes up with a basic list of names, the Justice Department's primary duty is to evaluate the candidates' personal, professional, and political qualifications. In performing this role the department may work closely with the White House staff, with the senators involved in the nomination, and with party leaders who may wish to have some input on the potential nominee.

State and Local Party Leaders

Regional party politicos have little to say in the appointment of Supreme Court justices, where presidential prerogative is dominant, and their role in the choice of appeals court judges is minimal. However, in the selection of U.S. trial judges their impact is formidable, especially when appointments occur in states in which neither senator is of the president's political party. In such cases the president need not fear that senatorial courtesy will be invoked against a district court nominee and thus will be more likely to consult with state party leaders rather than with the state's senators. For example, during the Kennedy and Johnson presidencies the Democratic mayor of Chicago, Richard J. Daley, personally approved every federal judge appointed in the Northern District of Illinois. In fact, sometimes during those years the president had to cater to factions *within* the local party machine. In 1966, for instance, leaders of the Italian faction of the Chicago Democratic party balked when it appeared that President Johnson would appoint a nonmachine Italian to "their" seat on the local federal bench. One such leader told Democratic senator Paul Douglas that the machine would even rather have another black, referring to a then-sitting black judge. President Johnson instead nominated a more acceptable Italian.[13]

Interest Groups

A number of pressure groups in the United States, representing the whole political spectrum from left to right, often lobby either for or against judicial nominations. Leaders of these groups—civil liberties, business, organized labor, civil rights—have little hesitation about urging the president to withdraw the nomination of someone whose political and social values are different from their own, or from lobbying the Senate to support the nomination of someone who is favorably perceived. When President Reagan nominated Sandra Day O'Connor for a Supreme Court position in 1981, a variety of interest groups clamored to make their views known. For example, the president of the National Organization for Women said her group was for the nomination, which she called "a major victory for women's rights." However, the conservative Moral Majority was not so pleased with Reagan's choice. Its leaders charged O'Connor with favoring abortion and objected to her support of the then-pending (later-defeated) Equal Rights Amendment. There is evidence that interest groups lobby for and against nominees at all levels of the federal judiciary. As one scholar has noted, pressure-group activity to influence the selection process "has long been characteristic of American politics." [14]

Other Judges

It is not unknown for judges and justices to suggest names of individuals who they believe would make good judges or to lobby behind the scenes for or against a candidate who has been nominated by the president. Chief Justice William Howard Taft did not hesitate to suggest to the Harding and Coolidge administrations of the 1920s the names of men who were "of a sound judicial temperament"—that is, men of conservative ideology who would vote the right way if appointed to the bench. Soon after he became chief justice, Taft related to a confidant that he had "established a very pleasant relationship with the Attorney General and with the President. The Attorney General assures me that he expects to talk with me all the time about the selection of Judges, and I am very sure of what he says." Within weeks Taft was writing the attorney general on a "Dear Harry" basis, and as one scholar has noted: "Hardly a vacancy occurred anywhere on the federal bench without the Chief Justice actively intervening." [15] Most efforts by sitting judges to influence the selection process are more restrained than Taft's, and most jurists probably never enter the fray. But there is evidence at all levels that some judges do indeed lobby, albeit discreetly, to influence the composition of the federal judiciary.

The American Bar Association

For the past four decades the Committee on the Federal Judiciary of the ABA has played a key role in evaluating the credentials of potential nominees for positions on the federal bench. The committee, composed of members from all the U.S. circuits, evaluates candidates on the basis of numerous criteria, including judicial temperament, age, trial experi-ence, character, and intelligence. A candidate approved by the commit-tee is rated "qualified," "well qualified," or "exceptionally well qualified." An unacceptable candidate is stamped with the "not qualified" label.

The traditional composition of the committee has made it the subject of some controversy. Because it has been made up largely of older, well-to-do, Republican, business-oriented corporation attorneys, some observers have argued that its evaluation of potential judicial candidates has been bi-ased in favor of its peers. There is a strong suspicion that the committee has seen being wealthy and conservative as positive traits and being liberal and outspoken as uncharacteristic of "a sound judicial temperament." It should come as no surprise, then, that the ABA's committee has generally worked more closely with Republican presidents than with Democratic administrations.

Bucking the recommendations of the committee is a risky business, and presidents are likely to think long and hard before nominating a candidate tagged with the "not qualified" label.[16] President Kennedy in 1962 successfully pushed for the appointment of Sarah T. Hughes (of the Northern District of Texas) despite opposition from the ABA, which argued that she was too old. Nevertheless it required lobbying from none other than the vice president (Lyndon Johnson) and the Speaker of the House (Sam Rayburn) to ease the nomination through.[17]

Some presidents have gone back and forth in terms of their willingness to be bound by the pronouncements of the ABA committee. For example, when he first took office, President Nixon indicated that he would appoint no one who did not have the blessing of the ABA. However, after Senate defeat of two of Nixon's Supreme Court nominees, Clement Haynsworth and G. Harrold Carswell, the ABA began to cast a more critical eye on Nixon's choices. (The ABA had approved the Haynsworth and Carswell nominations and felt somewhat humiliated when investigations by the press and the Senate turned up a variety of negative factors overlooked by the committee.) Late in 1971, when he was trying to fill two vacancies on the Supreme Court, Nixon brought up the possibility of nominating Senator Robert Byrd of West Virginia. Attorney General John Mitchell told Nixon that there would be a real problem se-curing ABA approval because Byrd had attended a "night law school" and had little experience as a practicing attorney. Nixon's reported reply to Mitchell indicates that the president's total confidence in the judgment of the ABA had waned. "Fuck the ABA," said Nixon. And indeed from that time on, the president refused to submit names to the ABA committee until *after* he had already selected and publicized them.

Since President Nixon and Watergate, two changes seem to have occurred in the ABA. First, it appears to have severed some of its close ties to the conservative establishment and taken stands on public policy issues that offend traditional dogma. For instance, it has come out for federal support of legal aid for the poor. Second, its impact on the judicial selection process may be a bit less now than in past decades. President Carter's setting up of the U.S. Circuit Judge Nominating Commission was seen in part as a successful end run around the bar association, and when President Reagan appointed Sandra O'Connor to the Supreme Court, the ABA was not even consulted.

The Senate Judiciary Committee

The rules of the Senate require its Judiciary Committee to pass on all nominations to the federal bench and to make recommendations to the Senate as a whole. Its role is thus to screen individuals who have already been nominated, not to suggest names of possible candidates. The committee by custom holds hearings on all nominations, at which time witnesses are heard and deliberations take place behind closed doors. In the case of district court appointments, the hearings are largely perfunctory because the norm of senatorial courtesy has for all intents and purposes already determined whether the candidate will pass senatorial muster. However, in the case of appeals court nominees—and surely in the instance of an appointment to the Supreme Court—the committee hearing is a serious proceeding.

Acting as a sort of watchdog of the Senate, the committee can affect the selection process in several ways. "First, it can delay Senate action on confirmation in the hope of embarrassing the president or to test his determination to make a particular appointment." As a general rule, the longer the delay, the poorer the nominee's chances are of securing approval. The Senate rejection of Nixon's two Supreme Court nominees, Haynsworth and Carswell, was the result, in part, of the elongated committee hearings, which permitted the opposition forces to gather negative data and flex their lobbying muscles. Second, the committee can simply recommend against Senate confirmation. Finally, committee opponents of the nomination might engage in an extensive Senate floor debate, which "affords still another opportunity for senators to seek to embarrass the administration by questioning the wisdom of a particular appointment." [18]

Historically the Judiciary Committee has had a distinctly southern and conservative flavor about it. As a result, it often did not look kindly upon appointees to the appeals courts and the Supreme Court who were thought to be too liberal—particularly on civil rights matters. Senator James Eastland of Mississippi, the powerful committee chair for many years, often exacted a terrible toll from presidents who sought to put integrationists on the upper federal courts. For example, when President Kennedy tried to secure the appointment of the black and liberal Thurgood Marshall for a seat on the appellate court bench, Senator Eastland refused to support the nomination unless he could get his old college roommate, William Harold Cox, a seat on the federal district court in Mississippi. Cox, who on the bench referred to blacks as "niggers" and "chimpanzees," is regarded as the worst of several racist judges Kennedy was "forced" to appoint in the South. As one black civil rights leader put it: "The brothers had to pay a lot of dues" to get Thurgood Marshall appointed to the bench.[19]

In 1979 the formidable Senator Eastland retired and in his place—in accordance with the sacrosanct norm of seniority—stepped the liberal Senator Edward Kennedy of Massachusetts. The Senate Judiciary Committee immediately felt the impact of its new chair, and changes followed in the role and orientation of the committee. As one leading judicial scholar noted, "Senator Kennedy's ascendancy to the chairmanship of the Judiciary Committee at the start of the 96th Congress presaged increased scrutiny of judicial nominees as individual senators, the committee, and the Senate institution resolved to re-examine their advice and consent role." [20] In his opening remarks to the committee, Kennedy indicated the direction toward which he would marshal the power and prestige of his chairmanship:

> The federal courts must become more representative of the people of this nation. Congress and the Administration must work together to insure that more women and more members of minority groups are appointed to the federal bench. A judicial branch in which only 5 per cent of the judges are women and only 2 per cent are black is unacceptable. I yield to none in the demand that federal judges who are nominated must be the best available candidates for the job. But excellence in the law is not restricted to candidates who by accident of birth are male or white. The sooner our judicial selection commissions and all other persons involved in the selection process accept this fact, remove their blinders, and expand their searches, the sooner we shall have a federal judiciary that truly meets all the tests of excellence in our society and that truly protects the rights of all citizens.[21]

Furthermore, Kennedy announced that so long as he was chairman, no judicial nomination would die because of the famous "blue slip" of senatorial courtesy. Rather, he insisted that all nominations must be considered by the full committee, and that the committee as a whole would decide whether to make a recommendation to the full Senate.

But the Kennedy reforms on the Judiciary Committee were short-lived. In the 1980 election the Republicans gained control of the Senate, and this resulted in the elevation to the Judiciary chairmanship of Strom Thurmond, the conservative GOP senator from South Carolina. Even before he formally assumed that position, Thurmond made it clear that he favored returning to "traditional" methods of selecting federal judges.[22] Since Thurmond began his chairmanship, it has in fact been business as usual—that is, the committee has retained its powerful role in the judicial selection process, but gone is any desire to make representativeness a characteristic of the U.S. judiciary.

The Senate

The final step in the judicial appointment process for federal judges is a majority vote by the Senate. As we have indicated, the Constitution states that the Senate must give its "advice and consent" to judicial nominations made by the president. Historically there have been two general views of the Senate's prescribed role. Presidents, from the time of George Washington, and a few scholars have taken the position that the Senate ought quietly to go along with the presidential choices unless there are overwhelmingly strong reasons to the contrary. Other scholars and, not unexpectedly, most senators have held to the views of Senator Birch Bayh of Indiana and Senator William Griffin of Michigan that the Senate "has the right and the obligation to decide in its own wisdom whether it wishes to confirm or not to confirm a Supreme Court nominee." [23] In practice the role of the Senate in the judicial confirmation process has varied, depending on the level of the federal judgeship that is being considered.

For district judges the norm of senatorial courtesy prevails. That is, if the president's nominee is acceptable to the senator(s) of the president's party in the state in which the judge is to sit, the Senate is usually happy to give its advice and consent with a quiet nod. For appointments to the appeals courts, as noted earlier, senatorial courtesy does not apply, since the vacancy to be filled covers more than just the state of one or possibly two senators. But it is customary for senators from each state in the circuit in which the vacancy has occurred to submit names of possible candidates to the president. An unwritten rule is that each state in the circuit should have at least one judge on that circuit's appellate bench, a practice often invoked when a vacancy involves a state's only representative on the circuit bench. So long as the norms are looked after and the president's nominee has reasonable qualifications, the Senate as a whole usually goes along with the recommendation of the chief executive.

It has been mainly with Supreme Court nominations that the Senate has been inclined traditionally to go toe-to-toe with the president if there is disagreement over the candidate's fitness for the High Court. Since 1789, presidents have sent the names of 137 persons to the Senate for its advice and consent. Of this number some 28 were either rejected or "indefinitely postponed" by the Senate, or the names were withdrawn by the president. Thus presidents have been successful about 80 percent of the time, and in fact their batting average seems to be improving, since as many as *one-third* of the nominations were rejected by the Senate in the last century. The record shows that presidents have met with the most success in getting their High Court nominations approved when (1) the nominee comes from a noncontroversial background and has middle-of-the-road political leanings—too far neither to the left or right, and (2) the president's party also controls the Senate or at least there is a majority that shares the president's basic attitudes and values.

Policy Links Between the Citizenry, the President, and the Federal Judiciary

Because this book is about policy making, it is appropriate to examine the links between the policy values of the elected chief executive and the decisional propensities of federal judges. If in electing one presidential candidate over another, the citizenry expresses its policy choices, is there evidence that such choices spill over into the kind of judges presidents appoint and the way those judges decide policy-relevant cases? For instance, if the people decide in an election that they want a president who will reduce the size and powers of the federal bureaucracy, does that president subsequently appoint judges who share that philosophy? And, equally important, when those judges hear cases that give them the opportunity either to expand or reduce the extent of a bureaucrat's power, do they opt for the reduction of authority? While we are a long way from having complete answers to these questions, recent evidence suggests the existence of some policy links.

We shall look at this phenomenon by exploring two separate sets of questions. First, what critical factors must exist for presidents to be able to obtain a judiciary that reflects their own political philosophy? Second, what empirical evidence is there to suggest that judges' decisions to some degree carry the imprint of the presidents who selected them?

The President and the Composition of the Judiciary

We suggest there are four general factors that determine whether chief executives can obtain a federal judiciary that is sympathetic to their political values and attitudes.

Presidential Support for Ideologically Based Appointments. One key aspect of the success of chief executives in appointing a federal judiciary that mirrors their own political beliefs is the depth of their commitment to do so. Some presidents may be content merely to fill the federal bench with party loyalists and pay little heed to their nominees' specific ideologies. Some may consider ideological factors when appointing Supreme Court justices but may not regard it as important for trial and appellate judges. Other presidents may discount ideologically grounded appointments because they themselves tend to be nonideological; still others may place factors such as past political loyalty ahead of ideology in selecting judges.

Dwight D. Eisenhower was a chief executive in the first category— that is, an almost apolitical president for whom ideological purity counted little. While his judicial appointees were indeed primarily Republican, upper middle-class types, there is no evidence to indicate that they were picked because their political philosophies matched Eisenhower's. As a result, the Eisenhower judges turned out to be a mixed bag; progressives and strong civil libertarians mingled with jurists of more conservative, law-and-order values.

As a president, Harry Truman had strong political views, but when selecting judges he placed personal loyalty to himself ahead of the candidate's overall political orientation. We noted earlier in this chapter how anxious Truman was to appoint Carroll O. Switzer to fill the judicial vacancy in Iowa. Truman wanted to reward Switzer for sticking with him in the 1948 presidential campaign when so many others had deserted the president, and he couldn't have cared less whether Switzer was a liberal or a conservative. Said Truman, "That guy Switzer backed me when everyone else was running away, and, by God, I'm going to see that he gets a judgeship!" Truman's premium on personal loyalty rather than ideology is generally reflected in the group of men he put on the bench. For example, there was scant linkage between Truman's personal liberal stance on civil rights and equal opportunity and his judicial selections: he appointed no blacks and no women at all, and at least three of his key southern district court appointees have been identified as being very unfriendly toward the cause of civil rights.[24]

If Eisenhower and Truman exemplify presidents who eschewed ideological criteria, Ronald Reagan provides a good example of a chief executive who has selected his judicial nominees with a clear eye toward their compatibility with his own conservative philosophy. During the first two years of his administration, Reagan appointed 87 judges to the district and appeals courts. Of these, 85 were Republicans and 81 were white males; the majority were well-off (half had net worths of over $400,000 and almost a quarter were millionaires); many had established records as political conservatives and as apostles of judicial self-restraint. For example, when Reagan district judge nominee D. Brock Bartlett appeared before the Senate Judiciary Committee, he stated that a judge's role "is not to attempt to impose his or her ideas about social policy." After the Judiciary Committee recommended Bartlett's confirmation, Senator Paul Laxalt (R-Nev.) was prompted to observe, "We're delighted we're finally starting to develop a Reagan team out there on the federal bench." [25] In fairness to President Reagan it should be pointed out, however, that he has not been the only modern president to pack the bench with those who shared his political and legal philosophies: both Presidents Johnson and Carter successfully appointed activist liberal judges.

The Number of Vacancies to Be Filled. A second element affecting the capacity of chief executives to establish a policy link between themselves and the judiciary is the number of appointments available to them. Obviously the more judges a president can select, the greater the potential of the White House to put its stamp on the judicial branch. For example, George Washington's influence on the Supreme Court was significant because he was able to nominate ten individuals to the High Court bench. Jimmy Carter's was nil, on the other hand, because no vacancies occurred during his term as president.

The number of appointment opportunities depends, of course, on several factors: how many judges and justices die or resign during the president's term, how long the president serves, and whether or not Congress passes legislation that significantly increases the number of judgeships. Historically the last factor seems to have been the most important in influencing the number of judgeships available, and, as one might expect, politics in its most basic form permeates this whole process. A study of proposals for new-judges bills in thirteen Congresses tested these two hypotheses: (1) "proposals to add new federal judges are more likely to pass if the party controls the Presidency and Congress than if different parties are in power" and (2) "proposals to add new federal judges are more likely to pass during the first two years of the President's term than during the second two years." The author concluded that his "data support both hypotheses—proposals to add new judges are about 5 times more likely to pass if the same party controls the Presidency and Congress than if different parties control, and about 4 times more likely to pass during the first two years of the President's term than during the second two years." He then noted that these findings serve "to remind us that not only is judicial selection a political process, but so is the creation of judicial posts." [26] Here, for instance, is a dramatic account of the impact of a new-judges bill passed during John Kennedy's presidency:

> Promptly upon Kennedy's election, Congress zipped through an omnibus judgeship bill giving the new president—and, of course, the politicians who helped elect him or whose friendship he now needed— an unprecedented store of judicial boodle to distribute. The act created 71 new judgeships. That wasn't all. Because of vacancies the Democratic Senate had not permitted Ike to fill, Kennedy during his first twenty months in office appointed 147 persons to the federal bench. By way of perspective, Harding, Coolidge and Hoover didn't have that many judgeships in their combined terms. In one slam-bang stretch of 47 days, from August 11 through September 27, 1961, 69 judges were nominated or appointed, an average of almost eleven per week. By midsummer 1962 almost 40 percent of federal judges were Kennedy appointees.[27]

Thus the number of vacancies that a president can fill—a function of politics, fate, and the size of the judicial workloads—is another variable that helps determine the impact a chief executive has on the composition of the federal judiciary.

The President's Political Clout. Another factor is the scope and proficiency of presidential skill in overcoming any political obstacles. One such stumbling block is the U.S. Senate, as we have noted previously. If the Senate is controlled by the president's political party, the White House will find it much easier to secure confirmation than if opposition forces control the Senate. Sometimes when the opposition is in power in the Senate, presidents are forced into a sort of political horse trading to get their nominees approved. For example, when the Democrats controlled the Senate during the Nixon and Ford administrations, those two presidents had to make a political deal for the district judgeships in California: the state's two Democratic senators were permitted to appoint one of their own for every three Republicans that were put on the bench.

The Senate Judiciary Committee is another roadblock between the will and political savvy of the president and the men and women who sit on the federal bench. Some presidents have been more adept than others in easing their candidates through the jagged rocks of the Judiciary Committee rapids. Both Presidents Kennedy and Johnson, for example, had to deal with the formidable committee chairman James Eastland of Mississippi, but only Johnson seems to have had the political adroitness to get most of his liberal nominees approved. Kennedy lacked this skill, and we have mentioned the kinds of judges he was often obliged to appoint.

The president's personal popularity is another element in the political power formula. Chief executives who are well liked by the public and command the respect of opinion makers in the news media, the rank-and-file of their political party, and the leaders of the nation's major interest groups, are much more likely to prevail over any forces that seek to thwart their judicial nominees. Personal popularity is not a stable factor and is sometimes hard to gauge, but there is little doubt that presidents' standing with the electorate helps determine the success of their efforts to influence the composition of the American judiciary. For example, in 1930, President Hoover's choice for a seat on the Supreme Court, John J. Parker, was defeated in the Senate by a two-vote margin. It is likely that had the nomination been made a year or so earlier, before the onset of the depression took Hoover's popularity by the throat, Parker might have gotten on the Supreme Court. Likewise, in 1968 President Johnson's low esteem among voters and the powers-that-be may have been partially responsible for Senate rejection of Johnson's candidate for chief justice, Abe Fortas, and also for the Senate's refusal to replace Fortas with Johnson's old pal Homer Thornberry. As one observer commented, "Johnson failed largely because most members of the Senate 'had had it' with the lame-duck President's nominations." [28] Conversely, President Eisenhower's success in getting approval for an inordinately large number of nominees dubbed "not qualified" by the ABA (some 13.2 percent) may be attributed, in part at least, to Ike's great popularity and prestige.

The Judicial Climate into Which the New Judges Enter. A final matter affects the capacity of chief executives to secure a federal judiciary that reflects their own political values: the current philosophical orientations of the sitting district and appellate court judges with whom the new appointees must interact. Since federal judges serve lifetime appointments during good behavior, presidents must accept the composition and value structure of the judiciary as it exists when they first come into office. If the existing judiciary already reflects the president's political and legal orientation, the impact of new judicial appointees will be immediate and substantial. On the other hand, if new chief executives face a trial and appellate judiciary whose values are radically different from their own, the impact of their subsequent judicial appointments will be weaker and slower to materialize. New judges must respect the controlling legal precedents and the existing constitutional interpretations that prevail in the judiciary at the time they enter it, lest they risk being overturned by a higher court. Such a reality may limit the capacity of a new set of judges to get in there and do their own thing—at least in the short run. Several examples bring this principle down to earth.

When Franklin Roosevelt became president in 1933, he was confronted with a Supreme Court and a lower federal judiciary that had been solidly packed with conservative Republican jurists by his three GOP predecessors in the White House. A majority of the High Court and most lower-court judges viewed most of Roosevelt's New Deal legislation as unconstitutional, and indeed it was not until 1937 that the Supreme Court began to stop overturning virtually all of FDR's major legislative programs.

To make matters worse, his first opportunity to fill a Supreme Court vacancy did not come until the fall of 1937. Thus, despite the ideological screening that went into the selection of FDR's judges, it seems fair to assume that, at least between 1933 and 1938, Roosevelt's trial and appellate judges had to restrain their liberal propensities in the myriad of cases that came before them. This may explain in part why the voting records of the Roosevelt court appointees is not much more liberal than that of the conservative judges selected by his three Republican predecessors; the Roosevelt team just didn't have much room to move in a judiciary dominated by staunch conservatives.

The decisional patterns of the Eisenhower judges further serve to illustrate this phenomenon. While we will momentarily point out that the Eisenhower appointees were more conservative than those selected by Presidents Truman and Roosevelt, the differences in the rulings they made are pretty small. One major reason was that the Eisenhower jurists entered a realm that from top to bottom was dominated by Roosevelt and Truman appointees, who were for the most part liberals. Ike's generally conservative judges didn't have much more room to maneuver than did Roosevelt's liberal jurists in the face of a conservative-dominated judiciary.

Bringing this line of reasoning up to date, President Reagan's impact on the judicial branch should be rather substantial. When he entered the White House, the Supreme Court was already teetering to the right because of Nixon's and Ford's conservative appointments. (Carter had no opportunity to appoint anyone to the High Court.) Despite Carter's liberal appointees on the trial and appellate court benches, Reagan still found a good many conservative Nixon and Ford judges on the bench when he took office. Thus he had and should continue to have a significant opportunity to shape the entire federal judiciary in his own conservative image.

Presidents' Values and Their Appointees' Decisions

We now know the conditions that must be met if presidents are to secure a judiciary in tune with their own policy values and goals. What evidence is there that presidents have in fact been able to do so? Or, to return to our original question, when the people elect a particular president, is there reason to believe that their choice will be expressed in the kinds of judges that are appointed and the kinds of decisions that those judges render?

To answer these questions we shall look at an investigation of the liberal-conservative voting patterns of the teams of district court judges appointed by 11 presidents during this century. This comprehensive study is the only one that covers enough presidents, judges, and cases to allow us to make some meaningful generalizations. In essence we shall see whether liberal presidents appointed trial judges who decided cases in a more liberal manner and whether conservative chief executives were able to obtain district court jurists who followed their policy views.

To begin, we will offer some examples to define the sometimes slippery terms liberal and conservative. In the realm of civil rights and civil liberties, liberal judges would generally take a broadening position—that is, they would seek in their rulings to extend these freedoms; conservative jurists, by contrast, would prefer to limit such rights. For example, in a case in which a government agency wanted to prevent a controversial person from speaking in a public park or at a state university, a liberal judge would be more inclined than a conservative to uphold the right of the would-be speech giver. Or in a case involving school integration, a liberal judge would be more likely to take the side of the minority petitioners. In the area of government regulation of the economy, liberal judges would probably uphold legislation that benefited working people or the economic underdog. Thus, if the secretary of labor sought an injunction against an employer for paying less than the minimum wage, a liberal judge would be more disposed toward the labor secretary's arguments, whereas a conservative judge would tend to side with business, especially big business. Another broad category of cases often studied by judicial scholars is that of criminal justice. Liberal judges are, in general, more sympathetic to the motions made by criminal defendants. For instance, in a case in which the accused claimed to have been coerced by the government into an illegal confession, liberal judges would be more likely than their conservative counterparts to agree that the government had acted improperly.

Table 4-3 indicates the percent of liberal decisions rendered by the district court appointees of Presidents Woodrow Wilson through Gerald

Table 4-3 The Percent of Liberal Decisions Rendered by the District Court Appointees of Presidents Wilson Through Ford, 1933-1977

Appointing president	Percent	Number
Woodrow Wilson	51	94
Warren Harding	41	538
Calvin Coolidge	43	630
Herbert Hoover	42	910
Franklin D. Roosevelt	47	2,827
Harry S Truman	41	3,008
Dwight D. Eisenhower	37	4,287
John F. Kennedy	40	4,368
Lyndon B. Johnson	51	5,750
Richard Nixon	37	3,539
Gerald R. Ford	44	197

Source: Data from Robert A. Carp and C. K. Rowland, *Policymaking and Politics in the Federal District Courts*, 65. Copyright © 1983 by the University of Tennessee Press and reprinted by permission.

R. Ford. Fifty-one percent of the decisions of the Wilson judges are liberal, which puts these jurists on a par with those of Lyndon Johnson for having the most liberal voting record. The liberal pattern of the Wilson judges is not surprising: Wilson was one of the staunchest liberal presidents of this century—particularly on economic issues. Moreover, he chose his judges on a highly partisan, ideological basis: 98.6 percent of his appointments to the lower courts were Democrats—still the record for any president in recent memory.

Succeeding Wilson in the White House were the three Republican chief executives of the 1920s, beginning with Harding's "return to normalcy" in 1921 and followed by the equally conservative Coolidge and Hoover. The right-of-center policy values of these three presidents (and the undisputed Republican domination of the Senate during their incumbencies) are mirrored in the decisional patterns of the trial judges they selected. The liberalism score drops by 10 points from Wilson to Harding, 51 to 41 percent, and stays around that same level for the Coolidge and Hoover judicial teams.

With Franklin D. Roosevelt's judges it's back to left-of-center. At 47 percent liberal, the Roosevelt jurists are five points more liberal than those of his immediate predecessor, Herbert Hoover. We have good evidence that FDR used ideological criteria to pick his judges and that he put the full weight of his political skills behind that endeavor. He once instructed his dispenser of political patronage, James Farley, in effect to use the judicial appointment power as a weapon against senators and representatives who were balking at New Deal legislation: "First off, we must hold up judicial appointments in States where the [congressional] delegation is not going along [with our liberal economic proposals]. We must make appointments promptly where the delegation is with us. Second, this must apply to other appointments. I'll keep in close contact with the leaders." [29]

At first blush the comparatively conservative voting record of the Truman judges seems a bit strange in view of Truman's personal commitment to liberal economic and social policy goals. Only 41 percent of the Truman judges' decisions were liberal, a full six points less than Roosevelt's jurists—and even a point below the Hoover nominees. As we noted earlier, however, Truman counted personal loyalty much more heavily than ideological standards when selecting his judges, and as a result many conservatives found their way into the ranks of the Truman judges. Indeed, even Truman's Supreme Court nominees were of a rather nondescript, conservative ilk:

> Harry Truman's first [Supreme] court appointment was a Republican senator from Ohio, Harold Burton—the only Republican ever selected by a Democratic President. His three other nominees were high-ranking Democratic politicians—Chief Justice Fred Vinson had been his Secretary of the Treasury, Tom Clark had served as Attorney General, and Sherman Minton was an Indiana senator. Truman's men generally held to the modest "judicial restraint" defended so brilliantly by Frankfurter, the court's intellectual eminence. Three of Truman's appointees—Vinson, Burton, and Minton—were among eight justices rated as "failures" in the 1971 poll of professors.[30]

Because of Truman's lack of interest in making policy-based appointments, coupled with the president's strong opposition in the Senate and general lack of popular support throughout much of his administration, his personal liberalism was generally not reflected in the policy values of his judges. Eisenhower's judges were more conservative than Truman's, as expected, but the difference is not very great. But we have already noted that Eisenhower paid little attention to purely ideological appointment criteria; in addition, his judges had to work in the company of an overwhelming Democratic majority in the whole federal judiciary. These factors must have mollified many of the conservative inclinations of the Eisenhower jurists.

The 40 percent liberalism score of the Kennedy judges represents a swing to the left. This is to be expected, and at first blush it may appear strange that John Kennedy's team on the bench was not even more left of center. However, we must keep in mind Kennedy's problems in dealing with the conservative, southern-dominated Senate Judiciary Committee; his lack of political clout in the Senate, which often made him a pawn of senatorial courtesy; and his inability to overcome the stranglehold of local Democratic bosses, who often prized partisan loyalty over ideological purity—or even competence—when it came to appointing judges.

Lyndon Johnson's judges moved impressively toward the left, and, as we noted his judges were as liberal as Wilson's and much more so than Kennedy's. We can account for this on the basis of the four criteria discussed earlier in this chapter that predict a correspondence between the values of chief executives and the orientation of their judges. Johnson knew well how to bargain with individual senators and was second to none in his ability to manipulate and cajole those who were initially indifferent or hostile to issues (or candidates) he supported; his impressive victories in Congress—for example, the antipoverty legislation and the civil rights acts—are monuments to his skill. Undoubtedly, too, he used his political prowess to secure a judicial team that reflected his liberal policy values. In addition, Johnson was able to fill a large number of vacancies on the bench, and his liberal appointees must have felt right at home ideologically in a judiciary capped by the liberal Warren Court.

If the leftward swing of the Johnson team is dramatic, it is no less so than the shift to the right made by the Nixon judges. Only 37 percent of the decisions of Nixon's jurists were liberal. Nixon, of course, placed enormous emphasis on getting conservatives nominated to judgeships at all levels; he possessed the political clout to secure Senate confirmation for most lower-court appointees—at least until Watergate, when the Nixon wine turned to vinegar; and the rightist policy values of the Nixon judges must have been prodded by a Supreme Court that was growing more and more conservative.

The 44 percent liberalism score of the Ford judges puts them right between the Johnson and Nixon jurists in terms of ideology. That Ford's jurists were less conservative than Nixon's is not hard to explain. First, Ford himself was much less of a political ideologue than his predecessor, as reflected in the way in which he screened his nominees and in the type of individuals he chose. (Ford's appointment of the moderate John Paul Stevens to the Supreme Court versus Nixon's selection of the highly conservative William H. Rehnquist illustrate the point.) Also, because Ford's circuitous route to the presidency did not enhance his political effectiveness with the Senate, he would not have had the clout to force highly conservative Republican nominees through a liberal, Democratic Senate, even if he had wished to.

What about the Carter and Reagan judges, whose voting patterns have not yet been systematically evaluated? There is evidence, albeit somewhat fragmentary and anecdotal, that the Carter district (and appellate) judges have been distinctly liberal, in contrast with Reagan's jurists, who are clearly marching to a more conservative drummer.[31] This should come as little surprise, given the four criteria we have discussed for a meeting of the minds between a president and the federal judiciary. Reagan, like Carter, has gone out of his way to select candidates who share his basic policy goals; like his predecessor, too, Reagan has filled a sizable number of vacancies (Carter, however, had no opportunity to appoint anyone to the Supreme Court); and both had a reasonable degree of political clout with Senates controlled by their respective parties. Finally, both were able to send ideological counterparts into a federal judiciary that contained a goodly number of like-minded jurists ready to receive them with open arms.

We have explored the degree to which presidents have been able to secure a judiciary that reflects their own policy values. The evidence indicates that if they are of a mind to, and have a little luck, chief executives can appoint judges who mirror many of the attitudes and values of the electorate. It is particularly significant that such data show up at the district court level, where presidential input is at its weakest because senatorial courtesy naturally muddies the selection process. But even among district court jurists we see the imprint of policy links between the people's choice and the actions of their appointed judges! If this is the case, the potential policy ties at the appeals court and Supreme Court levels should be even stronger, because the president has a much freer hand in selecting those jurists than U.S. trial judges.

The Judicial Socialization Process

The central focus of this chapter is on the federal judges and justices themselves. We continue our look at the judges by examining a critical period in their professional life—the judicial socialization process, the time during which new appointees learn to be judges.

When scholars use the term *socialization,* they are referring to the process whereby individuals acquire the values, attitudes, and behavior patterns of the ongoing social system. Factors that aid the process include family, friends, education, co-workers, religious training, political party affiliation, and the communications media. Social scientists also apply the term *socialization* to the process by which a person is formally trained to perform the specific tasks of a particular profession. It is the second meaning of the term, then, that will concern us.

Prior to looking at judges' on-the-job training, we must acknowledge that much significant socialization occurs *before* the judges first mount the bench. From their parents, teachers, exposure to the news media, and so on, future judges learn the rules of the political game as it is practiced in America. That is, by the time they are teenagers they have absorbed key values and attitudes that will circumscribe subsequent judicial behavior: "the majority should rule on general matters of public policy, but minorities have their rights, too"; "judges ought to be fair and impartial"; or "the Constitution is an important document and all political leaders should be bound by it." In college and law school future judges acquire important analytic and communications skills, in addition to the basic substance of the law. After a couple of decades of legal practice, the preparation for a judgeship is in its final stage; the future judge has learned a good bit about how the courts and the law actually work and has specialized in several areas of the law. Despite all this preparation, sometimes called "anticipatory socialization," [32] most new federal judges in America still have a lot to learn even after donning the black robe.

In many other countries preparing to be a judge is like preparing to be a physician, an engineer, or a pharmacist—that is, one goes to a particular professional school in which one receives many years of in-depth training and perhaps an on-the-job internship. Since 1959 in France, for example, all new would-be judges are intensively trained for a minimum of 28 months in the prestigious Ecole Nationale de la Magistrature; they enter judicial service only after passing rigorous, competitive examinations. Not only does the United States lack formalized training procedures for the judicial profession, but there is the naive assumption that being a lawyer for a decade or so is all the experience one needs to be a judge. After all, don't most lawyers, like judges, work in the courtroom? Isn't it enough for the lawyer-turned-judge just to mount the bench and put on a new hat? To the contrary, becoming a judge in America requires a good deal of *freshman socialization* (short-term learning and adjustment to the new role) and *occupational socialization* (on-the-job training over a period of years).

Let us examine what it is like to become a new judge and why socialization must continue well into the novice jurist's career. Typical new trial court appointees may be first-rate lawyers and experts in a few areas of the law in which they have specialized. As judges, however, they are suddenly expected to be experts on *all* legal subjects, are required to engage in judicial duties usually quite unrelated to any tasks they performed as lawyers (for example, sentencing), and are given a host of administrative assignments for which they have had no prior experience (for example, learning how to docket efficiently several hundred diverse cases).[33] The following statements by U.S. trial judges reveal what it was like for them as the new kid on the judicial block. (Virtually all the judges who were interviewed for this book were promised anonymity, and thus no footnotes will appear at the end of their quotations.)

> Before I became a federal judge I had been a trial lawyer dealing mainly with personal injury cases and later on with some divorce cases. Needless to say, I knew almost nothing about criminal law. With labor law I had had only one case in my life on this subject, and that was a case going back to the early days of World War II. In other words when I became a federal judge I really had an awful lot to learn about many important areas of the law.
>
> My legal background and experience really didn't prepare me very well for the kind of major judicial problems I face. For instance, most lawyers don't deal with constitutional issues related to the Bill of Rights and the Fourteenth Amendment; rather they deal with much more routine questions, such as wills and contracts. Civil liberties questions were really new to me as a judge, and I think this is true for most new judges.

At the appeals court level there is also a period of freshman socialization—despite the circuit judge's possible prior judicial experience—although former trial judges appear to make the transition with fewer scars. As a couple of appeals judges said of their first days on the circuit bench: "I was no blushing violet in fields I knew something about. How effective I was is another question." Even an experienced former trial judge recalled his surprise that "it takes a while to learn the job—and I'm not addressing myself to personal relationships. . . . That's a very different job." Another appeals judge, regarded by his peers as a leader from the beginning, said that he "remarked only yesterday that I don't know how I got through my first year." [34] During the transition time—the period of learning the appellate court ropes—circuit judges tend to speak less for the court than their more experienced colleagues; they often take longer to write opinions, defer more often to senior colleagues, or just wallow about in indecision.

The learning process for new Supreme Court justices is even harder—if the personal testimonies of justices as diverse as Benjamin Cardozo, Frank Murphy, Harlan F. Stone, Earl Warren, William Brennan, and Arthur Goldberg are to be believed. As one scholar has noted, "Once on the Court, the freshman Justice, even if he has been a state or lower federal court judge, moves into a strange and shadowy world." [35] Perhaps this is the metaphor that Chief Justice William Howard Taft had in mind when he confided that in joining the Court he felt that he had come "to live in a monastery." As with new appeals court judges, novice Supreme Court justices tend to defer to senior associates, to write fewer majority and dissenting opinions, and to manifest a good deal of uncertainty. New High Court appointees may have more judicial experience than their lower-court colleagues, but the fact that the Supreme Court is involved in broad judicial policy making—as opposed to the error correction of the appeals courts and the norm enforcement of the trial courts—may account for their initial indecisiveness.

Given the need on the part of all new federal jurists for both freshman and occupational socialization, where do they go for instruction? While there are many agents of socialization for novice judges, the evidence is pretty strong that the older, more experienced judges have the primary responsibility for this task: the system trains and nurtures its own. As one trial judge told us, "My prime sources of help were the two judges here in [X city]. They sent me various things even before I was appointed, and I was glad to get them." Another recalled, "I had the help I needed right down here in the corner of this building on this floor," pointing in the direction of another judge's chambers. One district judge gave a more graphic description of his "schooling":

> They [the other trial judges] let me sit next to them in actual courtroom situations, and they explained to me what they were doing at every minute. We both wore our robes and we sat next to each other on the bench. I would frequently ask them questions and they would explain things to me as the trial went along. Other times I would have a few free minutes and I would drop into another judge's courtroom and just sit and watch. I learned a lot that way.

For both the rotating appeals court judges and their trial court brethren, then, the lion's share of training comes from their more senior, experienced colleagues on the bench—particularly the chief judge of the circuit or district.[36] One scholar has noted that "the impact of chief judges was most noticeable on freshmen. . . . ('If all the judges are new, he'll pack a wallop out of proportion to one vote.')"[37] Likewise on the Supreme Court there is evidence that older associates, often the chief justice, play a primary part in passing on to novice justices the essential rules and values on which their very serious game is based.[38]

The fact that judges in America still require socialization even after their appointments is interesting in and of itself, but we might well ask: What is the significance of all this for the operation of our judicial-legal system? First, the agents of socialization that are readily available to the novice jurists allow the system to operate more smoothly, with a minimum of down time. If new judges were isolated from their more experienced associates, geographically or otherwise, it would take them much longer to learn the fine points of their trade and presumably there would be a greater number of errors foisted upon hapless litigants.

There is a second consequence of the socialization process. As noted in Chapter 1, the federal judicial system is a rather loose hierarchy that is constantly subjected to centrifugal and centripetal forces from within and without. The fact that the system is able to provide its own socialization—that the older, experienced jurists train the novices—serves as a sort of glue that helps bond the fragmented system together. It allows the judicial values, practices, and orientations of one generation of judges to be passed on to another. It gives continuity and a sense of permanence to a system that operates in a world where chaos and random behavior appear to be the order of the day.

The Retirement and Removal of Federal Judges

We have reached the final stage in our look at the judges themselves—the time when they cease performing their judicial duties, by choice, by ill health or death, or by the disciplinary actions of others.

Disciplinary Action

All federal judges appointed under the provisions of Article III of the Constitution hold office "during good Behavior," which means in effect for life or until they choose to step down. The only way they can be removed from the bench is by impeachment (indictment by the House of Representatives) and conviction by the Senate. In accordance with constitutional requirements (for Supreme Court justices) and legislative standards (for appeals and trial court judges), impeachment may occur for "Treason, Bribery, or other high Crimes and Misdemeanors." An impeached jurist would face trial in the Senate, which could convict by a vote of two-thirds of the members present.

The impeachment of a federal judge is a fairly rare event. Since 1789 the House has initiated such proceedings against only 10 jurists—although about an equal number of judges resigned just before formal action was taken against them. Of these 10 cases, only four resulted in a conviction, which removed them from office. Considering all the men and women who have sat on the federal bench during the past two centuries, that's not a bad record. (Four members of Congress have been convicted of felonies in a single session!)

Although outright acts of criminality on the bench are few, a gray area of misconduct may put offending judges somewhere in the twilight zone between acceptable and impeachable behavior. What to do with the federal jurist who hears a case despite an obvious conflict of interest, who consistently demonstrates biased behavior in the courtroom, who too often totters into court after a triple-martini lunch? A case in point is Judge

Willis Ritter, who used to sit on the federal bench in Salt Lake City. One observer described Ritter as

> ecumenically mean, which is to say he seems to dislike most persons who come into his court, be they defendant, government lawyer, private trial attorney, or ordinary citizen. Ritter is also selective about his fellow judges. He was once so estranged from another Utah federal judge that they wouldn't ride on the elevator together, much less speak; for a while the court clerk divided cases so that they didn't have to appear in the courthouse on the same day. . . . Ritter is one of the few federal judges in the nation who becomes so emotionally involved in his hearings that appeals courts often order him not to retry cases when they are reversed.[39]

One lawyer, who had managed to fall from Judge Ritter's graces, recalled an incident. As the lawyer was starting to present his case in open court, from out of the blue the judge began to hiss at him and continued to do so throughout the attorney's presentation. "Like a snake, he was going 'ssssss' all the time I was speaking," the astounded lawyer recounted later. "I never ever have been before a judge of this kind." [40]

But what to do with Judge Ritter and those of his ilk? Had Ritter committed impeachable offenses? Surely he had not been guilty of "Treason, Bribery, or other high Crimes and Misdemeanors," although one could well question whether he was indeed serving "during good Behavior." Historically, little was done in such cases other than issue a mild reprimand from colleagues (a useless gesture for a Judge Ritter) or impeachment (a recourse considered too drastic in most cases). In recent decades, however, actions have been taken to fill in the discipline gap. In 1966, for example, the Supreme Court upheld an action taken by the Tenth Circuit Judicial Council against U.S. District Judge Stephen S. Chandler of Oklahoma. The council had stripped him of his duties and authority (while permitting him to retain his salary and title) for a series of antics both on and off the bench that made Judge Ritter seem venerable by comparison.

In addition, on October 1, 1980, a new statute took effect on which Congress had labored for several years. Titled the Judicial Councils Reform and Judicial Conduct and Disability Act, the law contains two distinct parts.[41] The first provides for a Judicial Council in each circuit, composed of both appeals and trial judges and presided over by the chief judge of the circuit, and specifies that the council "shall make all necessary and appropriate orders for the effective and expeditious administration of justice within its circuit." The second part of the act establishes a statutory complaint procedure against judges. Basically, it permits an aggrieved party to file a written complaint with the clerk of the appellate court. The chief judge then reviews the charge and may dismiss it if it appears frivolous or for a variety of other reasons. If the complaint seems valid, the chief judge must appoint an investigating committee consisting of himself or herself and an equal number of trial and circuit judges. After an inquiry the committee reports to the council, which has several options: (1) the judge may be exonerated; (2) if the offender is a bankruptcy judge or magistrate, he or she may be removed; and (3) Article III judges may be subject to private or public reprimand or censure, certification of disability, request for voluntary resignation, or prohibition against further case assignments. However, removal of an Article III judge is not permitted; impeachment is still the only recourse. If the council determines that the conduct "might constitute" grounds for impeachment, it will notify the Judicial Conference, which in turn may transmit the case to the U.S. House of Representatives for consideration. Because this law has been on the books for only a short time, it is difficult to assess its effectiveness. However, it appears to fill in a wide gap in the disciplinary process between informal pressure on the one hand and outright impeachment on the other.

Disability of Justices

Perhaps the biggest problem has not been the removal of criminals and crackpots from the federal bench; rather, it has been the question of what to do with jurists who have become too old and infirm effectively to carry out their judicial responsibilities. As the former chief judge of the Fifth Circuit of Appeals John Brown tersely put it, "Get rid of the aged judges, and you get rid of most of the problems of the federal judiciary: drunkenness, incompetence, senility, cantankerous behavior on the bench." [42] For example, Justice William O. Douglas suffered a stroke while on the Supreme Court, but refused afterward to resign even when it was clear to all that he should do so. In 1974 Chief Justice Burger "believed Douglas was developing the paranoid qualities of many stroke victims. Douglas complained that there were plots to kill him and to remove him from the bench. Once he was wheeled in the Chief's chambers and maintained it was his. Rumors circulated among the staff that Douglas thought he was the Chief Justice." But he stayed on. A year later he was still interpreting the Constitution for over 200 million Americans although he "was in constant pain and barely had the energy to make his voice audible. He was wheeled in and out of conference, never staying the entire session, leaving his votes with Brennan to cast. Powell counted the number of times Douglas fell asleep. Brennan woke him gently when it came time to vote." Eventually Douglas resigned, but surely he remained on the bench longer than he should have. On the Court at the same time as Douglas were Justices John Harlan and Hugo Black. The latter, at 85, was in such poor health that Douglas was counseling *him* to resign. "But Black would not accept the advice." [43]

In contrast to Black, Harlan continued to run his chambers from his hospital bed. Nearly blind, he could not even see the ash from his own cigarette, but he doggedly prepared for the coming term. One day a clerk brought in an emergency petition. Harlan remained in bed as he discussed the case with the clerk. They agreed that the petition should be denied. Harlan bent down, his eyes virtually to the paper, wrote his name, and handed the paper to his clerk. The clerk saw no signature. He looked over at Harlan.

"Justice Harlan, you just denied your sheet," the clerk said, gently pointing to the scrawl on the linen. Harlan smiled and tried again, signing the paper this time. [44]

While the federal judiciary as a whole is not proportionally in the same state of ill health and advanced age as was the Supreme Court during the early 1970s, the problem of what to do with the aged or mentally disabled judge has not disappeared. Congress has tried with some success to tempt the more senior judges into retirement by making it financially more palatable to do so. Federal judges may now retire with full pay if they are 70 years old and have served on the bench for 10 years, or they may do so at age 65 if they have 15 years of service. Congress has also permitted judges to go on "senior" status instead of accepting full retirement: in exchange for a reduced caseload they are permitted to retain their office and staff and—equally important—the prestige and self-respect of being an active judge. Despite the congressional inducements to retire, "more vacancies occur as a result of death in harness, particularly at the higher levels, than in any other way." [45]

We conclude this discussion of judicial tenure on a more political note. There is some credible evidence that judges often time their resignations to occur when their party controls the presidency, so that they will be replaced by a jurist of similar political and judicial orientation. As one researcher concluded, "Among the Appeals and District judges there is a substantial contingent who bring to the bench political loyalties that encourage them, more often than not, to maneuver their departure in such a way that will maximize the chance for the appointment of a replacement by a president of their party." [46] We catch the flavor of this phenomenon in this account of an Iowa district judge's decision about retirement:

By 1948 Iowa Southern District Federal Judge Charles A. Dewey had decided that the time had come for him to retire. The seventy-one year old jurist had served on the federal bench for two full decades, and he felt that he had earned the right to his government pension. As a good Republican, however, he felt that it would be best to withhold his resignation until after the November election when "President Thomas E. Dewey" would be in a position to fill the vacancy with another "right-minded" individual like himself. Much to Judge Dewey's chagrin, his namesake did not receive the popular mandate in the presidential election, and Judge Dewey did not believe that he could carry on for another four years until the American people finally "came to their senses" and put a Republican in the White House. Therefore, shortly after the November election, Judge Dewey tendered his resignation.[47]

A similar note is sounded by former chief justice William Howard Taft, who clung to his High Court position lest he be replaced with someone whose policy values were more progressive than his own: "As long as things continue as they are, and I am able to answer in their place, I must stay in the Court in order to prevent the bolsheviki [that is, American Communists] from gaining control." [48]

These above illustrations provide further evidence that many jurists view themselves as part of a policy link between the people, the judicial appointment process, and the subsequent decisions of the judges and justices.

Summary

This chapter began with a collective portrait of the men and women who have served in the federal judiciary. We noted that despite the occasional maverick, the jurists have come from quite a narrow stratum within America's social and economic elite. The result is a corps of judges who share similar values and who therefore strive, with minimal coercion, to keep the judicial system functioning in a relatively harmonious manner. Though the formal qualifications for a seat on the bench are few, tradition has established several informal criteria, including a reasonable degree of professional competence, the right political affiliation and contacts, at least some desire for the job itself, and a bit of luck thrown in for good measure.

The judicial selection process itself includes a variety of participants, despite the constitutional mandate that the president shall do the appointing, with the advice and consent of the Senate. If presidents are to dominate this process and name individuals of similar policy values to the bench, several conditions must be met: chief executives must desire to make ideologically based appointments, they must have an ample number of vacancies to fill, they must be adroit leaders with political clout, and the existing judiciary must be attuned to their policy goals. If most of these conditions are met, presidents tend to get the kind of judges they want. In other words, there is an identifiable policy link between the popular election of the president, the appointment of judges, and the substantive contents of the judges' decisions.

Although much judicial socialization occurs before the judges don their black robes, a good deal of learning takes place after they assume the bench. Because both freshman and occupational socialization is performed by senior colleagues, the values and practices of one generation of judges are smoothly passed on to the next. Thus continuity in the system is maintained.

The disciplining and removal of corrupt or mentally unfit judges is still a problem, although it may be eased somewhat if recent congressional legislation proves effective. The fact that so many judges time their resignations so that a president of similar party identification and values may appoint a replacement is further evidence that the jurists themselves see a substantive policy link between the appointment process and the contents of many of their decisions.

Notes

1. For a more extensive study of this subject, particularly as it pertains to the U.S. appeals courts and the Supreme Court, see John R. Schmidhauser, *Judges and Justices: The Federal Appellate Judiciary* (Boston: Little, Brown, 1979), 55-58.
2. Debra Sharpe and Peggy Roberson, "Tower Backs Cobb for Federal Judge," *Beaumont Enterprise,* May 4, 1984, A1.
3. For a good discussion of President Carter's affirmative action policies for the federal judiciary, see Sheldon Goldman, "Should There Be Affirmative Action for the Judiciary?" *Judicature* 62 (1979): 488-496, and Sheldon Goldman, "Reagan's Judicial Appointments at Mid-Term: Shaping the Bench in His Own Image," *Judicature* 66 (March 1983): 335-347.
4. Schmidhauser, *Judges and Justices,* 49.
5. J. Woodford Howard, Jr., *Courts of Appeals in the Federal Judicial System* (Princeton, N.J.: Princeton University Press, 1981), 121.
6. Howard Ball, *Courts and Politics: The Federal Judicial System* (Englewood Cliffs, N.J.: Prentice-Hall, 1980), 201-202.
7. As quoted in Joseph C. Goulden, *The Benchwarmers: The Private World of the Powerful Federal Judges* (New York: Weybright and Talley, 1974), 33.
8. As quoted in Robert A. Carp and C. K. Rowland, *Policymaking and Politics*

in the Federal District Courts (Knoxville: University of Tennessee Press, 1983), 55.

9. As a standard procedure, the Senate Judiciary Committee sends to the senator(s) of the state in which a district court vacancy exists a request, printed on a blue form, to approve or disapprove the nomination being considered by the committee. If approval is not forthcoming, the senator simply retains the slip; but if there is no objection, the blue form is returned to the committee.

10. As quoted in Ball, *Courts and Politics,* 176.

11. Goulden, *The Benchwarmers,* 65. The reason why Kennedy was under pressure to appoint Cooper in the first place was that Cooper was the choice of Representative Emanuel Celler, titular leader of New York State's congressional delegation and chairman of the House Judiciary Committee.

12. For more information about the commission, see Larry C. Berkson and Susan B. Carbon, *The United States Circuit Judge Nominating Commission: Its Members, Procedure and Candidates* (Chicago: American Judicature Society, 1980).

13. Donald Dale Jackson, *Judges* (New York: Atheneum, 1974), 113.

14. John R. Schmidhauser, *The Supreme Court: Its Politics, Personalities, and Procedures* (New York: Holt, Rinehart and Winston, 1960), 21.

15. Walter F. Murphy, *Elements of Judicial Strategy* (Chicago: University of Chicago Press, 1964), 114.

16. The classic study of the role of the ABA is Joel B. Grossman, *Lawyers and Judges: The ABA and the Politics of Judicial Selection* (New York: Wiley, 1965).

17. For the humorous and interesting details of this controversy, see Goulden, *The Benchwarmers,* 61-62.

18. Harold W. Chase, *Federal Judges: The Appointing Process* (Minneapolis: University of Minnesota Press, 1972), 21, 23.

19. As quoted in Jackson, *Judges,* 122.

20. Elliot E. Slotnick, "Federal Appellate Judge Selection During the Carter Administration: Recruitment Changes and Unanswered Questions," *Justice System Journal* 6 (1981): 283.

21. As quoted in Elliot E. Slotnick, "Reforms in Judicial Selection: Will They Affect the Senate's Role? Part II," *Judicature* 64 (1980): 116.

22. *Tallahassee Democrat,* November 7, 1980, 11A.

23. As quoted in Ball, *Courts and Politics,* 167.

24. "Judicial Performance in the Fifth Circuit," *Yale Law Review* 73 (1963): 90-133.

25. Both quoted in the *Kansas City Times,* July 29, 1981, B6.

26. Jon R. Bond, "The Politics of Court Structure: The Addition of New Federal Judges," *Law & Policy Quarterly* 2 (1980): 182, 183, and 187.

27. Goulden, *The Benchwarmers,* 59.

28. Henry J. Abraham, *The Judicial Process,* 3d ed. (New York: Oxford University Press, 1975), 77.

29. James A. Farley, "Why I Broke with Roosevelt," *Collier's*, June 21, 1947, 13.
30. Jackson, *Judges*, 340.
31. For example, see Jon Gottschall, "Carter's Judicial Appointments: The Influence of Affirmative Action and Merit Selection on Voting on the U.S. Courts of Appeals," *Judicature* 67 (1983): 165-173, and Goldman, "Reagan's Judicial Appointments at Mid-Term," 335-347.
32. Howard, *Courts of Appeals in the Federal Judicial System*, 107.
33. New federal district judges with prior state court experience have a somewhat easier time of it, particularly in terms of the psychological adjustment to the judgeship and in dealing with some of the administrative problems. However, prior state court experience seems to be of little help in the jurists' efforts to become expert in *federal* law. See Robert A. Carp and Russell R. Wheeler, "Sink or Swim: The Socialization of a Federal District Judge," *Journal of Public Law* 21 (1972): 367-374.
34. All quoted in Howard, *Courts of Appeals in the Federal Judicial System*, 224.
35. Murphy, *Elements of Judicial Strategy*, 50.
36. For the best discussion of this phenomenon, see Howard, *Courts of Appeals in the Federal Judicial System*, Chapter 8.
37. Ibid., 229.
38. For examples of this, see Murphy, *Elements of Judicial Strategy*, 49-51.
39. Goulden, *The Benchwarmers*, 298.
40. Philip Hager, "Legal Leaders Seek Way to Unseat Unfit Federal Judges," *Houston Chronicle*, October 2, 1977, 1:6.
41. For more information about the act and its policy consequences, see Eric Neisser, "The New Federal Judicial Discipline Act: Some Questions Congress Didn't Answer," *Judicature* 65 (1981): 142-160.
42. As quoted in Goulden, *The Benchwarmers*, 292.
43. Bob Woodward and Scott Armstrong, *The Brethren* (New York: Simon and Schuster, 1979), 361, 392, 156.
44. Ibid., 157.
45. Henry J. Abraham, *The Judicial Process*, 4th ed. (New York: Oxford University Press, 1980), 43.
46. R. Lee Rainey, "The Decision to Remain a Judge: Deductive Models of Judicial Retirement" (Paper delivered at the annual meeting of the Southern Political Science Association, Atlanta, 1976), 16.
47. Robert A. Carp, "The Function, Impact, and Political Relevance of the Federal District Courts: A Case Study," Ph.D. dissertation, University of Iowa, 1969, 76.
48. As quoted in C. Herman Pritchett, *The Roosevelt Court: A Study of Judicial Votes and Values, 1937-1948* (New York: Macmillan, 1948), 18.

The Decision-Making Process 5

On what basis and for what reasons do federal judges rule the way they do on the motions, petitions, and judicial policy with which they must deal? We shall respond to this query by summarizing the theories and research findings of a large number of judicial scholars who have tried to find out what makes judges tick (Chapter 6 will examine the special case of decision making on the collegial appellate courts and the Supreme Court).

It is useful to begin with a brief discussion of the decision-making environment in which trial judges and their appellate colleagues operate. Because of the differing purposes and organizational framework of trial and appellate courts, judges of each type face particular kinds of pressures and expectations. As the chapter emphasizes, however, all federal jurists are subject to two major kinds of influences: the legal subculture and the democratic subculture. It is often difficult to determine, in any given case, the relative weight that any specific influence has on a judge. Studies have suggested, though, that when judges, especially trial judges, find no significant precedent to guide them—that is, when the legal subculture cupboard is bare—they tend to turn to the democratic subculture, an amalgam of determinants that includes their own political inclinations.

The Decision-Making Environment

At the base of the judicial hierarchy are the federal district judges, who conduct the actual trials and who make millions of separate decisions each year. Some pertain to legal points and procedures raised by litigants even before a trial begins, such as a motion by a criminal defendant's lawyer to exclude from trial a piece of illegally obtained evidence. During the actual course of the trial a judge must rule on scores of motions made by the attorneys in the case—for example, an objection to a particular question asked of a witness or a request to strike from the record a contested bit of testimony. Even after a verdict has been rendered, a trial judge may be beset with demands for decisions—for instance, the request by a litigant to reduce a monetary award made by a civil jury.

Trial judges can and occasionally do take ample time to reflect on their more important decisions and may consult with their staff or other judges about how to handle a particular legal problem. Nevertheless a significant portion of their decision making must be on the spur of the moment, without the luxury of lengthy reflection or discussion with staff or colleagues. As one trial judge told us: "We're where the action is. We often have to 'shoot from the hip' and hope you're doing the right thing. You can't ruminate forever every time you have to make a ruling. We'd be spending months on each case if we ever did that." (Again, virtually all of the judges interviewed for this study were promised anonymity.)

Decision making by members of the appeals courts and by the Supreme Court is different in several important respects. By the time a case reaches the appellate levels, the record and facts have already been established. The jurists' job is to review dispassionately the transcript of a trial that has already occurred, to search for legal errors that may have been committed by others. Few snap judgments are required. And while the appeals courts and the Supreme Court may occasionally hear oral arguments by attorneys, they do not examine witnesses and they are removed from the drama and confrontations of the trial courtroom. Another difference in the decision-making process between the trial and appellate levels is that the former is largely individualistic, while the latter is to some degree the product of group deliberation (discussed in Chapter 6).

Despite the acknowledged differences between trial and appellate judge decision making, there are many factors common to all federal jurists, and we shall examine several studies that have sought to explain why judges in general think and act as they do. As we shall see, the thrust of these scholarly attempts at explanation has differed. Some view judges as judicial computers who take in a volume of facts, law, and legal doctrines and spew out "correct" rulings—determinations that are virtually independent of the judges' values and attributes as human beings. Other researchers tend to explain judicial decision making in terms of the personal orientations of the judges themselves. A decision is seen not so much as the product of some unbiased, exacting thought process that judges acquire in law school but rather as the effects of the judge's life experiences, prejudices, and overall social values. As with most explanatory theories of human behavior, each of these approaches contains its fair share of the truth, but none accounts for the whole story of the activity in question.

One simple but comprehensive model for explaining judicial decision making was developed by Professors Richardson and Vines more than a decade ago.[1] These two judicial scholars argued that U.S. judges are influenced in their decision making by two separate but overlapping sets of stimuli: the legal subculture and the democratic subculture. We shall use their basic analytic framework, with updated research findings, to offer an account of how and why judges make decisions the way they do.

The Legal Subculture

In examining the legal subculture as a source of trial judge decision making, it is useful to focus on a number of specific questions. What are the basic rules, practices, and norms of this subculture? Where do judges learn these principles and what groups or institutions keep judges from departing from them? How often and under what circumstances do judges respond to stimuli other than those from the traditional legal realm?

The Nature of Legal Reasoning

In the popular television series *The Paper Chase* the formidable Professor Kingsfield promises his budding law students that if they work hard and turn their mush-filled brains over to him, he will instill in them the ability "to think like a lawyer." How *do* lawyers and judges think when they deliberate in their professional capacities? In one classic answer to this question, we are told that "the basic pattern of legal reasoning is reasoning by example. It is a three-step process described by the doctrine of precedent as follows: (1) similarity is seen between cases; (2) the rule of law inherent in the first case is announced; and (3) the rule of law is made applicable to the second case." [2]

Let us look at an example. The cases of *Lane v. Wilson* and *Gomillion v. Lightfoot* contained similar arguments and factual situations.[3] In the former case a black citizen of Oklahoma brought suit in federal court alleging that he had been deprived of the right to vote. In 1916 the legislature of that state had passed a law, ostensibly designed to give formerly disenfranchised black citizens the right to vote, that required them to register—but the registration period was only *12 days!* (White voters were for all practical purposes exempted from this scheme through the use of a "grandfather clause.") If blacks did not sign up within that short interval, never again would they have the right to vote. The Oklahoma legislature clearly realized that a 12-day period was wholly inadequate for blacks to mount a voter registration drive and that the vast majority would not acquire the franchise. The plaintiff in this case did not get on the registration rolls in 1916. When he was thereafter forbidden from ever voting, he brought suit claiming the Oklahoma registration scheme to be unconstitutional. The Supreme Court agreed with the plaintiff; in striking down the statute, it set forth this principle, or rule of law: "The Fifteenth Amendment nullifies sophisticated as well as simple-minded modes of discrimination." [4]

Two decades later another black citizen, Charles Gomillion, brought suit in the federal courts alleging a denial of his right to vote as secured by the Fifteenth Amendment. Here an Alabama statute altered the Tuskegee city boundaries from a square to a 28-sided figure, allegedly removing "all save only four or five of its 400 Negro voters while not removing a single white voter or resident." While not denying the right of a legislature to alter city boundaries "under normal circumstances," the Court saw through this thinly disguised attempt by the Alabama legislature to deny the suffrage to the black citizens of Tuskegee. Reasoning that the situation in *Gomillion* was analogous to that in the Oklahoma case, the Court used the precedent of *Lane v. Wilson* to strike down the Alabama law: "It is difficult to appreciate what stands in the way of adjudging a statute having this inevitable effect invalid in light of the principles of which this Court must judge, and uniformly has judged, statutes that, howsoever speciously defined, obviously discriminate against colored citizens. 'The Fifteenth Amendment nullifies sophisticated as well as simple-minded modes of discrimination.' *Lane v. Wilson*." Here is one example of the judicial reasoning process—of thinking like Professor Kingsfield's lawyer. Two cases are compared because the facts or principles are similar; a rule of law gleaned from the first case is applied to the second. This step-by-step process is the essence of proper and traditional legal reasoning.

Adherence to Precedent

A related value possessed by U.S. trial and appellate judges is a commitment to follow *precedents*—that is, decisions rendered on similar subjects by judges in the past. The sacred doctrine of *stare decisis* ("stand by what has been decided") is a cardinal principle of our common law tradition. In a series of interviews, federal district judges were asked to rate the importance of "clear and directly relevant" precedents in their decision-making process. Precedent attained a score of 90.44 on a 100-point scale, whereas the judge's "personal, abstract view of justice in the case" was ranked at only 60.69.[5] As for appellate court judges, a recent study of appeals courts in the Second, Fifth, and District of Columbia Circuits concluded that "adherence to precedent remains the everyday, working rule of American law, enabling appellate judges to control the premises of decision of subordinates who apply general rules to particular cases," [6] The U.S. Supreme Court, while technically free to depart from its own precedents, does so very seldom, for when "the Court reverses itself or makes new law out of whole cloth—reveals its policy-making role for all to see—the holy rite of judges consulting a higher law loses some of its mysterious power." [7]

Ideally, adherence to past rulings gives predictability and continuity to the law and reduces the dangerous possibility that judges will decide cases on a momentary whim or on a totally individualistic sense of right and wrong. Not all legal systems have placed such emphasis on stare decisis, however. In early Greek times, for example, the judge-kings decided each case on what appeared fair and just to them at the moment. When a judge-king resolved a dispute, the judgment was assumed to be the result of direct divine inspiration.[8] The early Greek model is thus the antithesis of the common law tradition. As we shall momentarily see, however, strict adherence to past precedent may be something of a legal fiction. We have long known that judges can and do distinguish among various precedents in creating new law. This helps to keep the law flexible and to account for changing societal values and practices. Indeed, many scholars have argued that the readiness of common law judges occasionally to discard or ignore precedents that no longer serve the public has contributed to the very survival of the common law tradition.

Constraints on Trial Judge Decision Making

Another significant element of the legal subculture—found under the heading of what one prominent scholar has called the "great maxims of judicial self-restraint" [9]—we have already examined, in Chapter 2. These maxims derive from a variety of sources—the common law, statutory law, legal tradition—but each one serves to limit and channel the decision making of the federal courts. Because we have discussed these various principles in detail, we shall merely reiterate here a few of the major themes of judicial self-restraint.

First, before a judge will agree even to hear a case, there must exist a definite "case" or "controversy" at law or in equity between bona fide adversaries under the Constitution. The case must involve the protection or enforcement of valuable legal rights, or the punishment, prevention, or redress of wrongs directly related to the litigants in the case. Allied with this maxim is the principle that U.S. judges may not render "advisory opinions"—that is, rulings on abstract, hypothetical questions. Also, all parties to a lawsuit must have "standing," or a substantial personal interest infringed by the statute or action in question.

The rules of the game also forbid federal jurists from hearing a case unless all other legal remedies have been exhausted. In addition, the legal culture discourages the federal judiciary from deciding "political questions," or matters that ought to be resolved by one of the other branches of government, by state governments, or by the voters. Federal judges are also obliged to give the benefit of the doubt to statutes and to official actions whose constitutionality is being questioned. A law or an executive action is presumed to be constitutional until proven otherwise (some judges adhere to this principle on economic issues but not on matters of civil rights and civil liberties, believing that on these matters the burden of proof is on the government). In this same realm federal judges feel bound by the norm that if they must invalidate a law, they will do so on as narrow a ground as possible or will void only that portion of the statute that is unconstitutional.

Finally, America's federal judges may not throw out a law or an official action simply because they personally believe it to be unfair, stupid, or undemocratic. In order for a statute or an official deed to be invalidated, it must be clearly unconstitutional. Of course, judges do not always agree about what is a "clearly unconstitutional" act, but most acknowledge that broad matters of public policy should be determined by the people through their elected representatives—not by lifetime appointees in black robes.

The Impact of the Legal Subculture: An Example

Because the principles that make up the legal subculture—reasoning, precedent, and restraint—tend to be abstract, it is useful to illustrate them with a real-life example. The 1964 case of *Evers v. Jackson Municipal Separate School District* is a case in point.[10] It was an uncomplicated school integration case in which a group of black children and their parents sought to enjoin the "district and its officials from operating a compulsory biracial school system." The facts and controlling precedents were clear enough: (1) Jackson, Mississippi, was overtly maintaining a segregated public school system; (2) the U.S. Supreme Court had ruled a decade previously in *Brown v. Board of Education* that such segregation was unconstitutional; and (3) the U.S. Court of Appeals for the Fifth Circuit, which has jurisdiction over Mississippi, had handed down a string of rulings ordering the integration process to go ahead.

The federal trial judge in this case, Sidney Mize, did not like the commands he heard from the legal subculture. Appointed to the federal bench back in 1937, Mize was an unabashed segregationist, as his written opinion in this case clearly shows. After discussing a score of alleged physical and mental differences between blacks and whites, Mize argued further that

> in the case of Caucasians and Negroes, such differences may be directly confirmed by comparative anatomical and encephalographic measurements of the correlative physical structure of the brain and of the neural and endocrine systems of the body. The evidence was conclusive to the effect that the cranial capacity and brain size of the average Negro is approximately ten per cent less than that of the average white person of similar age and size, and that brain size is correlated with intelligence.[11]

On a more positive and benign note, Judge Mize also argued, "From the evidence I find that separate classes allow greater adaptation to the differing educational traits of Negro and white pupils, and actually result in greater scholastic accomplishments for both." [12]

It seems clear where this decision is headed. But wait: enter the legal subculture. After 14 single-spaced printed pages of argument against the integration of the Jackson schools, Mize yielded to the requirements of legal reasoning, respect for precedent, and judicial self-restraint. Almost sheepishly he concluded his decision with these unexpected words:

> Nevertheless, this Court feels that it is bound by what appears to be the obvious holding of the United States Court of Appeals for the Fifth Circuit that if disparities and differences such as that reflected in this record are to constitute a proper basis for the maintenance of separate schools for the white and Negro races it is the function of the United States Supreme Court to make such a decision and no inferior federal court can do so.[13]

Mize then quietly enjoined the school district and its officials from operating a compulsory biracial school system: the legal subculture tiptoed to victory.

Wellsprings of the Legal Subculture

We have examined some of the major threads of the tapestry of America's legal subculture; we will now point briefly to the institutions that instill and maintain the legal values in this country—"the law schools, the bar associations, the judicial councils, and other groups that spring from the institutionalization of the 'bench and the bar.' " [14]

"The purpose of law school," we are told, "is to transform individuals into novice lawyers, providing them with competency in the law, and instilling in them a nascent self-concept as a professional, a commitment to the values of the calling, and that esoteric mental state called 'thinking like a lawyer' " [15] The world just does not look the same to someone on whom law school has worked its indoctrinating magic. Facts and relationships in the human arena that had formerly gone unnoticed suddenly become "compelling" and "controlling" to the fledging advocate. Likewise other facets of reality that previously had been important in one's world view are now dismissed as "irrelevant and immaterial."

Besides the indoctrination that occurs in law school, the values of the legal subculture are maintained by the state and national bar associations[16] and by a variety of professional-social groups whose members are from both bench and bar—for example, the honorary Order of the Coif. We have already documented in Chapter 4 how the values and practices of jurists are handed down from one generation to another. Thus the traditions and tenets of the American legal subculture are well tended by powerful support groups. They are rightly accorded ample deference if one is to understand judicial decision making in America.

The Limits of the Legal Subculture

Despite the taut nature of judicial reasoning and the importance of stare decisis and of judicial self-restraint, the legal subculture does not totally explain the behavior of American jurists. If "objective facts" and "obvious controlling precedents" were the only stimuli to which jurists responded, then the judicial decision-making process would be largely mechanical and all judicial outcomes would be quite predictable. Yet even the legal subculture's most loyal apologists would concede that judges often distinguish among precedents and that some judges are more inclined toward self-restraint than others.

To understand the thinking of judicial decision makers and the evolution of the law, we must consider more than law school curricula and the canons of the bar associations. One of the first great minds to realize this was Justice Oliver Wendell Holmes, Jr., who over a century ago wrote that

> the life of the law has not been logic; it has been experience. The felt necessities of the time, the prevalent moral and political theories, intuitions of public policy, avowed or unconscious, even the prejudices which judges share with their fellow-men have had a good deal more to do than syllogism in determining the rules by which men should be governed. The law embodies the story of a nations's development through many centuries, and it cannot be dealt with as if it contained only the axioms and corollaries of a book of mathematics. In order to know what it is, we must know what it has been, and what it tends to become. . . . The very considerations which judges most rarely mention, and always with an apology, are the secret root from which the law

draws all the juices of life. I mean, of course, considerations of what is expedient for the community concerned.[17]

By about the 1920s a whole school of thought had developed that argued that judicial decision making was as much the product of human, extralegal stimuli as it was of some sort of mechanical legal thought process. Adherents of this view, who were known as "judicial realists," insisted that judges, like other human beings, are influenced by the values and attitudes learned in childhood. As one of these "realists" put it, a judge's background "may have created plus or minus reactions to women, or blonde women, or men with beards, or Southerners, or Italians, or Englishmen, or plumbers, or ministers, or college graduates, or Democrats. A certain facial twitch or cough or gesture may start up memories, painful or pleasant." [18]

Since the late 1940s, the study of the personal, extralegal influences on decision making has become more rigorous. Often calling themselves "judicial behavioralists," modern-day advocates of the realist approach have improved on it in two ways. First, they have tried to test empirically many of the theories and propositions advanced by the realist school and, second, they have attempted to relate their findings to more scientifically grounded theories of human behavior. Thus, while a realist might have asserted that a Democratic judge would probably be more supportive of labor unions than a Republican jurist, a judicial behavioralist might go a step further by taking a generous random sample of labor union-versus-management decisions and statistically determining whether Democratic judges are significantly more likely to back the union position than their GOP counterparts. Thus it is one thing to intuitively ascribe a cause for human behavior; it is another to subject an assertion to careful empirical analysis.

In the next section we shall discuss the many extralegal stimuli that the realists and behavioralists have shown to impinge upon trial judge decision making. In the last section of the chapter, we shall explore questions such as these: Which is the more compelling explanation for judicial decision making—the one provided by the legal subculture model or the one offered by the realist-behavioralist school? Does the efficacy of the model depend on the type of case(s) we are attempting to analyze? Does the way that judges view their judicial role help to determine which mode of explanation is the more compelling?

The Democratic Subculture

We know that the legal subculture has an impact on American jurists. There is evidence, too, that popular, democratic values—manifested in a variety of ways through many different mediums—have an influence as well. Indeed, some scholars have argued that the only reason why federal courts have survived in the American political system is that they have learned to bend when the democratic winds have blown—that is, that judges have tempered rigid legalisms with commonsense popular values and have maintained "extensive linkages with the democratic subculture":

> Very often, legal elites such as bar associations and judicial councils are more noticeable spokesmen for the federal judiciary than are the spokesmen of the democratic subculture. However, representatives of the democratic subculture, such as members of political parties, members of social and economic groups, and local state political elites, can also be observed commenting on controversial questions. In matters like staffing the courts, determining their structure and organization, and fixing federal jurisdiction, democratic representatives have access through Congress and through other institutions that are influential in establishing judicial policy. Although Congress provides a main channel to the federal courts, access for democratic values is also obtained through the President, the attorney general, and through nonlegal officials who deal with the judiciary. In addition, the location of federal courts throughout the states and regions renders them unusually susceptible to local and regional democratic forces.[19]

In our discussion of the democratic subculture, we shall focus on the influences most often observed by students of the American court system—political party identification, localism, public opinion, and the legislative and executive branches of government.

The Influence of Political Party Affiliation

Do judges' political party affiliation affect the way they decide certain cases? The question is straightforward enough, but those who reply to it are by no means unanimous in their response. To most attorneys, judges, and court watchers among the general public, the question rings with outright impertinence, and their answer is usually something like this: after taking the sacred judicial oath and donning the black robe, a judge is no longer a Republican or a Democrat. Former affiliations are (or at least certainly should be) put aside as the judge enters a realm in which decisions are the product of evidence, sound judicial reasoning, and precedent rather than such a base factor as political identification. Or, as one student of American courts quipped in his perceptive book *Judges,* "Most judges would sooner admit to grand larceny than confess a political interest or motivation." [20]

Despite the cries of indignation from those who contend that the legal subculture explains virtually all judicial decision making, a mounting body of evidence strongly suggests that judges' political identification does indeed affect their behavior on the bench. Studies have shown that other personal factors—such as religion, sex, race, pre-judicial career, and the level of prestige of their law school education—may also play a role. However, only political party affiliation seems to have any significant and consistent capacity to explain and predict the outcome of judicial decisions.[21] One prominent student of American politics explains why there may be a cause-and-effect relationship between judges' party allegiance and their decisional patterns:

> If judges are party identifiers before reaching the bench, there would be a basis for believing that they—like legislators—are affected in their issue orientations by party. . . . Furthermore, judges are generally well educated and the vote studies show that the more educated tend to be stronger party identifiers, to cast policy preferences in ideological terms, to have clearer perceptions of issues and of party positions on those issues, to have issue attitudes consistent with the positions of the party with which they identify, and to be more interested and involved in politics. For judges, even more than for the general population, party may therefore be a significant reference group on issues.[22]

District Court Judges.   In examining what we have learned about the relationship between party affiliation and court decision making, we can begin with an observation that should come as no surprise: as a whole, Democratic judges and justices are generally more liberal than their Republican colleagues. In a study of over 27,000 published district court decisions between 1933 and 1977, it was determined that Democratic judges took the liberal position 46 percent of the time whereas Republican jurists did so in only 39 percent of the cases (see Table 5-1). Thus for almost a half-century, the Democrats' ratio of liberal-to-conservative opinions has been 1.33 times greater (more liberal) than the Republican ratio has been.[23] While the overall differences cannot be called overwhelming, neither can we dismiss them as inconsequential.

As Table 5-1 suggests, differences between Republicans and Democrats depend considerably on what type of cases we are talking about. In looking at partisan voting patterns in nineteen separate case categories, the study noted that "differences between judges from the two parties were greatest for cases involving state and local government efforts to regulate the economic lives of their citizens, race relations cases, disputes involving interpretation of the Fourteenth Amendment (excluding racial matters), and cases involving conviction for criminal offenses."

On the other hand, "partisan differences were almost totally absent in cases involving the interpretation of Indian laws and treaties, suits

Table 5-1 Liberal Decisions of Federal District Judges in Order of Magnitude of Partisan Difference for Nineteen Types of Cases, 1933-1977

Type of case	Overall	Demo-crats	Repub-licans	Partisan difference	Odds ratio
Local economic regulation	67%	75%	57%	18%	2.28
Race discrimination	51	57	42	15	1.90
Fourteenth Amendment[a]	42	48	34	14	1.81
Criminal conviction	38	43	30	13	1.75
U.S. habeas corpus pleas	27	29	20	9	1.63
Freedom of religion	52	56	46	10	1.52
Freedom of expression	52	57	47	10	1.48
U.S. commercial regulation	68	71	64	7	1.39
Criminal court motions	27	30	24	6	1.35
State habeas corpus pleas	23	25	20	5	1.32
Alien petitions	40	42	35	7	1.31
Union vs. company	47	50	45	5	1.20
Employee vs. employer	38	40	35	5	1.20
Union members vs. union	55	57	53	4	1.14
Environmental protection	61	62	59	3	1.14
Indian rights and law	49	51	49	2	1.10
Fair Labor Standards Act	57	57	55	2	1.08
Rent control, excess profit	61	61	59	2	1.05
Voting rights cases	48	46	50	−4	0.86

[a] Women's rights cases are included in this category rather than listed as a separate issue area, since data on the women's rights category are only for the years after 1973.

Source: Robert A. Carp and C. K. Rowland, *Policymaking and Politics in the Federal District Courts*, 38. Copyright © 1983 by the University of Tennessee Press and reprinted by permission.

brought by the secretary of labor (or the National Labor Relations Board...) under the Fair Labor Standards Act, disputes involving rent control and excessive profits, and, finally, cases dealing with reapportionment and the right to vote."[24] In voting rights cases, the GOP jurists were actually more liberal than the Democrats by 4 percentage points. In all the other case types examined in this study, however, Republican judges tended to follow the tradititional conservative views of their party.

Partisan differences among federal trial judges also vary a good deal from one time period to another. Between 1933 and 1953, partisan differences among the judges averaged 4 percentage points. This disparity dropped to a mere 1 percent between 1953 and 1969, whereas between

1969 and 1977 it jumped to 11 percent. (It had been as high as 17 percentage points in 1972.) [25]

All these facts and figures would become more meaningful if we could enter into the minds of typical Republican and Democratic judges and view the world from their perspectives. The closest we can come is to report the partial contents of interviews with two lifelong members of their respective parties. The two jurists, sitting in the same city and on the same day, discussed a subject that in recent decades has divided Republican from Democratic judges—their philosophy of criminal justice and, more specifically, their views about sentencing convicted felons. The rank-and-file Democrat (appointed by Lyndon Johnson) said in part:

> You know, most of the people who appear before me for sentencing come from the poorer classes and have had few of the advantages of life. They've had an uphill fight all the way and life has constantly stepped on them. . . . I come from a pretty humble background myself, and I know what it's like. I think I take all this into consideration when I have to sentence someone, and it inclines me towards handing down lighter sentences, I think.

One hour later a lifelong Republican (appointed by Richard Nixon) addressed the same issue but with quite a different twist at the end:

> When I was first appointed, I was one of those big law-and-order types. You know—just put all those crooks and hippies in jail and all will be right with the world. But I've changed a lot. I never realized what poor, pathetic people there are who come before us for sentencing. My God, the terrible childhoods and horrendous backgrounds that some of them come from! Mistreated when they were kids and kicked around by everybody in the world for most of their lives. Society has clearly failed them. As a judge there's only one thing you can do: *send them to prison for as long as the law allows because when they're in that bad a state there's nothing anyone can do with them. All you can do is protect society from these poor souls for as long as you can.* [Emphasis added.]

While we would not contend that all Republican and all Democratic trial judges think precisely in these terms, we believe that something of the spirit of partisan differences is captured in these two quotations.

Appeals Court Judges. As for partisan variations in the voting patterns of U.S. appeals court judges, here, too, there is evidence that the judges' (prior) party affiliation tempers their decision making to some degree.[26] In 1966 a study was published that explored the decision-making process of circuit judges in all U.S. courts of appeals. The author found that party affiliation was "associated with voting behavior, notably when the issues involved economic liberalism," and that other background variables "such as religion, socio-economic origins, education, and age were found to be almost entirely unrelated to voting behavior." The author cautions us, however, not to believe that party identification explains more than just a small portion of appellate court decision making. He stresses the point that we emphasized in the previous chapter—namely, that U.S. federal jurists are more alike than different, that they are not for the most part split into warring ideological camps. This first comprehensive survey concluded that "on balance, the findings underscore the absence of a sharp ideological party cleavage in the United States but also give support to the contention that the center of gravity of the Democratic party is more 'liberal' than that of the Republican party." [27]

About a decade later Goldman updated his earlier study, but the conclusions did not vary greatly. He found Republican appeals court judges to be more conservative than their Democratic colleagues and that "the party split was most pronounced on economic issues." (That is, GOP jurists were a bit more likely than their Democratic counterparts to oppose government efforts to regulate the economy and to support business in its judicial tussles with labor.) [28] Again, however, partisan differences were considered to be only a modest predictor of appellate court decision making.

Supreme Court Justices. Does political party affiliation affect the way members of the U.S. Supreme Court decide some of their cases? Although scholars have found this to be a hard subject to investigate, the evidence suggests a mild but positive "yes." The research hurdle stems, in part, from the fact that at any given time there are only nine justices on the Court, and it is virtually impossible to generalize about the behavior of groups this small. Moreover, numerous political parties have been represented on the Court in its nearly two-century history, and the definitions of *Federalist, Democrat, Whig, Republican, liberal,* and *conservative* have varied so over time that generalizations become very difficult. For example, prior to the 1920s most mainstream Democrats opposed civil rights for blacks; since that era most champions of the civil rights movement have been Democrats. In the jargon of the trade: the variables are so numerous and the n's (number of justices) are so small that statistically significant observations are virtually impossible to make.

Despite the methodological problems involved, some judicial scholars have gone where even angels fear to tread and have sought to explore this subject. In a comprehensive study of the relationship between party affiliation and the liberal-conservative voting patterns of the justices in this century, one scholar found that, between 1903 and 1939, party identification was "clearly a good cue for selecting judicial decision-makers with the proper values"—that is, on matters of support for the economic underdog, Democratic justices were more liberal than their Republican colleagues. Since 1940 the greater liberalism of Democratic Court members has extended as well to matters of civil rights and liberties, thereby reaffirming "the concept that judges are not random samples of their group." But even this scholar concedes, as did those who studied partisan voting by the appeals court and trial judges, that the relationships are weak:

> The inability to predict at high rates of probability is not surprising when one considers the assumptions that must be made and the variety of other influences on the Court such as political and environmental pressures, social change, precedent, reasoned argument [the "legal subculture" for these last two], intracourt social influences and idiosyncrasy.[29]

A more elaborate and revealing study of voting patterns over time of members of the Supreme Court was published in 1981.[30] It analyzed the voting behavior of 25 justices who had served on the Court between 1946 and 1978. The justices' decisional patterns on economic matters and on civil rights and liberties cases were related to some 20 possible explanatory variables. The study found strong correlations between liberal voting and the following attributes: (1) being a Democrat, (2) being appointed by a President other than Nixon or Truman, (3) having judicial rather than prosecutorial experience prior to becoming a justice, and (4) having had a long record of previous judicial service rather than a short tenure. The author was able to account for 87 percent of the variance in split decisions on civil liberties cases and 72 percent for economic regulation cases. (Both of these percentages are extraordinarily high for social science research.)

An Appraisal. Let us stop for a moment to look back on what we have said. Our basic point is that the political party affiliation of the judges and justices can well make a difference in the way they decide cases. Of all the background variables studied, it seems to be the most compelling and consistent. But a word of caution is in order, too. While evidence for partisan influence on judicial behavior is convincing, it by no means suggests that Democrats always take the liberal position on all issues while Republicans always opt for the conservative side. Rather, we are talking about tendencies—that is, where the decision is a close call, a Democrat on the bench tends to be more liberal than a GOP judge. When controlling precedents are absent or ambiguous or when the evidence in the case is about evenly divided, Democrats more than Republicans are inclined to be supportive of civil rights and liberties, to support government regulation that favors the worker or the economic underdog, and to turn a sympathetic ear toward the pleas of criminal defendants.

The Impact of Localism

A wide range of influences are included in the term *localism,* and we shall regard it as a broad second category of factors that affect judicial decision making. An accumulating body of literature suggests, in fact, that judges are influenced by the traditions and mores of the region in which their courts are located or, in the case of Supreme Court justices, by the geographic area in which they were raised. Indeed, for trial and appeals court judges geographical differences define both the legal and the democratic subcultures, as well as the nature of the questions that they must decide. Historically, such judges have had strong ties with the state and the circuit in which their courts are situated, and on many issues judicial decision making reflects the parochial values and attitudes of the region. As two leading students of the subject have noted:

> A persistent factor in the molding of lower court organization has been the preservation of state and regional boundaries. The feeling that the judiciary should reflect the local features of the federal system has often been expressed by state officials most explicitly. Mississippi Congressman John Sharp Williams declared that he was "frankly opposed to a preambulatory judiciary, to carpetbagging Nebraska with a Louisianian, certainly to carpetbagging Mississippi or Louisiana, with somebody north of Mason and Dixon's line." [31]

Why should judges in one district or circuit decide cases differently from their colleagues in other localities? Why should a Supreme Court justice make decisions differently from colleagues who hail from other parts of the United States? [32] Richardson and Vines have put the matter succinctly:

> Since both district and appeals judges frequently receive legal training in the state or circuit they serve, the significance of legal education is important. If a federal judge is trained at a state university, he is exposed to and may assimilate state and sectional political viewpoints, especially since state law schools are training grounds for local political elites. . . . Other than education, different local environments provide different reactions to policy issues, such as civil rights or labor relations. Indeed, throughout the history of the lower court judiciary there is evidence that various persons involved in judicial organization and selection have perceived that local, state, or regional factors make a difference and have behaved accordingly. [33]

Moreover, as we noted in Chapter 4, trial and appellate judges tend to come from the same district or state in which their courts are located, and the vast majority were educated in law schools in the same state as their district or circuit. (For example, two-thirds of all district judges in one study were born in the same state as their court, and 86 percent of all circuit judges attended a law school in their respective circuits.) [34] Also, the strong local ties of many judges tend to develop and mature even after their appointment to the bench.[35]

In their identification with their regional base, judges in fact are similar to other political decision makers. We have long known that public attitudes and voting patterns on a wide range of issues vary from one section of America to another.[36] As for national political officials, there is evidence that regionalism affects the voting patterns of members of Congress on many important issues—for example, civil rights, conservation, price controls for farmers, and labor legislation.[37] Furthermore, sectional considerations have their impact within each political party—for instance, northern Democrats are more liberal than their southern counterparts on many significant issues.

Regionalism at the Three Judicial Levels. We noted in Chapter 1 that when President George Washington appointed the first Supreme Court, half of its members were northerners and the other half were southerners. Surely Washington's choice was more than just a symbolic gesture to give a superficial balance to the Court. Washington, who had successfully led a group of squabbling, dissident former colonies during the Revolutionary War, understood that the attitudes and mores of his fellow citizens differed widely from one locale to another and that justices would not be immune from these parochial influences. Indeed, studies of the early history of the High Court reveal that sectionalism did creep into its decision-making patterns—particularly along North-South lines. For example, from a study of Supreme Court voting patterns in the sectional crisis that preceded the Civil War, we note that the four justices who were most supportive of southern regional interests were all from the South, whereas those jurists from the northern states usually favored the litigants from that region.[38]

In this century, too, there is evidence for the belief that where the justices come from tempers their decision making to some degree.[39] A fairly recent and dramatic manifestation of this principle is found in President Richard Nixon's famous "southern strategy." After the appointment of Warren Burger as chief justice in 1969,

> pressure had been building on Nixon to name a southerner to the Court. Though he had never publicly promised a southern nominee, Nixon's intentions were never seriously doubted. Aware that a judge in the South enjoyed a prestige unrivaled in any other section of the

country, Nixon advisors believed that he could do southerners no higher favor than to appoint one of their own to the highest court in the land. Even before Nixon assumed office, he had successfully identified with the southern cause. "The one battle most white southerners feel they are fighting is with the Court and Nixon has effectively identified himself with that cause," wrote election analyst Samuel Lubell. "Only Nixon can change the makeup of the Court to satisfy southern aspirations." [40]

Nixon then nominated Clement Haynsworth, Jr., of South Carolina, who was turned down by the Senate. He then sent forth the name of G. Harrold Carswell of Florida, but this nomination met the same fate as Haynsworth's. An angry Nixon then stated, "As long as the Senate is constituted the way it is today, I will not nominate another southerner." [41]

While political leaders and much of the general public believe that there is a relationship between the justices' regional backgrounds and their judicial decisions, scholars have had difficulty in documenting this phenomenon. First, links between the justices' regional heritage and their subsequent voting behavior are very difficult to pinpoint, and they exist at most for probably a few regionally sensitive issues. Also, there is reason to believe that after Supreme Court justices are appointed and move to Washington, over time they may take on a more national perspective, loosening to a significant degree the attitudes and narrow purview of the region in which they were raised and educated. For example, in his early days in Alabama, Hugo Black had been a member of the Ku Klux Klan, but after his judicial appointment in 1937, Justice Black became one of the most articulate advocates of civil rights ever to sit on the Supreme Court.

Some evidence exists that regionalism pervades the federal judicial system at the appeals court level as well. One recent study noted regional differences on such important questions as rights of the consumer, pleas by criminal defendants, petitions by workers and by blacks, public rights in patent cases, and immigration litigation. The author of this study concluded that "regionalism is an inescapable adjunct of adjudicating appeals in one of the oldest regional operations of federal power in existence." He observed that while the appeals courts may adhere to national standards, such norms are nevertheless "regionally enforced. In the crosswinds of office and constituencies, Courts of Appeals may mediate cultural values—national and local, professional and political—in federal appeals." [42]

Federal district judges appear to reflect their sectional heritage in decisional patterns even more distinctly than their colleagues on the appellate bench. In an analysis of trial judge decision making between 1933 and 1977, one research team compared the ratio of liberal to conservative opinions for northern and southern judges (see Table 5-2). They learned that the northerners were 1.29 times more liberal than their colleagues in the South. Equally interesting, it was found that North-South sectional differences have been increasing over the years. Prior to 1954 the ratio was 1.14; it jumped to 1.22 between 1954 and 1969; and after 1969 the figure mounted to 1.41. East-West differences among the district judges have been almost negligible. On questions of criminal justice and of civil rights and liberties, northern judges have again been somewhat more liberal than their southern colleagues, and the differences have been increasing over time. For issues involving government regulation of the economy and of labor, the northerners were also a bit more liberal, but with this category of issues sectional variances have been *declining* since 1933.

Regional differences within the parties have also been observed over the years—mainly between judges in the North and South. For the past half century northern Democrats have been the most liberal group of judges. This is followed by southern Democrats, northern Republicans and then southern Republicans. The difference between southern Republicans and northern Democrats is 16 percentage points, that is, northern Democrats are 48 percent more liberal than southern Republicans.[43]

Variances in Judicial Behavior Among the Circuits. Not only does judicial decision making vary from one region of the land to another, but studies reveal that, for numerous reasons, each of the circuits has its own particular way in which its appellate and trial court judges administer the law and make decisions. One reason, of course, is that circuits tend to follow sectional lines that mark off historical, social, and political differences. Another reason is that the circuit courts of appeals tend to be idiosyncratic, and thus the standards and guidelines they provide the trial judges will reflect their own approach.[44] Let us look at an example. On October 1, 1981, the Eleventh Circuit Court of Appeals came into existence when Congress split the Fifth Circuit. One of the many decisions the new Eleventh Circuit faced was which law it would follow. In a recent interview Chief Judge John C. Godbold explained how this problem was solved:

> We selected a case where the law of the old Fifth was materially different from the law of some of the other circuits, and we voted it *en banc* to decide the question of choice of law. We heard the case *en banc* the morning of October 2, 1981, the second day we were in existence,

Table 5-2 Liberal Decisions of Federal District Judges, Controlled for Region: All Cases, Criminal Justice, Civil Rights and Civil Liberties, and Labor and Economic Regulation Cases, 1933-1977

	1933-1953	1954-1968	1969-1977	All years
All cases				
North (%)	46	42	47	45
South (%)	43	37	38	39
α	1.14	1.22	1.41	1.29
East (%)	46	42	43	43
West (%)	44	39	44	43
α	1.08	1.08	0.90	0.99
Criminal justice				
North (%)	26	23	31	27
South (%)	27	21	24	24
α	0.93	1.12	1.40	1.22
East (%)	23	23	27	25
West (%)	29	23	30	27
α	0.66	0.94	0.89	0.83
Civil rights and liberties				
North (%)	39	39	53	47
South (%)	45	42	45	44
α	0.79	0.88	1.39	1.12
East (%)	39	39	51	55
West (%)	42	41	49	54
α	0.80	0.86	1.00	0.91
Labor and economic regulation				
North (%)	58	64	61	61
South (%)	49	55	55	53
α	1.48	1.40	1.30	1.40
East (%)	62	65	61	63
West (%)	51	58	58	55
α	1.59	1.32	1.08	1.34

Source: Robert A. Carp and C. K. Rowland, *Policymaking and Politics in the Federal District Courts*, 97. Copyright © 1983 by the University of Tennessee Press and reprinted by permission.

because we had all been in New Orleans the day before closing down the old Fifth. We announced our decision later that day. In it we said, we choose the law of the old Fifth not only in this case but for all cases.[45]

Studies of liberal-conservative voting patterns over time have shown that trial judge decision making varies a good deal from one circuit to another. In the First Circuit, for example, which covers several New England states, 51 percent of the judges' decisions have been liberal. In the Fourth Circuit, on the other hand (Maryland, North and South Carolina, Virginia, and West Virginia), only 34 percent of the judges' decisions have been liberal. Also, "variances in judicial voting patterns from one circuit to another seem to have increased over time, and this trend appears to have accelerated." [46]

Variances in Trial Judge Behavior Among the States. At first blush it may appear strange to argue that U.S. judicial decisions vary significantly state by state, since the state is not an official level of the federal judicial hierarchy, which advances from district to circuit to nationwide system. Still, direct and indirect evidence suggests that each state is unique in the way its federal judges administer justice. There are several reasons why this is so. First, a state, like a circuit or a region, is often synonymous with a particular set of policy-relevant values, attitudes and orientations. One would automatically expect, for instance, that on some issues U.S. trial and appellate judges in Texas would act differently from Massachusetts jurists, not so much because they are from different states but because they are from different political, economic, legal, and cultural milieus. Second, many judges regard their states as meaningful boundaries and behave accordingly. For example, a U.S. trial judge in Louisiana told us, "One thing I frequently discuss with the other judges here is sentencing matters. Judge _____ has been a big help with this. I wouldn't want to hand down a sentence which is way out of line with what the other judges are doing here in this state for the same crime." [47] Comments from a jurist indicate that the same phenomenon occurs in the U.S. Eighth Circuit. For instance, in Iowa the federal trial judges

> were anxious that their sentencing practices be reasonably similar, particularly where the facts of a case were almost identical. They . . . believed that if a person committed a federal crime in Iowa, the criminal should expect nearly equal treatment regardless of whether he was tried in the Northern or Southern federal districts of the state. This mutual belief is nicely illustrated in these remarks made by Judge Graven to Judge Riley in 1954:
>
> "I have coming before me at Sioux City for sentencing on December 14 one . . . who apparently was splitting $20 and passing them. I am informed that there is a similar charge against him in the Southern District which is being transferred to this District under Rule

20 and that it is expected that that charge will also be disposed of at Sioux City on December 14th.

"I note that you have two defendants who were associates of Mr. _____ coming up before you for sentencing. Since all the defendants committed the same crimes and presumably have much the same background, I would not want my sentence of Mr. _____ to be out of line with the sentence you impose. If you impose your sentences before December 14th at 10:00 a.m., I wish you would let me know what your sentences are." [48]

Third, we would note the impact upon federal judicial behavior of diversity of citizenship cases—suits that comprise a quarter of the district courts' civil business and about a sixth of civil appeals to circuit courts (see Chapter 2). Because the Supreme Court requires the lower courts to apply *state* rather than federal law in such cases, it behooves U.S. trial judges to keep abreast of and sensitive to the latest developments in state law. The effect may be the same for circuit judges as well. For example, when three-judge appellate panels are appointed for diversity of citizenship cases, there is a tendency to name circuit judges from states whose law governs. As one scholar observed: "A 'slight local tinge' thus colored diversity opinions as part of a general tendency of members to defer to colleagues most knowledgeable about the subject." [49]

We would also note that quantitative studies of federal trial judges' voting behavior substantiate the proposition that there are meaningful differences on a state-by-state basis. In fact, such differences have been increasing since the late 1960s. Also, it has been observed that in both circuits that cross North-South boundaries, the Sixth and the Eighth, the district courts in the border and southern states are markedly more conservative than in the other states.[50] This suggests that local and regional values—as personified by the state—have a greater influence on trial judge decision making than the circuit as a whole.

Urban-Rural Variances in Judicial Behavior. We shall examine one final aspect of the impact of localism on judicial decision making: whether the judge grew up in, or now holds court in, a large city or a rural setting. There is good reason to believe that decision making by urban-oriented judges in America is somewhat more liberal than judicial behavior by small town, rural-directed jurists. First, as documented by social scientists in attitude surveys of the overall population and in numerous studies of the voting behavior of legislators from urban and rural areas, the values and attitudes of urban areas tend to be more liberal.[51] Second, since, as we have noted, trial and appellate court judges often preside over courts in the same environments in which they were born and socialized, big-city jurists probably bring to the bench the liberalism they have grown up with, while their rural counterparts have been less exposed to the pluralism of metropolitan areas and thus have a more homogeneous, conservative view.

A third reason to associate liberal decision making in America's larger cities with the judges who sit there is the presence of articulate, well-financed liberal judicial lobbying groups. Whether they appear as litigants or as *amici* ("friends of the court"), liberal groups are more likely to be based in metropolitan areas, where they in turn sponsor a good deal of litigation. Labor unions, gay rights activists, the American Jewish Congress, the National Association for the Advancement of Colored People, and women's rights groups are examples of organizations that have strong bases in urban America. Just because these lobbying groups are more active in urban centers does not mean, of course, that the cities will automatically become centers of judicial liberalism. Still, there can be no victories for liberal causes until the appropriate cases are heard in court. Progressive-minded jurists in small towns would have little effect if they were not presented with cases through which they could express their liberal orientation. Likewise, conservative judges in the big cities would be under little intellectual pressure to render liberal decisions were they not often confronted with teams of well-organized attorneys representing liberal causes. Thus, while the mere presence of activist groups does not cause liberal decision making, their efforts at least create the opportunities for liberal decisions to be rendered.

Finally, the anonymity that the larger cities provide U.S. trial and appellate judges makes it psychologically easier for them to go out on a limb and render innovative, often unpopular, liberal decisions.[52] This was vividly illustrated by a district judge in Houston as he compared himself with a colleague in a small East Texas community not known for its progressive values:

> It's not so bad for us here when we have to hand down one of those bombshell rulings. The press covers it and some of the right wing groups squawk, and some people cuss you out on the local [radio] call-in shows that night, but in a day or so it blows over and some other story comes along to take its place.... I mean, when I leave the courthouse at night, I step outside and nobody even knows who I am. But now with Judge _____ up in _____ city, it's different. Everyone in town calls him the "red judge." He's had death threats made on him, and at one time had to be under special guard. He can't even go into a supermarket without people pointing him out. It must be hell for him up there.

The propositions about urban versus rural decision making seem to be borne out by empirical studies. We have learned that since the turn of the century justices on the Supreme Court who were raised in larger cities have been more liberal on economic matters than their colleagues bred in more pastoral settings. This has also been true on the dimension of civil rights and liberties since the 1940s.[53] Although liberal-conservative differences on the urban-rural scale have not yet been systematically documented for appeals judges, there is evidence to show that judicial administration varies greatly depending on whether the circuit is rural or contains many urban centers.[54] For federal trial judges we have good cause to assert that urban jurists are more liberal than their colleagues in the smaller cities and towns. For instance, for the years 1933 to 1977, 41 percent of the decisions were liberal in rural districts with only one judge, whereas 46 percent were liberal in the larger cities where two judges presided. The phenomenon has been even more dramatic when one looks at the South. Here 38 percent of the decisions were liberal in districts where only one judge sat, while in cities with seven or more judges the liberal percentage was 49 percent.[55] Thus the urban-rural dichotomy is one final aspect of the effect of localism on the behavior of judges in the United States.

The Impact of Public Opinion

If one were to approach a typical judge or justice and ask if public opinion affected the decisions made from the bench, the jurist might well respond with a fair measure of indignation. We might well hear an answer something like this: "Look, as a judge with a lifetime appointment, I'm expected to be free from the pressures of public opinion. That's part of what we mean when we say that we're a 'government of laws—not of men.' When I decide a case, I look at the law and the facts. I don't go out into the streets and take some sort of public opinion poll to tell me what to do."

Despite judges' likely protestations to the contrary, there is reason to believe that to some degree and on certain issues U.S. judges do temper their decision making with public opinion. Before we look at the specific evidence for this, let us outline our intuitive reasons for asserting some role for public opinion. First, judges as human beings, as parents, as consumers, as residents of the community are themselves part of public opinion. Putting on a black robe may stimulate a greater concern for responsible, objective decision making, but it does not void a judge's membership in the human race. As one judicial scholar has noted, "since judges often have been born, reared, and recruited from a local political system, it seems likely that public opinion would have an effect, especially in issues that are *locally visible and controversial.* Even with lifetime appointments . . . public opinion still might seep into judicial decisions via judges' personal experiences and attitudes." [56] A keen example of a judge's sensitivity to local public opinion was provided by a New Orleans jurist who related one aspect of a pending school integration case. He noted that he lives "in a white, middle class suburb and my neighbors feel pretty strongly against busing and I have to be careful not to express my thoughts on the matter in front of them. My wife gets this kind of 'static' from the neighbors all the time." [57] In another instance, when the media reported that U.S. district judge William Overton was involved in a decision that overturned Arkansas's creation-science law, the judge received over 500 letters, most of them highly critical. (The Arkansas law required that the teaching of evolution in schools be accompanied by the teaching of creation science, a theory that life is of recent, supernatural, sudden origin, as related in the Book of Genesis; Overton's position was that the law violated the principle of separation of church and state.) The judge was so overwhelmed by the outpouring of negative public opinion that he took the unusual step of making the letters available to reporters and to the University of Arkansas at Little Rock. "How many monkeys are in your family tree?" asked one angry letter-writer from Richmond, Virginia. "Repent!" And another follower of the Prince of Peace from Benton, Arkansas, sent a clipping that included a picture of three persons who filed suit, and wrote: "I hope the souls of you and these 3 goons rot in Hell for eternity." [58]

A second reason for suggesting the influence of public opinion on judicial behavior is that in many instances it is actually supposed to be an official factor in the decision-making process. For example, when it came to implementing the famous *Brown v. Board of Education* school desegregation ruling, the Supreme Court refused to set strict national guidelines for how their ruling was to be carried out. Rather, it was left up to individual federal district judges to implement the High Court decision based on the judges' determination of local moods, conditions, and traditions. [59] Likewise when the Supreme Court ruled that it was permissible for federal courts to hear cases involving malapportionment of state legislatures, it refused to indicate how its decision was to be carried out. Instead it was in effect left to the lower federal judiciary to implement the ruling in accordance with the way they viewed local needs, conditions, and the state political climate. [60] A further example may be found in the obscenity rulings of the Burger Court, in which the justices determined that federal courts should use community values and attitudes in determining what materials are obscene. [61]

Thus, not only is it humanly impossible for judges to rid themselves of the influence of public opinion, but indeed for many important types of cases judges are obliged to consider the attitudes and values of the public. This does not mean they go out and take opinion polls whenever they face a tough decision, but it does mean that public opinion is often one ingredient in the decision-making calculus.

Third, Supreme Court justices and federal judges in general are surely aware that ultimately their decisions cannot be carried out unless there is a reasonable degree of public support for them. As one Supreme Court scholar has noted, "Presumably, the more favorably people view the Court and its work, the more likely they are to carry out the Court's policies rather than to impede them.[62] It has been an open secret for a long time that when the Court is about to hand down a bombshell decision likely to be unpopular among many groups of Americans, the author of the majority opinion takes great pains to word the decision in such a way as to generate popular support for it—or at least to salve the wounds of those potentially offended by it. Examples of High Court decisions in which the author is thought to have written as much for the public at large as for the usual narrow audience of lawyers and lower court judges include the following: *Marbury v. Madison,* in which the Court claimed for itself the right to declare acts of Congress unconstitutional; *Brown v. Board of Education,* which called for an end to racial segregation in the public schools; *Roe v. Wade,* in which the Court upheld a woman's right to an abortion; and *United States v. Nixon*—the Watergate case—in which the justices ordered the president of the United States to yield to the authority of the courts.[63]

The *empirical* evidence for the impact of public opinion is suggestive but hardly conclusive, in part because social scientists have only recently begun to examine this phenomenon and because the proposition is very difficult to prove. Nevertheless, several studies have provided some concrete evidence of a link between public opinion and judicial decision making. For example, during the war in Vietnam, some scholars tried to determine whether popular support for the war was related to the severity of federal sentences in draft evasion cases. While not all studies reached identical conclusions, one found a close relation between public opinion that American involvement in Vietnam was a mistake and the tendency of judges to give probation rather than a prison term to draft evaders. Also, federal judges in states that generally are more liberal and innovative in policy making handed down lighter sentences in draft evasion cases.[64] Another study conducted during the Vietnam era found that as opposition to the war increased among the American people, federal judges were more and more likely to grant requests for conscientious objector status.[65]

Finally, a study of California state (not federal) courts noted that sentencing in marijuana cases often changed in severity soon after a popular referendum was held on reducing criminal penalties for personal use of the drug. For example, judges who had given light sentences prior to the referendum sometimes gave harsher sentences if the local vote was in favor of maintaining criminal penalties. Conversely, harsh-sentencing jurists sometimes became more lenient when the vote indicated that the public favored reducing the penalties.[66]

Thus despite the traditional notion of the blindfolded justice weighing only the facts in a case and the relevant law, there is commonsense and statistical support for the assertion that jurists do keep their eyes (and ears) open to public opinion.

The Influence of Congress and the President

We shall now look at one final set of stimuli that the democratic subculture may bring to bear on the behavior of U.S. judges—the chief executive and Congress. Perhaps the most obvious link between the values of the democratic subculture and the output of the federal courts lies in the fact that the people elect the president and members of the Senate, and the president appoints judges and justices with the advice and consent of the Senate. We have already noted, in Chapter 4, the substantial capacity of the chief executive and certain key senators to influence what kind of men and women will sit on the bench, but even after judges have been appointed, the president and the Congress may have an impact on the content and direction of judicial decision making.

First, as we discussed in Chapter 2, to a very large degree the jurisdiction of the federal trial and appellate courts is determined by the Congress of the United States. Congress has the authority to decide which types of issues may become appropriate matters for judges to resolve. For example, the Wagner Act passed by Congress in 1935, prohibited employers from engaging in several unfair labor practices, all of which would have disrupted trade union organizing. In doing so Congress in effect expanded the jurisdiction of the federal courts to hear a large number of labor-management disputes that previously had been outside the purview of the federal judiciary. Conversely, Congress may restrict the jurisdiction of the federal courts. In response to popular dissatisfaction with many court rulings on busing, abortion, school prayer, and so on, Congress, with the indirect support of the president, has been considering passage of a number of bills that would restrict the right of the courts to render decisions on these subjects.[67] Even if Congress does not actually pass such legislation, one may speculate that the threat to do so may cause the federal courts to pull in their horns when it comes to deciding cases in ways that are not in accord with the will of the president or Congress.

Second, there is evidence that judicial decision making is likely to be bolder and more effective if it has the active support of at least one, and ideally both, other branches of the federal government.[68] School integration is a case in point. When the federal courts began to order desegregation of the public schools after 1954, we know that they met with considerable opposition—primarily from those parts of the country most affected by the Supreme Court ruling in the *Brown* case. It is doubtful whether the federal courts could have overcome this resistance without the support given them (sometimes reluctantly) by the president and Congress. For example, in 1957 Arkansas governor Orville Faubus sought to obstruct a district judge's order to integrate Little Rock's Central High School. President Eisenhower then nationalized the National Guard and in effect used federal bayonets to implement the judge's ruling. President Kennedy likewise used federal might to support a judge's decision to admit a black student to the University of Mississippi in the face of massive local resistance. Congress also lent its hand to federal desegregation rulings. For instance, it voted to withhold federal aid to school districts that refused to comply with district court desegregation decisions. Surely White House and congressional support emboldened the Supreme Court and the lower judiciary to carry on with their efforts to end segregation in the public schools.

Sometimes presidential and congressional actions may in fact *lead* rather than just implement judicial decision making. One study analyzed the impact on trial judge behavior of the 1937 Supreme Court decisions that permitted much greater government regulation of the economy.[69] As expected, federal district judge support for government regulation increased markedly after the Supreme Court gave its official blessing to the government's new powers. However, it was also learned that district court backing for labor and economic regulation had been building *before* the Supreme Court's decisions: pro-regulation decisions by U.S. trial judges went from 44 percent in 1936 to 67 percent in 1937—a change of 23 points. The authors attributed this at least in part to the fact that prior to 1937 the president and Congress were strongly pushing legislation in response to public opinion that favored an expanded federal role in labor and economic regulation.[70]

Another example is found in the willingness of the lower federal judiciary to support the petitions of those who sought classification as conscientious objectors. In 1965 the Supreme Court liberalized the definition of what constitutes a valid conscientious objector status. The Court ruled that to attain such status, it was no longer necessary to believe in a "Supreme Being" as such, but that one could possess any belief that occupied "a place in the life of its possessor parallel to that filled by the orthodox belief in God." [71] The district courts did not respond to this High Court ruling with any noticeable increase in pro-conscientious objector rulings: the percentage of decisions in favor of conscientious objectors, which was 40 percent in 1965, actually decreased to 18 percent in 1966 and remained at that same level throughout the following year. However, in 1967 Congress amended the Selective Service Act and deleted the statutory reference to a "Supreme Being." Between 1967 and 1968—more than two years after the Supreme Court decision—the percentage of district court decisions in favor of conscientious objector petitions jumped from 18 to 59 percent.[72] There is reason to believe that this change in judicial decision making was spurred in part by the lead of Congress.

Thus the Supreme Court and the lower courts are not, and cannot be, immune to the will of Congress and of the chief executive as they go about their judicial business. Not only does the President, with the advice and consent of the Senate, select all members of the federal judiciary, but to a large degree the Congress prescribes the jurisdiction of the federal courts and often the qualifications of those who have standing to sue in these tribunals. Moreover, many court decisions cannot be meaningfully implemented without the support of the other two branches of government—a fact not lost on the judges and justices themselves. Sometimes, too, the courts appear to follow the lead of the president and Congress on various public policy matters. Whichever set of circumstances is the case, it is clear that the legislative and executive branches of government constitute an important source of nonjudicial influence on court behavior.

The Subcultures as Predictors

Earlier in the chapter we indicated that there is scholarly divergence over the question of whether judicial decision making is essentially the product of facts, laws, and precedent (the legal subculture), or whether the various extralegal factors we have examined carry more weight (the realist-behavioralist view). In other words, are court decisions better explained by understanding the facts and law that impinge upon a given case, or by knowing which newspaper the judge reads in the morning or how the judge voted in the last election?

The clue to answering the question lies in knowing what kind of case the judge is being asked to decide. In our discussion of the nature and scope of the federal judicial workload, in Chapter 2, we indicated that the vast majority of the trial judge's cases and much appellate judicial business involve routine norm enforcement decisions. In cases in which the law and the controlling precedents are clear, the victor will be the side that is able to marshal the best arguments to show that the law and precedents favor its position. In other words, in the lion's share of cases the legal subculture model best explains and predicts judicial decision making. When traditional legal cues are unclear, ambiguous, or absent, however, then judges are obliged to respond to the democratic subculture for guidance in their decision making. We will examine the types of situations in which the legal subculture model might give way to the democratic subculture as an explicator of judicial behavior.

When the Legal Evidence Is Contradictory

It is probably fair to say that in a majority of cases the facts, evidence, and controlling precedents distinctly favor one side or another. In such instances the judge is clearly obliged to decide for the party with the stronger case. Not to do so would violate the judge's legal training and mores; it would subject a trial or appeals court judge to reversal by a higher court, an event most jurists find embarrassing; and it would render the Supreme Court vulnerable to the charge that it was making up the law as it went along—an impression not flattering to the High Court justices. On the other hand, judges often find themselves in situations in which the facts and evidence are about equally compelling on either side, or in which there are about an equal number of precedents to sustain a finding for either party. As one U.S. trial judge in Houston told us:

> There are days when you want to say to the litigants, "I wish you guys would've settled this out of court because I don't know what to do with you." If I grant the petition's request, I can often modify the relief requested [in an attempt to even out the decision], but still one side has got to win and one side has got to lose. I could cite good precedents on either side, and it's no good worrying about the appeals court because there's no telling what they would do with it should the judge's decision be appealed.

In such situations the judge has little choice but to turn to his or her value-set to determine how to resolve the case. We can assume that decision making is affected by local attitudes and traditions or by the judge's perception of the public mood or the will of the current Congress or administration.

As we shall see in Chapter 7, since the advent of the Burger Court in 1969, an inordinate number of the Supreme Court's decisions have been regarded as "ideologically imprecise and inconsistent," often sustained by weak, five-to-four majorities. This state of affairs has surely increased the likelihood that trial and appellate judges will respond to stimuli from the democratic rather than the legal subculture. That is, the confusion created by the Burger Court in setting forth ambiguous or contradictory guidelines has meant that the lower federal courts—and perhaps even members of the Supreme Court—have been forced to rely on (or have felt free to give vent to) their own personal ideas about how the law should read. As one study concluded, "With the decline of the fact-law congruence after 1968 the ... [lower federal judiciary] became more free to take their decision-making cues from personal-partisan values rather than from guidelines set forth by the Higher Court." [73]

When a Case Involves New Areas of the Law

There is a second situation that causes researchers to set aside the legal subculture model and turn to the democratic subculture approach—when jurists are asked to resolve new types of policy questions for which statutory law and appellate court guidelines are virtually absent. Since about 1937 most new and uncharted areas of the law have been in the realms of civil liberties and criminal justice rather than in the area of labor and economic regulation. As we noted in Chapter 1, since 1937 the federal courts have leaned toward self-restraint and deference to the elected branches when it comes to ordering the economic lives of the American people.[74] Moreover, in recent decades Congress has legislated, often with precision, in the areas of economic regulation and labor relations, and this has further restricted the discretion of judges in these fields. As a result, the noose of the legal subculture has been drawn tightly around trial judges' necks in this realm, and there is little room for creative decision making or for responding to the tug of the heart rather than to the clear command of the law. Thus, since New Deal days the legal rather than the democratic subculture has been the better predictor of trial and appellate judge decision making for labor and economic regulation cases.

Since the 1930s the opposite trend has been true for issues involving criminal justice and civil rights and liberties:

> The "great" and controversial decisions of the Stone, Vinson, Warren, and Burger Courts focused primarily on issues of civil liberties and of the rights of criminal defendants, and it is precisely those sorts of issues which evoked the greatest partisan schisms among the justices. Research has shown that ... [the lower courts] were by no means immune to the debates and divisions which racked the nation's High Court; they, too, seem to have split along "political" lines more often on criminal justice and on civil rights matters than they did with other sorts of cases.[75]

The ambiguity (or perhaps the constant state of flux) of the law on matters such as the rights of criminal defendants, First Amendment freedoms, equal protection of the law, and so on, has given the federal jurists greater opportunity to respond than in the labor and economic realms, where their freedom of action has been more circumscribed. Put another way, since the 1930s the democratic rather than the legal subculture model has become increasingly important as a predictor of judicial behavior on Bill of Rights matters.

A series of interviews with a wide range of district and appellate court judges lends further credence to this notion. In one study the trial judges were asked about their willingness to "innovate," that is, their inclination to make new law in areas where appellate court or congressional guidelines were ambiguous or nonexistent. After asking why judges create new law through judicial innovation, the interviewer noted:

> One answer is that the courts innovate because other branches of government ignore certain significant problems which, to individual judges, cry out for attention. Accordingly, the individual district judge innovates in an attempt to fill a legal vacuum, as one judge commented, "The theory is that judges should not be legal innovators, but there are some areas in which they have to innovate because legislatures won't do the job. Race relations is one of these areas. . . ." Other areas mentioned as needing judicial innovation because of legislative inaction were housing, equal accommodations, and criminal law (especially habeas corpus).[76]

Picking up on the thread of these interviews, a more recent study of decisional patterns and variations in district judge decision making showed that "the subjects that . . . [the Kitchin study] found to represent the greatest areas of freedom in judicial decision making are the very same subjects that we find to maximize partisan voting differences among the district judges. In situations where judges are more free to take their decision-making cues from sources other than appellate court decisions and statutes, they are more likely to rely on their personal-partisan orientations."[77]

A cross section of appellate judges was recently asked: "When precedents are absent or ambiguous, what do you do?" Seventy-four percent replied that their own personal conception of the "dictates of justice" would be "very important" in their coming to grips with such a situation and another 17 percent said that such personal dictates would be "moderately important." Not a single appeals judge indicated that such dictates would be "not important." The interviewer concluded that "when judges are free to choose, personalities, predilections, and group relations perforce fill the void."[78]

Let us look at a relatively new area of the law in which appellate court and congressional guidelines are few and thus lower-court judges must fend for themselves—the definition of obscenity. Prior to 1957 there were no Supreme Court decisions of note on the matter of obscenity. In that year the nation's High Court ruled that obscenity was not protected by the First Amendment and said that it could be defined as material that dealt with sex "in a manner appealing to prurient interest." [79] Seven years later the Supreme Court said that in determining what appealed to the prurient interest of the average person, hypothetical "national standards" were to be used,[80] but then nine years after that the Court changed its mind and ruled that "state community standards" could be employed." [81] But what is obscenity? No one seems to know with any greater certainty today than Justice Potter Stewart did in 1964 when he confessed that he could not intelligibly define obscenity but that "I do know it when I see it." [82] Given the reluctance or the inability of Congress and the Supreme Court to define obscenity, U.S. trial and appellate judges have little choice but to look to their own personal values and perceptions of the local public need in order to determine what kinds of books, films, and plays the First Amendment protects in their respective districts and circuits.

Judge's Role Conception

In our discussion of which better explains judicial decision making—the rules of the legal subculture or stimuli from the democratic subculture—there is one additional factor to consider—how judges conceive of their judicial role. Judicial scholars often talk about judges falling into one of three basic decision-making categories regarding whether or not judges should make law when they decide cases. "Law makers" are those who take a broad view of the judicial role. These jurists, often referred to as "activists" or "innovators" contend that they can and must make law in their decisions, because the statutory law and appellate or Supreme Court guidelines are often ambiguous or do not cover all situations and because legislative intent is frequently impossible to determine. In one study of federal district judges, 14 percent were classified in this category, whereas in an investigation of appeals court judges 15 percent were associated with this role.[83]

At the other end of the continuum are the "law interpreters," who take a very narrow, traditional view of the judicial function. Sometimes called "strict constructionists," they don't believe that judges should substitute judicial wisdom for the rightful power of the elected branches of government to make policy. They tend to eschew making innovative decisions that may depart from the literal meaning of controlling precedents. In the Kitchin study, 52 percent of the U.S. trial judges were found to be "law interpreters," while only 26 percent of the appeals court judges were so designated.[84] This finding is consistent with our discussion in Chapters 1 and 2 that federal district judges are more concerned with routine norm enforcement, whereas the appellate judges' involvement—and their perception of it—is with broader questions of judicial policy.

Midway between the "law interpreters" and the "law makers" are judges known as "pragmatists" or "realists," who believe that on occasion they are indeed obliged to make law, but that for most cases a decision can be made by consulting the controlling law or appellate court precedents. Studies have indicated that a third of federal district judges assume this moderate role, while a full 59 percent of their appellate court colleagues do so.[85] Comparing federal jurists with state judges, one scholar has noted, "Federal judges appear to take the pragmatist or realist view more often, which may reflect their opportunities to make a larger number of innovative decisions." [86]

Thus, whether or not judicial decisions are better explained by the legal or the democratic model depends not only on the nature of the cases and the state of the controlling law and precedents; it depends to some degree on how the individual judges evaluate these factors. In virtually every case that comes before them, judges have to determine how much discretion they have and how they wish to exercise it. This is obviously a subjective process, and, as one research team put it, "activist judges will find more discretion in a given fact situation than will their more restrained colleagues." [87]

Summary

Federal judges make millions of decisions each year, and scholars have sought to explain the thinking behind these decisions. Two schools of thought provide an explanation. One theory is based on rules and procedures of the legal subculture. Judges' decisions, according to this model, are the product of traditional legal reasoning and adherence to precedent and to judicial self-restraint. Another school of thought, the realist-behavioralist approach, argues that judges are influenced in their decision making by such factors as party affiliation, local values and attitudes, public opinion, and pressures from Congress and the president. We asserted that in the vast majority of cases the legal subculture model is the more accurate predictor of judicial decision making. However, stimuli from the democratic subculture often become useful in accounting for judges' decisions (1) when the legal evidence is contradictory or equally compelling on either side; (2) if the situation involves new areas of the law and significant precedents are absent; and (3) when judges are inclined to view themselves as activist law makers rather than as law interpreters.

Notes

1. Richard J. Richardson and Kenneth N. Vines, *The Politics of Federal Courts* (Boston: Little, Brown, 1970).
2. Edward H. Levi, *An Introduction to Legal Reasoning* (Chicago: University of Chicago Press, 1948), 1-2.
3. *Lane v. Wilson*, 307 U.S. 268 (1939) and *Gomillion v. Lightfoot*, 364 U.S. 339 (1960).
4. *Lane v. Wilson*, 307 U.S. 275 (1939).
5. William Kitchin, *Federal District Judges* (Baltimore: Collage Press, 1978), 71.
6. J. Woodford Howard, Jr., *Courts of Appeals in the Federal Judicial System: A Study of the Second, Fifth, and District of Columbia Circuits* (Princeton, N.J.: Princeton University Press, 1981), 187.
7. Walter F. Murphy, *Elements of Judicial Strategy* (Chicago: University of Chicago Press, 1964), 204.
8. Henry Sumner Maine, *Ancient Law* (Boston: Beacon Press, 1963), 3-19.
9. Henry J. Abraham, *The Judicial Process*, 4th ed. (New York: Oxford University Press, 1980), 373-400.
10. *Evers v. Jackson Municipal Separate School District*, 232 F. Supp. 241 (1964).
11. *Evers v. Jackson Municipal Separate School District*, 232 F. Supp. 247 (1964).
12. *Evers v. Jackson Municipal Separate School District*, 232 F. Supp. 249 (1964).
13. *Evers v. Jackson Municipal Separate School District*, 232 F. Supp. 255 (1964).
14. Richardson and Vines, *The Politics of Federal Courts*, 8-9.
15. Steven Vago, *Law and Society* (Englewood Cliffs, N.J.: Prentice-Hall, 1981), 307.
16. For a good, current bibliography on this subject, see Vago, *Law and Society* 316-319.
17. Oliver Wendell Holmes, Jr., *The Common Law* (Boston: Little, Brown, 1881), 1-2.
18. Jerome Frank, *Courts on Trial: Myth and Reality in American Justice* (Princeton, N.J.: Princeton University Press, 1950), 151.
19. Richardson and Vines, *The Politics of Federal Courts*, 10.
20. Donald Dale Jackson, *Judges* (New York: Atheneum, 1974), 18.
21. Some studies suggest that age, socioeconomic status, and religion may influence some judges on some of their cases, but the associations are weak. For example, see Sheldon Goldman, "Voting Behavior on the United States Courts of Appeals Revisited," *American Political Science Review* 69 (1975): 491-506; John R. Schmidhauser, "The Justices of the Supreme Court: A Collective Portrait," *Midwest Journal of Political Science* 3 (1959): 1-57; and Donald Leavitt, "Political Party and Class Influences on the Attitudes of

Justices of the Supreme Court in the Twentieth Century" (Paper delivered at the annual meeting of the Midwest Political Science Association, Chicago, 1972). Other studies suggest that these background factors have virtually no explanatory power—e.g., Howard, *Courts of Appeals in the Federal Judicial System,* chap. 6. For a more detailed discussion of this subject and a literature review, see Robert A. Carp and C. K. Rowland, *Policymaking and Politics in the Federal District Courts* (Knoxville: University of Tennessee Press, 1983), chap. 2.

22. David W. Adamany, "The Party Variable in Judges' Voting: Conceptual Notes and a Case Study," *American Political Science Review* 63 (1969): 59.

23. For a more extensive discussion of the "odd ratio" and methodology used in this study, see Carp and Rowland, *Policymaking and Politics in the Federal District Courts,* 33-34.

24. Carp and Rowland, *Policymaking and Politics in the Federal District Courts,* 37, 38.

25. Ibid., 34-36.

26. For a good review of the literature on this subject, see Goldman, "Voting Behavior on the United States Courts of Appeals Revisited," 491, note 2. Also, see Howard, *Court of Appeals in the Federal Judicial System,* chap. 6.

27. Sheldon Goldman, "Voting Behavior on the United States Courts of Appeals, 1961-1964," *American Political Science Review* 60 (1966): 384.

28. Goldman, "Voting Behavior on the United States Courts of Appeals Revisited," 505. Goldman's second article also found that the variable of the judge's age was of some significance: older judges tended to be somewhat more conservative than their younger colleagues.

29. Leavitt, "Political Party and Class Influences on the Attitudes of Justices of the Supreme Court in the Twentieth Century," 18-19.

30. C. Neal Tate, "Personal Attribute Models of the Voting Behavior of U.S. Supreme Court Justices: Liberalism in Civil Liberties and Economic Decisions, 1946-78," *American Political Science Review* 75 (1981): 355-367.

31. Richardson and Vines, *The Politics of Federal Courts,* 71.

32. For a more elaborate discussion of this phenomenon, see Carp and Rowland, *Policymaking and Politics in the Federal District Courts,* chap. 4.

33. Richardson and Vines, *The Politics of Federal Courts,* 73.

34. Ibid., 72.

35. For example, see Robert A. Carp and Russell Wheeler, "Sink or Swim: The Socialization of a Federal District Judge," *Journal of Public Law* 21 (1972): 359-393. Also, Robert A. Carp, "The Influence of Local Needs and Conditions on the Administration of Federal Justice" (Paper delivered at the annual meeting of the Southwestern Political Science Association, Dallas, 1971).

36. For example, see Angus Campbell et al., *The American Voter* (New York: Wiley, 1960); Everett Carll Ladd, Jr., and Charles D. Hadley, *Transformations of the American Party System,* 2d ed. (New York: Norton, 1978); V. O. Key, Jr., *Public Opinion and American Democracy* (New York: Knopf,

1967); and Samuel A. Stouffer, *Communism, Conformity, and Civil Liberties* (New York: Doubleday, 1955).

37. Barbara Hinckley, *Stability and Change in Congress* (New York: Harper & Row, 1978); Randall B. Ripley, *Congress: Process and Policy,* 2d ed. (New York: Norton, 1978); V. O. Key, Jr., *Politics, Parties, and Pressure Groups,* 5th ed. (New York: Crowell, 1964), especially chaps. 9 and 24; and J. H. Fenton, "Liberal-Conservative Divisions by Sections of the United States," *Annals* 344 (1962): 122-127.

38. John R. Schmidhauser, "Judicial Behavior and the Sectional Crisis of 1837-1860," *Journal of Politics* 23 (1961): 615-640. To be more precise, Schmidhauser found that justices' party affiliation and their geographic orientation were highly interrelated. Because the four justices who were most supportive of southern regional interests were all southern Democrats and since the two justices with the strongest pro-northern voting patterns were northern Whigs, Schmidhauser concluded that the effects of party and region were virtually inseparable.

39. Leavitt, "Political Party and Class Influences on the Attitudes of Justices of the Supreme Court in the Twentieth Century."

40. James F. Simon, *In His Own Image* (New York: David McKay, 1973), 103-104.

41. Ibid., 123.

42. Howard, *Courts of Appeals in the Federal Judicial System,* 55, 79, 156.

43. Carp and Rowland, *Policymaking and Politics in the Federal District Courts,* 98.

44. For example, see Sheldon Goldman, "Voting Behavior on the United States Courts of Appeals, 1961-1964," 370-385.

45. *The Third Branch* 15 (June 1983): 8. The formal opinion in the case, *Bonner v. City of Prichard, Alabama,* 661 F. 2d 1206, was released on November 3, 1981.

46. Carp and Rowland, *Policymaking and Politics in the Federal District Courts,* 101, 102.

47. Carp and Wheeler, "Sink or Swim," 376.

48. Carp, "The Influence of Local Needs and Conditions on the Administration of Federal Justice," 17-18.

49. Howard, *Courts of Appeals in the Federal Judicial System,* 234.

50. For example, see Carp and Rowland, *Policymaking and Politics in the Federal District Courts,* 106-116.

51. For example, see Key, *Public Opinion and American Democracy;* Leon Epstein, "Size and Place and the Two-Party Vote," *Western Political Quarterly* 9 (1956): 138-150; and John Wahlke et al., *The Legislative System* (New York: Wiley, 1962).

52. We do not mean to suggest that it is impossible to render innovative *conservative* decisions. It is just that during the past several decades the vast majority of the highly unpopular judicial decisions have been of a liberal nature—e.g., the release of an obviously guilty criminal on a legal technical-

ity, an order to a state university to grant recognition to a campus gay organization, a ruling that a local obscenity ordinance is too vague.

53. Leavitt, "Political Party and Class Influences on the Attitudes of Justices of the Supreme Court in the Twentieth Century," 19.

54. Howard, *Courts of Appeals in the Federal Judicial System,* chaps. 2 and 3.

55. Carp and Rowland, *Policymaking and Politics in the Federal District Courts,* 133, 137.

56. Henry R. Glick, *Courts, Politics, and Justice* (New York: McGraw-Hill, 1983), 247.

57. Carp and Wheeler, "Sink or Swim," 373.

58. "Arkansas Judge Who Struck Down Creation-Science Law Condemned in Hundreds of Letters," *Houston Chronicle,* August 6, 1982, 1:9.

59. *Brown v. Board of Education,* 349 U.S. 294 (1955).

60. *Baker v. Carr,* 369 U.S. 186 (1962).

61. *Miller v. California,* 413 U.S. 15 (1973).

62. Lawrence Baum, *The Supreme Court,* 2d ed. (Washington, D.C.: CQ Press, 1985), 128.

63. The full citations are as follows: *Marbury v. Madison,* 1 Cranch 137 (1803); *Brown v. Board of Education,* 347 U.S. 483 (1954); *Roe v. Wade,* 410 U.S. 113 (1973); and *United States v. Nixon,* 418 U.S. 683 (1974).

64. For example, see Glen T. Broach et al., "State Political Culture and Sentence Severity in Federal District Courts," *Criminology* 16 (1978): 373-382.

65. Ronald Stidham and Robert A. Carp, "Trial Courts' Responses to Supreme Court Policy Changes: Three Case Studies," *Law & Policy Quarterly* 4 (1982): 215-235.

66. James H. Kuklinski and John E. Stanga, "Political Participation and Government Responsiveness: The Behavior of California Superior Courts," *American Political Science Review* 73 (1979): 1090-1099.

67. However, many constitutional scholars argue that the right of the federal courts to hear such cases stems directly from Article III of the Constitution and that therefore Congress could not legally curtail court jurisdiction over these subjects except by initiating an amendment to the Constitution.

68. For example, see Stephen L. Wasby, *The Impact of the United States Supreme Court* (Homewood, Ill.: Dorsey Press, 1970), especially 255-256; Harrell R. Rodgers, Jr., and Charles S. Bullock III, *Coercion to Compliance* (Lexington, Mass.: Heath, 1976).

69. *National Labor Relations Board v. Jones and Laughlin Steel Corp.,* 301 U.S. 1 (1937) and *West Coast Hotel Co. v. Parrish,* 300 U.S. 379 (1937).

70. Stidham and Carp, "Trial Courts' Responses to Supreme Court Policy Changes," 218-222.

71. *United States v. Seeger,* 380 U.S. 166 (1965).

72. Stidham and Carp, "Trial Courts' Responses to Supreme Court Policy Changes," 222-227.

73. Carp and Rowland, *Policymaking and Politics in the Federal District Courts,* 37.

74. However, on matters of *local* economic regulation, voting differences among judges are still sharp (See Table 5-1). Only at the national level have federal judges tended to refrain from substituting their own views for those of elected officials.
75. Carp and Rowland, *Policymaking and Politics in the Federal District Courts*, 39.
76. Kitchin, *Federal District Judges*, 104.
77. Carp and Rowland, *Policymaking and Politics in the Federal District Courts*, 40.
78. Howard, *Courts of Appeals in the Federal Judicial System*, 165, 166-167.
79. *Roth v. United States* and *Alberts v. California*, 354 U.S. 476 (1957).
80. *Jacobellis v. Ohio*, 378 U.S. 184 (1964).
81. *Miller v. California*, 413 U.S. 15 (1973).
82. *Jacobellis v. Ohio*, 378 U.S. 197 (1964).
83. Kitchin, *Federal District Judges*, 107.
84. Ibid.
85. Ibid.
86. Glick, *Courts, Politics, and Justice*, 261.
87. Carp and Rowland, *Policymaking and Politics in the Federal District Courts*, 14.

Decision Making: The Special Case of Collegial Courts

6

Until now we have treated decision making by federal judges at all levels as if it were essentially the product of identical influences—those from the legal and the democratic subcultures. To a substantial degree this was a valid approach to take. After all, Supreme Court justices adhere to the same legal reasoning process as do their colleagues on the district court bench; U.S. trial judges may be influenced in close cases by their political party affiliation just as are members of the appeals courts. But before an analysis of judicial decision making can be complete, we need to recognize one vital difference between trial courts on the one hand and the appeals courts and the U.S. Supreme Court on the other. The former render decisions that are largely the product of a single individual, whereas the latter two are *collegial* courts, in which decision making is the product of group interaction. As one former trial judge, now a member of an appellate court, described it:

> The transition between a district judge and circuit judge is not an easy one, primarily because of, shall I say, the autocratic position occupied by the district court judge. He is the sole decider. He decides as he sees fit, and files the decision in a form as he sees fit. *A Court of Appeals decides by committee.* One of the first traumas I had was when opinions were sent back by the other judges asking me to add this sentence, change that, etc., to get concurrence. I admit at the beginning I resisted that. It was pride. I learned it was a joint project, but it was a very difficult thing. I see the same in others. [1] [Emphasis added.]

What are the extra ingredients that go into a decision made by the nine-member Supreme Court or by a three-judge appellate panel? What is the essence of the dynamics of multijudge decision making that distinguishes it from a judgment made by a single jurist? We shall discuss several theoretical approaches that have attempted to get a handle on this interesting but slippery subject.

Cue Theory

As we have noted, so long as U.S. trial and appeals courts have jurisdiction over a case, the judges must render some type of decision on the merits; they have little discretion as to the composition of their dockets. If the judges view a particular case as presenting a trivial question, they will not spend time agonizing over it, but they are still obliged to provide some kind of formal ruling on the substance of the matter. Not so with the Supreme Court. Recall from Chapter 2 that of the approximately 5,000 petitions presented to the Court each year, the justices agree to hear only a few hundred on the merits—and only about half of those carry with them full-blown written opinions. The Judiciary Act of 1925 gave the Supreme Court almost total control over its own docket—that is, the justices themselves decide which issues they want to tackle in a given term and which ones are not ripe for adjudication or must be summarily dismissed for "want of a substantial federal question." The importance of this is that what the Supreme Court decides *not* to rule on is often as significant as the cases it does summon forth for its scrutiny.

Judicial scholars have sought to identify the reasons why some petitions are culled out for special attention and why the rest never receive those important four votes that are needed for the Supreme Court to grant certiorari and decide the case. A pioneering study of this question was conducted by a research team during the early 1960s.[2] Analysts began by examining the Court's official reasons for granting certiorari as set forth in Rule 17, which specifies that the Court might hear a case if (1) an appeals court has decided a point of local law in conflict with local decisions, (2) a court of appeals has departed from "the usual course of judicial proceedings," (3) a conflict is perceived between a lower-court decision and a Supreme Court precedent, (4) a conflict exists on a point of law among the various federal circuits, or (5) there exists a really important question on which the Court feels it must have the final word.

The research team tested these official reasons by comparing the cases for which certiorari was granted with those in which review was denied. To their surprise (or maybe not), the official reasons did not prove to be a very accurate or useful guide to the Court's decision making. For example, in over 50 percent of the cases that were selected for review, the Court's official reason for its actions was that the cases were "important"—a nebulous adjective at best. The researchers thought they could do better. They set out to identify certain key characteristics of those cases for which review was and was not granted. They hoped to develop some predictive statements that were more precise and reliable than Rule 17. The result was cue theory.

Cue theory is based on the assumption that the Supreme Court justices have neither the time nor the desire to wade through the myriad of pages in the thousands of petitions presented to them each year. Therefore, it is logical to assume that they must have developed some sort of shortcut to help them select the petitions that are interesting and important. The justices must, researchers hypothesized, look for cues in each petition—readily identifiable characteristics that trigger a positive response in the justices as they skim through the cumbersome assemblage of legal documents. After all, we ourselves have our own particular cue theories as we go about our daily lives. We wouldn't read through a four-page circular on a local store's white sale, for instance, if we already had an ample supply of bedding material. Just as we look for cues in sorting through the daily mail, so, too, do justices on the Supreme Court as they sort through the daily arrival of petitions for certiorari. At least this is what the research team reasoned.

The results of the team's hypotheses and investigations were encouraging. Of the several possible cues they tested for, three were found to contain substantial explanatory power. In order of importance they were (1) whether the U.S. government was a party to a case and was asking for Court review, (2) whether a civil rights or civil liberties issue was involved, and (3) whether there was dissension among the judges in the court that had previously heard the case (or disagreement between two or more courts and government agencies). If a case contained all three cues, there was an 80 percent chance that certiorari would be granted; if none were present, the chance dropped to a mere 7 percent. Clearly the researchers had developed a useful model to explain this one aspect of Supreme Court behavior.

During the past two decades judicial scholars have further tested, elaborated on, and revised cue theory. Some studies have found a relationship between the way the justices voted on a grant of certiorari and their eventual vote on the merits of the case at conference.[3] More recent studies have suggested that a fourth cue has considerable explanatory power—the ideological direction of the lower-court decision.[4] In comparing the Warren Court (1953-1969) and the Burger Court (1969-present) on certiorari voting, the analysts reached several conclusions. First, during the liberal Warren Court era, the justices were more likely to review economic cases that had been decided in a *conservative* manner by the lower court[5]—especially when the U.S. government was seeking Court review. Second, and conversely, the more conservative Burger Court has tended to review *liberal* lower-court economic decisions. Third, the Burger Court has been readier to scrutinize a civil libertarian position taken by a lower court than a lower-court decision limiting civil liberties.

Cue theory, then, is one predictor of High Court voting behavior. It is interesting to note the way the 1970s studies shed light on the 1960s research: the earlier team observed that the justices were likely to review cases involving civil rights or civil liberties issues. The later analysts found that the justices would most probably hear such cases when lower-court rulings had gone against the ideological grain of the Court's majority. As one contemporary judicial scholar has summarized the certiorari behavior of the Court during the past several decades:

> Cues may change over time as political issues change throughout the country and as new justices come to the Court with their own ideas about public policy and law. During the 1950s, civil liberties were most important and made up a large part of the Court's total workload. In addition, during the 1950s and most of the 1960s, underdog appellants such as aliens, minorities, criminal defendants, laborers, and other have-nots were more successful in obtaining a hearing than during the 1970s, when the Supreme Court was shifting to more conservative policies under justices appointed by Republican President Richard Nixon. In recent years, upperdogs such as governments at all levels, businesses, and corporations have received more attention by the Supreme Court.[6]

In the remainder of the chapter we will examine several models of appellate court behavior that seek to explain how these collegial bodies make decisions once a case has been docketed. The models are small-group theory, attitude theory and bloc-formation analysis, and fact pattern analysis.

Small-Group Analysis

As applied to the judiciary, most small-group research is based on the thesis that judges want to influence the judgments of their colleagues and to be on the winning side as often as possible. This school of thought assumes that judges' positions are not written in stone from the start but are susceptible to moderation or even to a 180-degree turn on occasion. More specifically, scholars believe that a good deal of interaction takes place among justices from the time a case is first discussed in conference to the moment the final decision is rendered in open court some weeks or months later. One researcher, in fact, has referred to the justices' openness to change as "fluidity." [7]

It has been no secret that the way judges relate to one another affects their behavior on the court. Examination of the personal papers of members of the Supreme Court, interviews with appellate court jurists, and reminiscences of former law clerks all reveal the impact of group dynamics on voting behavior and on the content of written opinions.[8] Two characteristics in particular seem to carry weight as justices seek to influence their colleagues—personality and intellect. Judges who are considered to be warm, good-hearted, fair-minded, and so on seem able to put together winning coalitions and to hammer out compromises a bit more effectively than colleagues who have a reputation for condescension, self-righteousness, hostility, or vindictiveness.[9] This reflection on human nature should come as no surprise. A student who had served on his university's multimember student court gave us an illustration of this phenomenon, and while a student tribunal is certainly not the U.S. Supreme Court, we think the dynamics involved are similar:

> We had this guy on the court . . . who was one of these people that you just kind of naturally take to. I mean, he had a good sense of humor and was real decent and outgoing. I don't think he was that much of a "brain" or anything, but you always felt that he honestly wanted to do the right thing. Well, when we were split on some case—especially on matters of what punishment to hand down—and he suggested a way out, I think we all listened pretty carefully to what he thought was fair. He was just that sort of person.

The other personal attribute that is part of small-group dynamics is the knowledge and intellectual capacity of the individual judge.[10] A justice with a superior intellect or wide experience in a particular area of the law has a good deal more clout than a jurist who is seen as an intellectual lightweight. As one appeals court judge observed:

> Personality doesn't amount to so much as opinion-writing ability. Some judges are simply better than others. Some know more, think better. It would be strange if among nine men all had the same ability. Some simply have more respect than others. . . . That's bound to be so in any group. The first thing, is the judge particularly broad and experienced in the field? A couple of judges are acknowledged masters in admiralty. What they think carries more weight. I don't have much trouble being heard on criminal law or state government. I've been there. Ex-district judges on Courts of Appeals certainly carry more weight in discussion of trial procedures, instructions to juries, etc. Every judge is recognized for a particular proficiency obtained before or after his appointment. It saves enormous spadework and drudgery [to assign opinions accordingly]. No one could develop an expertise in all these fields.[11]

The techniques or strategies that justices use in their conscious (or even unconscious) efforts to maximize their impact on multijudge courts can be grouped into three general categories: persuasion on the merits, bargaining, and threat of sanctions. While the tactics overlap and are inherently interrelated, we shall take a look at their central focuses, which are in fact different.

Persuasion on the Merits

This aspect of small-group dynamics takes us right back to the *legal subculture* discussed in Chapter 5. Quite simply, it means that because of their training and values, judges are open to persuasion based on sound legal reasoning bolstered by legal precedents. Unless judges have taken a hard-and-fast position from the start, most can be swayed by an articulate and well-reasoned argument from a colleague with a differing opinion.

One study of the Supreme Court concluded that the justices

> can be persuaded to change their minds about specific cases as well as about broad public policies, and intellectual persuasion can play an important role in such shifts. . . . Time and time again positions first taken at conference are changed as other Justices bring up new arguments. Perhaps most convincing in demonstrating the impact of intellectual factors are the numerous instances on record in which the Justice assigned the opinion of the Court has reported back to the conference that additional study had convinced him that he and the rest of the majority had been in error.[12]

For example, Justice Robert Jackson, hardly a wilting violet when it came to holding fast to a judicial point of view, once commented: "I myself have changed my opinion after reading the opinions of the other members of this Court. And I am as stubborn as most. But I sometimes wind up not voting the way I voted in conference because the reasons of the majority didn't satisfy me."[13]

Judges on the appeals courts appear to be just as willing to have their positions altered by arguments well seasoned by the spices of precedent and sound judicial reasoning. After long interviews with appellate judges in three circuits one scholar noted, "If one generalization held, it was that circuit judges perceived the core elements of leadership to be intellectual integrity and professional skill." One such judge put it this way when asked about the small-group dynamics on his court: "Yes, there is leadership, if you will, but leadership influenced by legal knowledge, legal insight, practical judgment, and ability to articulate them persuasively!"[14]

The persuasion-on-merits phenomenon can't be pushed too far, however. If the facts and legal arguments are straightforward enough, a justice may simply not be open to change. And judges who are deeply committed to a specific point of view or whose egos are sufficiently great will probably be impervious to legal arguments not consistent with their own views. For instance, at the present time Justices Thurgood Marshall and William Brennan are profoundly and morally opposed to the principle of capital punishment and have often said so in their opinions. It is doubtful that any amount of legal reasoning or any calling up of "sacred precedents" could alter their belief that executions constitute "cruel and unusual punishment" by contemporary standards.

Bargaining

Bargaining may sound like a strange word to use in talking about the personal interactions of judges on collegial courts. When students first hear the term, they often think of the vote-trading technique called *logrolling* that legislators sometimes use. For example, one lawmaker might say to another, "If you vote for a new federal dam in my district, I'll vote to build a couple of new post offices in yours." Is this what happens with judges, too? Is there evidence that they sometimes say to one another, "If you vote for me in this case, I'll decide with you in one of your 'pet cases' "? In fact, there is virtually *no* evidence for this in the U.S. judiciary. Bargaining does indeed take place, but it is more subtle and does not involve vote swapping. While some bargaining occurs in the give-and-take that goes on in conference, when the initial votes are taken, most is focused on the scope and contents of the majority (or even the dissenting) opinion.

To understand how the bargaining process works, it is important to realize that usually much more is at stake in the outcome of a decision than merely whether party A or party B wins. Judges also have to discuss such questions as these: How broad should the decision be—that is, should we suggest in our written opinion that this case is unique, or should we open the gates and encourage other suits of this nature? Should we overturn what appears to be the obviously controlling precedent, or should we "distinguish around" it and let the precedent stand? Should we base our decision on constitutional grounds, or should we allow the victor to win on more technical and restrictive grounds? In other words, most decisions at the appellate level are not zero-sum games in which the winner automatically takes all; there are almost always important supplementary issues to be talked about or to be bargained for.

A landmark case of the 1970s provides a good example. In 1973 the Supreme Court handed down a joint decision on the matter of abortion.[15] To most citizens the only issue the Court had to decide was whether abortion was legal or not. While that may have been the bottom-line question, many other issues were in fact at stake, and the bargaining over them among the majority justices was intense.[16] What is human life and when does it begin? Should the decision rest on the Ninth Amendment or should it be based on the due process clause of the Fourteenth Amendment? Does a fetus have any constitutional rights? Is it a greater health risk to a woman to have an abortion or to deliver a child after carrying it to full term? Can a woman decide to have an abortion on her own or does a physician have to concur; and if so, how many doctors need concur? And this by no means completes the list!

For the abortion case the justices spent over a year trying to hammer out a decision that would be acceptable to a majority. Draft opinions were sent around, altered, and changed again as the official opinion writer, Justice Harry Blackmun, tried to accommodate all views—or at least not to offend someone in the majority so strongly that he would join the dissenters. Woodward and Armstrong noted in *The Brethren* that the law clerks "in most chambers were surprised to see the Justices, particularly Blackmun, so openly brokering their decision like a group of legislators."[17] But the law clerks themselves were not immune to the bargaining process. In the Supreme Court's cafeteria, law library, and gymnasium the clerks asked one another whether "your Justice" could go along with this or that compromise or related that "my Justice" would never support an opinion containing such and such an offensive clause.

With a significant portion of appeals and Supreme Court cases, then, bargaining is the name of the game—it is one way in which a group of jurists, in a unanimous or majority opinion, are able to present a united front. One classic study that focused on the Supreme Court has observed:

> For Justices, bargaining is a simple fact of life. Despite conflicting views on literary style, relevant precedents, procedural rules, and substantive policy, cases have to be settled and opinions written; and no opinion may carry the institutional label of the Court unless five Justices agree to sign it. In the process of judicial decision-making, much bargaining may be tacit, but the pattern is still one of negotiation and accommodation to secure consensus. Thus how to bargain wisely— not necessarily sharply—is a prime consideration for a Justice who is anxious to see his policy adopted by the Court. A Justice must learn not only how to put pressure on his colleagues but how to gauge what amounts of pressure are sufficient to be "effective" and what amounts will overshoot the mark and alienate another judge. In many situations a Justice has to be willing to settle for less than he wants if he is to get anything at all. As Brandeis once remarked, the "great difficulty of all group action, of course, is when and what concession to make.[18]

Appellate judges do most of their face-to-face bargaining at the three-judge conferences and then iron out the details of the opinion later on using the telephone and short memos. As with Supreme Court decision making, a threat to dissent can often result in changes in the way the majority opinion is drafted. For example,

> When a conservative minority sought to amend a middle-of-the-road compromise by which the 5th circuit achieved unanimity in the Mississippi school case, for example, a former legislator reportedly threatened to bolt to the left. "They came back into the fold in a hurry," a colleague remarked. "So you see, the judicial process is like legislation. All decisions are compromises." [19]

Threat of Sanctions

Besides persuasion on the merits and bargaining, there is one other tactic that jurists use in their efforts to maximize their impact on the multimember appellate tribunals—the threat of sanctions. Basically there are three sanctions that a judge or justice can invoke against colleagues: the vote, the willingness to write a strong dissenting opinion, and "going public."

The Judge's Vote. The threat to take away one's vote from the majority, and thus dissent, may cause the majority to mollify its views. For example, back in 1889 Justice Horace Gray sent this subtle (or perhaps not so subtle) message to Justice Samuel Miller:

> After a careful reading of your opinion in *Shotwell v. Moore,* I am very sorry to be compelled to say that the first part of it . . . is so contrary to my conviction, that I fear, unless it can be a good deal tempered, I shall have to deliver a separate opinion on the lines of the enclosed memorandum.
>
> I am particularly troubled about this, because, if my scruples are not removed, and Justices Field, Bradley and Lamar adhere to their dissent, your opinion will represent only four judges, half of those who took part in the case.[20]

His back against the wall because of his narrow majority, Justice Miller was obliged to yield to his colleague's costly "scruples."

For the most part the potential effect of a threat to dissent from the majority depends on how small that majority is. Thus if the initial vote among a three-judge appellate panel were three-to-zero, the threat of one member to dissent would not be all that serious; there would still be a two-to-one majority. Conversely, if at a preliminary Supreme Court conference there were a five-to-four vote, the threat by one of those five to defect would be taken seriously indeed by the remaining four.

Sometimes, however, the impact of one's vote is not merely a function of how divided the court is. On occasion the perceived need for unanimity among the court may be so strong that *any* justice's threat to vote against the prevailing view may have a disproportionate effect. We know now, for example, that prior to the 1954 *Brown* decision, a majority on the Supreme Court opposed segregation in the schools. Chief Justice Warren and the other liberals believed, though, that a simple majority was not enough to confront the expected backlash if segregation were struck down; only a *unanimous* Court, they felt, could have any chance of seeing its will prevail throughout the nation. Therefore, the liberal majority bided its time during the early 1950s until the moment came when all nine judges were willing to take on the malignant giant of racial segregation.

A more recent example occurred when President Richard Nixon declined to turn over the now-famous tape recordings to the federal prosecutor. His refusal was challenged in the courts, and when the case reached the nation's highest tribunal, it became clear that only a unanimous Court could effectively rebuke the chief executive and avert what was fast becoming a constitutional crisis. The colorful language of *The Brethren* tells the tale. When the eight justices (Justice Rehnquist had disqualified himself) met in conference to discuss the case, Justice

> Brennan saw the consensus immediately. The President did not have a single vote. Even more encouraging, there was reason to believe that the gaps among the Justices could be bridged. A single opinion seemed within reach. That would be the greatest deterrent to a defiant President. Brennan decided to float again his suggestion of a single opinion, authored by, and signed by, all eight. Someone had to steer a middle ground between Powell and White—the emerging antagonists on the question of standards for Presidents and other citizens. The Court could erupt into a confusing mixture of opinions, concurrences and dissents. The Chief was not capable of preventing that, Brennan believed.
>
> Brennan spoke up. The Nixon challenge had to be met in the strongest way possible. An eight-signature opinion would do it. With the memos now in circulation, they could bang out an opinion in a week of concentrated effort. Each Justice might be given a section to work on, and they could convene in a few days to measure progress. Brennan reminded them of the impact of nine signatures on the Little Rock school opinion. It had been one of the Court's finest moments. The country would benefit from such a show of strength now.[21]

Thus while the impact of the threat to abandon the majority is usually in direct proportion to the closeness of the vote, there are occasions when a majority will pay top dollar to keep any judge or justice from breaking ranks.

The Willingness to Write a Strong Dissent.   There are dissents and there are dissents. Appellate court jurists who intend to vote against the majority must decide whether to write a lengthy, assertive dissenting opinion or merely to dissent without opinion. For jurists who are not regarded by other justices—or by the public at large—as being prestigious or articulate, the threat to write a dissenting opinion may be taken with the proverbial grain of salt. If, however, potential dissenters are respected jurists with a reputation for a keen wit or for often being right in the long run, the situation is quite different. The other judges may be willing to alter their views to accommodate potential dissenters' positions or at least to dissuade them from attacking the majority position. As one court observer has noted:

> There are factors which push the majority Justices, especially the opinion writer, to accept accommodation. An eloquent, tightly-reasoned dissent can be an upsetting force. Stone's separate opinions during the thirties pointed up more sharply the folly of the conservative Justices than did any of the attacks on the Court by elected politicians. The majority may thus find it profitable to mute criticism from within the Court by giving in on some issues.[22]

Thus the second sanction—the threat to write a dissenting opinion— depends on the circumstances for its effectiveness. Sometimes it may be regarded as no more than a nuisance or the fruit of judicial egomania; on other occasions it may be viewed as likely to weaken the impact of the majority opinion.

The Threat to 'Go Public.'   On rare occasions an appellate judge may use the ultimate weapon against colleagues—public exposure. Such strong medicine is usually administered only when a jurist believes a colleague (or a group of judges) has violated the basic rules of the game; the judge then threatens to hang out the dirty linen for all to see. For example, one appeals court judge told how, as a newcomer to the bench, he had threatened public exposure to force a senior colleague to withdraw an opinion filed without his consent, a possibility he had been warned against by another judge on the court: "It was my first sitting as a circuit judge," he recalled. "It was not a major case. But there was strong give and take!" [23]

In 1967, Judges John Danaher and Warren Burger (soon to be Chief Justice Burger) accused three of their appellate court colleagues of consciously attempting to foist on the Washington, D.C., Circuit a minority position on criminal procedures.[24] Ironically, some four years later it was Burger who was threatened with public exposure by a Supreme Court colleague who felt that Burger was trying to turn his minority status on a case into a majority position.

The incident occurred as follows. When the vote had been taken at conference on the abortion case, Chief Justice Burger was in the minority (the case was *Roe v. Wade,* considered jointly with *Doe v. Bolton*). According to Supreme Court practice, this would have meant that the senior member of the majority—in this case William O. Douglas—would have been assigned to speak for the Court. Ignoring Court protocol, Burger assigned the official opinion writing to his alter ego Harry Blackmun. This enraged Douglas. But the pot didn't really boil over until several months later when Burger lobbied from his minority status to have the case postponed until the next term. (Douglas wanted the decision to come down immediately.) These extracts from *The Brethren* capture something of the drama of the confrontation:

> This time Douglas threatened to play his ace. If the conference insisted on putting the cases over for reargument, he would dissent from such an order, and he would publish the full text of his dissent. Douglas reiterated the protest he had made in December about the Chief's assigning the case to Blackmun, Burger's response and his subsequent intransigence. . . . Douglas . . . continued: "When, however, the minority seeks to control the assignment, there is a destructive force at work in the Court. When a Chief Justice tries to bend the Court to his will by manipulating assignments, the integrity of the institution is imperiled."

Douglas's pen then became more acid:

> Borrowing a line from a speech he had given in September in Portland, Douglas then made it clear that, despite what he had said earlier, he did in fact view the Chief and Blackmun as Nixon's Minnesota Twins. "Russia once gave its Chief Justice two votes; but that was too strong even for the Russians." [25]

Douglas was ultimately prevailed upon to refrain from publishing this petulant opinion, but the illustration remains a classic example of the third sanction that one jurist can use against another—the threat to go public.

Despite the availability of the several sanctions, it should be noted that they are usually invoked with varying degrees of hesitation—lest a judge or justice acquire a reputation for intransigence. For example, with regard to a justice's willingness to write a dissenting opinion, one perceptive scholar has noted:

Although dissent is a cherished part of the common law tradition, a Justice who persistently refuses to accommodate his views to those of his colleagues may come to be regarded as an obstructionist. A Justice whose dissents become levers for legislative or administrative action reversing judicial policies may come to be regarded as disloyal to the bench.[26]

Or, putting it in more human terms, one appeals court judge observed that "you have to keep on living with each other. In the next case the situations may be reversed." [27]

The Special Role of the Chief Justice and of the Chief Judges

As indicated in previous chapters, the chief justice of the U.S. Supreme Court and the chief judges of the several courts of appeals have a number of special duties and responsibilities. At this point we shall examine their respective roles insofar as they constitute one more ingredient in the recipe for small-group interaction.

The Chief Justice. The Constitution makes only passing reference to this official whose stature has come to loom so large in the eyes of the American people. Despite the constitutional slight, the chief justice can have considerable impact on the decision-making process. The key seems to be whether the chief justice possesses the capacity and the will to use the formal and informal powers that have accrued to the office during the past two centuries.

The chief justice's greatest potential for leadership is at the conference where the cases are discussed and where the initial votes are taken among the justices. Because the chief has the primary responsibility for setting the agenda of the conference and traditionally is the first to offer an opinion about each case, the potential for influencing both the format and the tone of the deliberation is significant. As noted earlier, one scholar has identified two types of roles for justices at conference: social leader and task leader. The social leader "attends to the emotional needs of his associates by affirming their values as individuals and as Court members, especially when their views are rejected by the majority. Ordinarily he is the best liked member of the Court. . . . In terms of personality, he is apt to be warm, receptive and responsive." The task leader, on the other hand, is the intellectual force behind the conference deliberations, focusing on the actual decision and trying to keep the Court consistent with itself. Danelski describes how the two roles complement each other:

> As presiding officer of the conference, the Chief Justice is in a favorable position to assert task and social leadership. His presentation of cases is an important task function. His control of the conference's process

makes it easy for him to invite suggestions and opinions, seek compromises, and cut off debate which appears to be getting out of hand, all important social functions.[28]

The chief justice also has a key role in setting up what is called the *discuss list*—that is, those special petitions selected out of the many to which the Court will give full consideration. The chief's law clerks obviously must help with this task, but the chief guides their judgment. This special activity helps determine which cases the Court will consider as a group and which are to be summarily dismissed.

The final power of the chief justice is the assignment of opinions— that is, to designate who will write the official decision of the Court.[29] As noted earlier, this task falls to chief justices only if they are in the majority when the vote on a case is taken at conference; otherwise the most senior justice in the majority selects the opinion writer. The chief justices have the greatest control over an opinion when they assign it to themselves, and traditionally they have retained many important cases for that reason.[30] It will be recalled that in such cases as *Marbury v. Madison, Brown v. Board of Education,* and *United States v. Nixon,* the chief justice used his option to speak as the official voice of the Court.

Chiefs who choose not to write the opinion may assign it to that member of the majority whose views are closest to the dissenters', with the hope that some of the minority may subsequently switch their votes to the majority view. Or, as has most often been the case in recent decades, chief justices will assign the opinion to an ideological alter ego so that the grounds for the decision will be favorable to their own.

Since Warren Burger has been chief justice, a new and somewhat unhappy wrinkle has appeared in this overall process of opinion assignment. Using his option of being the last to vote on a case in conference, Burger occasionally sits back and waits to see how the vote is headed and then automatically joins the majority position—regardless of whether he had supported that position during the discussion of the case. This has increased Burger's control over opinion assignment but at some real cost to the internal harmony within the Court. We get a flavor of this from the perspective of Justice William O. Douglas:

> It took Douglas several moments to grasp the pattern of the assignments, and then he was flabbergasted. The Chief had assigned four cases in which Douglas was sure the Chief was not a member of the majority. These included the two abortion cases, which the Chief had assigned to Blackmun. He could barely control his rage as he ran down the list. Was there some mistake? He asked a clerk to check his notes from the conference. Douglas kept a docket book in which he recorded his tabulation of the votes. It was as he suspected. . . . "God, I miss

Hugo," Douglas lamented to friends whenever Burger manipulated assignments. "Burger would never have dared pull that if Hugo were around." As senior Associate Justice, Black had helped keep the Chief within bounds. To Douglas's dismay, that role now fell almost exclusively to him.[31]

Despite the considerable influence that a chief justice may have on the Court's small group, the crucial factor, as previously indicated, seems to be whether the chief has both the *capacity* and the *desire* to exert such potential authority. For example, the first great chief justice, John Marshall, possessed both these traits, and they helped fill the intellectual vacuum of the Court during the early 1800s:

> Marshall, like the majority of justices in the court's history, was an experienced politician. . . . He guided the court in a series of sweeping decisions . . . through force of personality and a talent for negotiation. Justice William Johnson, a Jefferson appointee, grumbled to his patron about Marshall's dominance. Wondering why Marshall invariably wrote the Court's opinions, Johnson reported to Jefferson that he had "found out the real cause. [William] Cushing was incompetent. [Samuel] Chase could not be got to think or write. [William] Paterson was a slow man and willingly declined trouble, and the other two judges [Marshall and Bushrod Washington] you know are commonly estimated as one judge." [32]

While John Marshall had the skill and the desire to influence the Court, not all of his successors possessed these traits. For instance, the nation's chief justice between 1941 and 1946, Harlan Fiske Stone, had neither the talent nor the will for either task leadership or social leadership. As his biographer sadly wrote of him, "He was totally unprepared to cope with the petty bickering and personal conflict in which his court became engulfed." [33]

The Chief Judges of the Appeals Courts. As with the Chief Justice, the leadership potential of the administrative circuit heads is determined, in part, by their intellectual and negotiating skills and by their desire to put them to use. In reality, however, their potential effect on their respective circuits is probably less than the potential impact of the chief justice on the Supreme Court. First, since most appellate court decisions are made by three-judge panels on a rotating basis, the chief judge is not likely even to be a part of most circuit decision making. Second, the circuits are more decentralized than the Supreme Court. Finally, the chief judge is not nearly so prominent a figure in the eyes of the public or of other government decision makers. Or, as one former chief judge said about the job: "The only advantage is that the title sounds more imposing if you are speaking in public or writing an article. Otherwise it's a pain in the ass." [34]

Much of a chief judge's work is administrative (such as docketing cases, keeping financial records, adjusting the caseloads), but it is also true that administration and policy making are not mutually exclusive endeavors. As the chief judge of the former U.S. Fifth Circuit once acknowledged: "So many times judicial problems slop over into administrative problems and vice versa" that the real questions are when and where this effect occurs. Commenting on the influence of the chief judges, one observer has said:

> As with strong presidents [or "as with strong chief justices," he might have added] . . . the spillover depends on the personality of the chief and the countervailing force of experienced colleagues. The impact of chief judges was most noticeable on freshmen and the composition of three-judge district courts. ("If all the judges are new, he'll pack a wallop out of proportion to one vote.") Southern judges made no bones about packing three-judge district courts in race relations cases. ([The liberal] "Tuttle was not about to set up a three-judge court with [segregationists like] Cameron and Cox on it; this occurs no more.") Of all administrative powers, plainly the most potent instruments of policy leadership involve the assignment of work.[35]

Evidence of Small-Group Interaction

In discussing small-group dynamics, we have argued that it involves persuasion on the merits by one judge toward another, bargaining among the appellate jurists, and the threat of sanctions, such as a judge's vote, a willingness to write a strong dissent, and the threat to "go public." We have also contended that the chief justice of the Supreme Court and the chief judges of the appeals courts can potentially affect the decision making of their respective small judicial groups. The evidence we have cited for this so far has largely been anecdotal or subjective, but there are some more rigorous empirical data for our arguments—at least for the Supreme Court.

One study compared the justices' initial votes at conference with the final votes as they appeared in the published reports for the years 1946 to 1956.[36] Any change in the two sets of votes was attributed to small-group interaction. The findings tell us several things. First, there were vote changes in about 60 percent of all cases. Most of these changes occurred when a justice who had not participated in the first vote or who had been a dissenter opted to join the majority position. But when one considers all votes for all cases, the justices changed positions only 9 percent of the time. In such instances of vote change, the initial majority position lost out in only 14 percent of the cases. Thus, there is evidence, both anecdotal and quantitative, that the output of multijudge courts is affected by small-group dynamics, although few ultimate outcomes appear to be altered by it. Be that as it may, we would argue that most small-group interaction involves the drawing up of the majority opinion, in setting forth its perimeters and corollaries. As of this date scholars lack a precise measure of the impact of such dynamics, but it seems fair to say it is considerable.

Attitude Theory and Bloc-Formation Analysis

Many judicial scholars have been dissatisfied with small-group analysis, arguing that the fruits of such exploration are barely worth their efforts. While not denying that personal interactions make a difference in some cases and perhaps play a key role in a handful of decisions, they contend that the richest ore for explaining judicial behavior can be found in other mines. After all, as the conclusion to the previous section notes, justices' positions change on all cases as the result of personal interactions only 9 percent of the time and such changes produce a majority loss in only 14 percent of the cases. This means that small-group dynamics make a bottom-line hit on the Court only about 1 percent of the time (.09 x .14 equals .0126)—hardly an overwhelming phenomenon.

A decision-making model that claims greater explanatory power deals with the discovery of the justices' basic, judicially relevant attitudes and with the coalitions, or *blocs,* formed by jurists who share similar attitudes.[37] This approach rests on the assumption that judges—particularly appellate jurists—view cases primarily in terms of the broad political, socioeconomic issues they raise and that they generally respond to these issues in accordance with their own personal values and attitudes. The "official reasons" the justices give for their decisions (found in their published opinions) are regarded as "mere rationalizations." For example, let us suppose that Judge X strongly believes that the government should never tamper with freedom of the press. If a case comes before the court in which censorship is the central issue, then Judge X will go with his convictions and vote on the side of the news media. His written opinion may be full of impressive legal citations, quotations from eminent law reviews, or lofty discussions of the importance for democracy of a maximum of freedom of expression. But all this, the attitude scholars contend, is only a rationalization after the fact. The *real* reason for Judge X's vote was that he strongly dislikes the concept of government censorship.

The attitude theorists do not claim that their decision-making models explain everything, nor do they deny that judges must often decide cases *against* the grain of their personal values. For instance, a justice may be a strong environmentalist, but if a pro-environment petitioner has absolutely no standing to sue, it is not likely that the justice will yield to the tug of the heart. Nevertheless, supporters of the judicial attitude approach contend that it can explain a significant portion of judicial behavior and that it is well worth the research time and effort that such studies require.

Let us now examine some specific questions about this approach: Where do judicial attitudes originate? How does one learn about a judge's attitudes? What are some of the techniques that have been used to study attitudinal behavior and bloc formation? What have these techniques uncovered in terms of substance?

First, as noted in Chapters 4 and 5, appellate jurists acquire their relevant attitudes from the same sources that people in general do: from parents and friends, from educational institutions, from the media, from political activities, and so on. Thus, there is clearly an overlap between the attitude theorists and those who study judicial background characteristics. The difference is that the latter want to know *from where* the justices acquire their values, while the attitude theorists concentrate on measuring the effects of judges' values—regardless of their origin—on collegial decision making. The attitude scholars acknowledge that some beliefs change during the course of a jurist's tenure on the bench, but still they postulate "that attitudes are 'relatively enduring.' "[38]

Second, how can one compile a judge's attitudes in order to test for their manifestations in collegial court decisions? Unfortunately, judges have shown no willingness to answer the sort of in-depth questionnaires that might reveal judicially significant attitudes—particularly on matters that relate to issues that may come before them in court. Likewise judges are reluctant to give speeches, grant interviews, or write articles that bare their judicial souls. Judges consider such behavior inappropriate and many resist making it easy for reporters and social scientists to suggest a link between their personal values and the way they decide cases.

For the most part, scholars have turned to the contents of written opinions to categorize judges' primary values. Thus a justice who writes a strong opinion attacking government interference with the free operation of the marketplace is said to have a conservative economic attitude. This sort of approach has opened the researchers to the charge that they have created a tautology: a justice writes several conservative economic opinions; is classified as an economic conservative; and lo and behold, aggregate analysis of his or her voting patterns reveals that the judge is a conservative on economic issues. Such theorists respond that this criticism is unfair because the patterns they have uncovered have proved to be consistent over time and susceptible to duplication by other researchers using similar methodologies. The next section will examine some of the research techniques that have been useful in measuring judicial attitudes and, in particular, the degree to which these attitudes cause like-minded judges to vote as blocs on similar cases.

Content Analysis

One important method used by attitude theorists is *content analysis*—they search through hundreds of appellate court opinions for certain key words or phrases that indicate a particular judicial attitude.[39] For example, a judge whose opinions contain numerous references to "personal freedom" is probably going to be more of a civil libertarian than one whose published decisions are strewn with continual references to "law and order." Such an approach has been greatly enhanced by the advent of the computer; it has been possible to lay bare the attitudinal dimensions of scores of judges who jointly have rendered thousands of opinions.

Bloc Analysis

The publication in 1948 of *The Roosevelt Court: A Study in Judicial Politics and Values, 1937-1947* is regarded as the first attempt to study, in a rigorous, quantitative manner, voting blocs on the Supreme Court. The author discovered two basic attitudinal coalitions on the Court: those who voted to sanction the liberal economic reforms of Roosevelt's New Deal and those who believed that such measures were unconstitutional. During the 1950s and beyond, the analysis of voting blocs based on similar attitudes became more sophisticated.[40] For example, researchers not only tested for the existence of a cohesive bloc on the Court, but they began to introduce such factors as an index of interagreement—that is, a mean agreement score of the justices in the bloc.

The dean of the attitude-bloc approach, Glendon Schubert, looked at the state of the art in 1974:

> Sociometric analysis of interagreement in voting behavior, which focused upon a pool of all the votes of all of the justices, in cases decided on the merits during a stipulated period, showed ... that the Court characteristically divided into a liberal bloc and conservative bloc. But bloc analysis also showed that there were usually some justices who did not seem to affiliate with either bloc, and there seemed to be a considerable amount of inconsistent voting, even among the bloc members—inconsistent, that is, in the sense that in some decisions one or more justices would vote with members of the "opposing" bloc rather than with members of their own bloc. The latter findings were perplexing, and it was not until the introduction of more powerful

research tools that they were understood. At first through linear cumulative scaling and subsequently through factor analysis and multidimensional scaling, studies of the voting behavior of Supreme Court justices have shown that there are three major attitudinal components of judicial liberalism and conservatism.

The three types of attitude dimensions developed by Schubert were political, social, and economic. The political liberal supports civil rights and liberties, while the conservative is more supportive of the law-and-order position. The social liberal upholds the egalitarian position on matters of voting, citizenship, and ethnic status; a counterpart is more inclined to oppose equal access to the polity and the economic structure. Finally, the economic liberal is less of a defender of private property and vested interests than is a conservative colleague.[41]

The courts of appeals have also been subjected to bloc analysis during the past two decades, and there, too, researchers have been able to identify groups of judges with similar voting patterns on the same issue dimension.[42]

Scaling

Almost simultaneously with the development of bloc analysis came the application of scaling techniques to the study of judicial behavior on collegial courts.[43] *Scaling* is founded on several basic assumptions. One is that there exists an underlying attitudinal continuum of beliefs about a given subject—for example, support for civil rights and liberties. In principle the stronger one's support for these freedoms, the higher one would fall on the scale. On a hypothetical 10-point scale a justice who was only moderately supportive of civil rights and liberties might be assigned a score of 3, whereas a justice who always voted on the libertarian side would be given a score of 10.

Scaling also assumes that there is a cutoff point somewhere along the scale for each justice—that is, the point at which the case stimuli will be so low that the justice will vote against rather than for the particular attitude dimension being studied. Judicial behavioralists like to use scaling because it permits them to predict how a judge or justice might vote (or would have voted) in any given case. For example, let us assume that Justice X can be assigned a six on a 10-point civil rights scale (with 1 representing unqualified support for civil rights and 10 indicating total opposition to this cause). Then let us suppose that a case comes up in which the stimuli to vote for the civil rights position is only a 4. We would predict that the justice would *not* vote for the liberal position because the stimuli to do so had not reached his threshold of 6. Scales are said to be accurate if their predictions are correct about 90 percent of the time, and to the delight of scholars most scales do meet this level of reliability.

Since 1946 two types of scales have worked particularly well in the analysis of non-unanimous Supreme Court decisions: the C scale (Glendon Schubert's scale for civil rights and liberties) and the E scale (Schubert's scale for matters in which an economic underdog is in litigation against a well-to-do opponent). Improving on his earlier analysis and techniques, Schubert developed what he called a "psychometric model." [44] In such a model justices hypothetically respond (in their votes) to various stimuli found in the cases. The key elements are (1) the nature of the stimulus and where it falls on the value continuum, and (2) the particular judge's attitude and where it appears on the value scale.

The use of the techniques of content analysis, bloc analysis, and scaling have greatly enhanced the capacity of judicial scholars to explain and predict the behavior of judges on collegial courts. One researcher, Harold Spaeth, has gained for himself a fair amount of popular acclaim for his accurate radio and newspaper predictions of pending Supreme Court decisions and votes. Using the very research techniques we have discussed here, he has scored hits on over 9 out of 10 predictions of judicial behavior. [45]

Fact Pattern Analysis

There is another model for explaining the behavior of judges on collegial courts—*fact pattern analysis*. At first blush this approach seems to resemble that of the traditional legal subculture understanding of judicial decision making discussed in Chapter 5, because its central thesis is that the facts of a case are the primary determinants as to how the case will be resolved. Recall that the legal subculture model contends that a judge will resolve an issue in favor of that side which is able to marshal the stronger set of factual evidence and legal precedents. While fact pattern scholars also believe that the facts of a case determine its outcome, they quickly part company with the traditional approach after that point.

Several basic assumptions of the fact pattern approach set it apart from other models of judicial behavior. First, when fact pattern scholars refer to the "facts of a case," they have in mind quite a different set of items from the legal subculture adherents. "Facts" to these scholars include such elements as the gender of the litigants, whether an attorney in a criminal case is court-appointed or privately retained, the social status of the parties, and whether the petitioner is a member of a racial minority. According to traditional scholars, such information is not supposed to affect the outcome of a case, but to the fact pattern theorists, cases are often won or lost because of just such extrajudicial variables. Let us look at an example.

One classic study using this approach focused on the voting behavior of Supreme Court justice Felix Frankfurter. The author found that Frankfurter was favorably disposed toward a petitioner in cases containing certain basic facts, or "signs," as the writer called them. The signs included the terms *confession-counsel,* meaning that the defendant's confession may not have been voluntary; *Negro,* indicating the minority status of the accused; and *state,* suggesting an insensitivity to correct criminal procedure. Referring to these signs, the study noted that there was

> a positive association between the presence of each and a favorable vote for civil liberties by Frankfurter in both years. Frankfurter's favorable vote was cast with the appearance of the 'Negro' sign in 13 of 15 cases; with the appearance of the 'state' sign 28 of 47 times; and with the appearance of the 'confession-counsel' factor in 8 cases out of 9. These figures alone suggest that Frankfurter's willingness to draw negative inferences against a governmental unit in civil liberty cases might have been affected by the presence of these factors, with the presence of one or more of them improving the chances of a favorable vote.[46]

A second theoretical underpinning of fact pattern researchers is that they do not begin their analysis with any assumption

> regarding the existence or nonexistence of consistent patterns in the acceptance of facts or in decisions based on facts. Whether or not consistency does exist in a given area of adjudication is determined by the use of the methods. If consistent patterns cannot be identified, it must be concluded that judicial action in the given area of law cannot be understood in terms of the dependence of decisions on facts. If, on the other hand, consistent patterns are found, an important implication of the proposed methods is apparent. Should it be possible to predict only later cases from earlier cases, the underlying pattern of consistency could be explained in terms of stare decisis. But if earlier cases could be predicted from later ones, adherence to precedent would have to be explained in terms of an independent—although convergent—recognition and acceptance of similar standards of justice by different judges at different times. Thus not only the existence of consistent patterns but also the basis for their consistency can be evaluated.[47]

Finally, the fact pattern scholars believe that to explain judicial behavior they must learn how to weight each of the key facts of a case and also to learn how the facts combine to have the greatest (and the least) effect on any given judge. This is obviously a time-consuming and complicated procedure because the researcher is usually dealing with scores of possible facts and an enormous variety of possible weightings—

combinations that literally run into the billions. Using sophisticated mathematical equations and the computer, fact pattern scholars have advanced into the unknown with considerable success. One of its key exponents explains how:

> Each case is represented by an equation, in which an index denoting the acceptance or rejection of a fact by an appellate court is set equal to the combination of appearances, nonappearances, and denials of the fact at the preceding stages. The weights of the fact at the various stages—in the sense of how persuasive its appearance at the respective stages is toward its acceptance by the appellate court—are the *unknowns* in the equations. As the equations are solved, the weights are determined. To be sure, the complex procedures which are required for the solutions of the equations again necessitate the use of a computer, especially because there is a separate system of equations for each fact. By using the weights in a case not previously encountered, one can predict for each fact an acceptance or rejection that would be consistent with the established pattern of past cases.[48]

Fact pattern analysis, as with the other approaches to collegial court decision making, does not claim to explain the whole of judicial behavior. But as with the other models discussed in this chapter, it has provided some key insights during the past several decades as to how and why appellate judges act as they do.[49]

Summary

We began this chapter with the observation that decision making by judges on collegial, appellate courts is in some key ways different from the behavior of judges acting alone on trial benches. Because of these differences scholars have devised theories and research techniques to capture the special reality of decision making by jurists on the U.S. appeals courts and the Supreme Court. We took a close look at the discretionary review process of the Supreme Court and noted that the issues it decides *not* to rule on are often as substantively important as those cases it selects for full review. In this context we discussed the importance of cue theory—the attempt by scholars to learn the characteristics of those few cases chosen from the many for Supreme Court consideration.

We then focused on three separate theoretical approaches to explain and predict the decision making of multijudge courts: small-group analysis, attitude and bloc-formation analysis, and fact pattern analysis. Each of these has its own working assumptions and research techniques used to glean the explanatory data. Although it is tempting to speculate on which of these several approaches provides the best insights into appellate court behavior, it is probably fairest to say that the jury of judicial scholars is still out on this query.

Notes

1. From an interview with an appeals court judge as quoted in J. Woodford Howard, Jr., *Courts of Appeals in the Federal Judicial System* (Princeton, N.J.: Princeton University Press, 1981), 135.
2. Joseph Tanenhaus et al., "The Supreme Court's Certiorari Jurisdiction: Cue Theory," in *Judicial Decision-Making*, ed. Glendon Schubert (New York: Free Press, 1963), 111-132.
3. For example, see S. Sidney Ulmer, "The Decision to Grant Certiorari as an Indicator to Decision 'On the Merits,' " *Polity* 4 (1972): 429-447.
4. For example, see Donald R. Songer, "Concern for Policy Outputs as a Cue for Supreme Court Decisions on Certiorari," *Journal of Politics* 41 (1979): 1185-1194, and S. Sidney Ulmer, "Selecting Cases for Supreme Court Review: An Underdog Model," *American Political Science Review* 72 (1978): 902-910.
5. Virginia C. Armstrong and Charles A. Johnson, "Certiorari Decisions by the Warren & Burger Courts: Is Cue Theory Time Bound?" *Polity* 15 (1982): 141-150.
6. Henry R. Glick, *Courts, Politics, and Justice* (New York: McGraw-Hill, 1983), 217.
7. J. Woodford Howard, Jr., "On the Fluidity of Judicial Choice," *American Political Science Review* 62 (1968): 43-57.
8. For example, see Walter F. Murphy, *Elements of Judicial Strategy* (Chicago: University of Chicago Press, 1964); Bob Woodward and Scott Armstrong, *The Brethren: Inside the Supreme Court* (New York: Simon and Schuster, 1979); Howard, *Courts of Appeals in the Federal Judicial System*; Alpheus T. Mason, *Harlan Fiske Stone: Pillar of the Law* (New York: Viking Press, 1956).
9. In the parlance of judicial scholars, this is referred to as the *social leadership* function. See David J. Danelski, "The Influence of the Chief Justice in the Decisional Process," in *Courts, Judges, and Politics*, 3d ed., ed. Walter F. Murphy and C. Herman Pritchett (New York: Random House, 1979), 695-703. We will have more to say about Danelski's characterizations a little later in the chapter.
10. This is termed the *task leadership* function. See Danelski, "The Influence of the Chief Justice in the Decisional Process."
11. Howard, *Courts of Appeals in the Federal Judicial System*, 230-231.
12. Murphy, *Elements of Judicial Strategy*, 44.
13. As quoted in Murphy, *Elements of Judicial Strategy*, 44.

14. As quoted in Howard, *Courts of Appeals in the Federal Judicial System*, 231.
15. *Roe v. Wade*, 410 U.S. 113 (1973) and *Doe v. Bolton*, 410 U.S. 179 (1973).
16. Woodward and Armstrong, *The Brethren*, chaps. entitled "1971 Term" and "1972 Term."
17. Ibid., 233.
18. Murphy, *Elements of Judicial Strategy*, 57.
19. Howard, *Courts of Appeals in the Federal Judicial System*, 209.
20. As quoted in Charles Fairman, *Mr. Justice Miller and the Supreme Court 1862-1890* (Cambridge, Mass.: Harvard University Press, 1939), 320.
21. Woodward and Armstrong, *The Brethren*, 309.
22. Murphy, *Elements of Judicial Strategy*, 63-64.
23. As quoted in Howard, *Courts of Appeals in the Federal Judicial System*, 209.
24. *Ross v. Sirica*, 380 F. 2d 557 (D.C. Cir. 1967).
25. Woodward and Armstrong, *The Brethren*, 187, 188.
26. Murphy, *Elements of Judicial Strategy*, 61.
27. As quoted in Howard, *Courts of Appeals in the Federal Judicial System*, 209.
28. Danelski, "The Influence of the Chief Justice in the Decisional Process," 696.
29. For an excellent discussion of this subject, see David W. Rohde and Harold J. Spaeth, *Supreme Court Decision Making* (San Francisco: Freeman, 1976), chap. 8.
30. Elliot E. Slotnick, "The Chief Justice and Self-Assignment of Majority Opinions: A Research Note," *Western Political Quarterly* 31 (1978): 219-225.
31. Woodward and Armstrong, *The Brethren*, 170-171.
32. Donald Dale Jackson, *Judges* (New York: Atheneum, 1974), 329.
33. As quoted in Danelski, "The Influence of the Chief Justice in the Decisional Process," 698.
34. As quoted in Howard, *Courts of Appeals in the Federal Judicial System*, 228.
35. Howard, *Courts of Appeals in the Federal Judicial System*, 229. In a few instances the chief judges have been accused of "stacking" the three-judge panels, which are supposed to operate on a more or less random, rotational basis. For example, see *Armstrong v. Bd. of Educ. of Birmingham*, 323 F. 2d 333, 352-361 (5th Cir. 1963); 48 F.R.D. 141, 182 (1969). See also, Burton M. Atkins and William Zavoina, "Judicial Leadership on the Court of Appeals: A Probability Analysis of Panel Assignment in Race Relations Cases on the Fifth Circuit," *American Journal of Political Science* 18 (1974): 701-711.
36. Saul Brenner, "Fluidity on the United States Supreme Court: A Reexamination," *American Journal of Political Science* 24 (1980): 526-535.
37. For a good discussion of the attitude approach to the study of judicial decision making, see Rohde and Spaeth, *Supreme Court Decision Making*, chap. 4, and Glendon Schubert, *The Judicial Mind Revisited* (New York: Oxford University Press, 1974). Also see James L. Gibson, "From Simplicity to Complexity: The Development of Theory in the Study of Judicial Behavior," *Political Behavior* 5 (1983): 7-50.

38. Rohde and Spaeth, *Supreme Court Decision Making,* 75.
39. For example, see Glendon Schubert, "Jackson's Judicial Philosophy: An Exploration in Value Analysis," *American Political Science Review* 59 (1965): 940-963, and Werner F. Grunbaum, "A Quantitative Analysis of the 'Presidential Ballot' Case," *Journal of Politics* 34 (1972): 223-243.
40. For example, see Glendon Schubert, *Quantitative Analysis of Judicial Behavior* (New York: Free Press, 1959) and S. Sidney Ulmer, "The Analysis of Behavior Patterns in the United States Supreme Court," *Journal of Politics* 22 (1960): 629-653.
41. Schubert, *Judicial Policy Making,* 160-161.
42. For example, see Sheldon Goldman, "Conflict on the U.S. Courts of Appeals 1965-1971: A Quantitative Analysis," *University of Cincinnati Law Review* 42 (1973): 635-658, and Charles M. Lamb, "Warren Burger and the Insanity Defense: Judicial Philosophy and Voting Behavior on a U.S. Court of Appeals," *American University Law Review* 24 (1974): 91-128.
43. For a good discussion of scaling and its application to judicial studies, see Joseph Tanenhaus, "The Cumulative Scaling of Judicial Decisions," *Harvard Law Review* 79 (1966): 1583-1594.
44. Schubert, *The Judicial Mind Revisited.*
45. "Computer Helps Predict Court Rulings," *New York Times,* August 15, 1971, 1:75, and "Court Handicappers: Computer Predictions of Supreme Court Decisions," *Newsweek,* August 12, 1974, 53.
46. S. Sidney Ulmer, "The Discriminant Function and a Theoretical Context for Its Use in Estimating the Votes of Judges," in *Frontiers of Judicial Research,* ed. Joel B. Grossman and Joseph Tanenhaus (New York: Wiley, 1969), 365.
47. Fred Kort, "Quantitative Analysis of Fact-Patterns in Cases and Their Impact on Judicial Decisions," in *American Court Systems,* ed. Sheldon Goldman and Austin Sarat (San Francisco: Freeman, 1978), 334.
48. Ibid., 332.
49. For other examples of fact pattern studies, see S. Sidney Ulmer, "Supreme Court Behavior in Racial Exclusion Cases: 1935-1960," *American Political Science Review* 56 (1962): 325-330; Stuart S. Nagel, *The Legal Process from a Behavioral Perspective* (Homewood, Ill.: Dorsey Press, 1969), chaps. 10-13; and Reed C. Lawlor, "Personal Stare Decisis," *Southern California Law Review* 41 (1967): 73-118.

Implementation and Impact of Federal Judicial Policies

7

In the two previous chapters we have focused on decision making by federal judges. In this chapter we extend the discussion to examine what happens *after* a decision is reached. Decisions made by federal judges are not self-executing, and a wide variety of individuals—other judges, public officials, even private citizens—may be called upon actually to implement or carry out a court's decisions. As we study the implementation process we will look at the various actors involved, their reactions to judicial policies, and the methods by which they may respond to a court's decision.

Depending upon the nature of the court's decision, the judicial policy may have a very narrow or a very broad impact. A suit for damages incurred in an automobile accident would directly affect only the persons involved, or perhaps their immediate families. On the other hand, the famous *Gideon v. Wainwright* decision has directly affected literally millions of people in one way or another.[1] In *Gideon* the Supreme Court held that states must provide an attorney for indigent defendants in felony trials. As you can see, scores of people—defendants, judges, lawyers, taxpayers—have felt the effects of that judicial policy. As we discuss the implementation process, then, we will also look at the impact on society of judicial policy making.

As noted above, a wide range of public officials, and even private citizens, may play a role in implementing a judicial policy. Lower-court judges, however, are so frequently involved in enforcing a higher court's decision that they deserve especially careful attention. Therefore, we begin our analysis of the implementation process with the lower-court judges.

The Impact of Upper-Court
Decisions on Lower Courts

As we noted in Chapter 1, Americans often view the appellate courts, notably the U.S. Supreme Court, as most likely to be involved in policy making. The trial courts, on the other hand, are frequently seen as norm enforcers rather than policy makers. Given this traditional view, the picture that often emerges is one in which the Supreme Court makes a decision that is then implemented by a lower court. In short, some envision a judicial bureaucracy with a hierarchy of courts much like superiors and subordinates.[2] Recent studies, however, have cast doubt on the bureaucracy theory, arguing instead that "most of the work of the lower courts seems less dependent on the Supreme Court than ... bureaucracy [theory] would indicate." [3] In other words, we now realize that lower-court judges have a great deal of independence from the appellate courts and may be viewed as "independent actors ... who will not follow the lead of higher courts unless conditions are favorable for their doing so." [4]

For example, it is well known that not all federal district judges immediately enforced the Supreme Court's public school desegregation decision.[5] Instead, some judges allowed school districts to engage in a variety of tactics ranging from evasion to postponement of the Supreme Court mandate.[6]

Lower-Court Discretion

Why do the lower-court judges have so much discretion when it comes to implementing a higher court's policy? In part, the answer may be found in the structure of our judicial system. You will recall from our discussions in Chapters 1 and 3 that the federal judiciary has always been characterized by independence, decentralization, and individualism. Federal judges are protected by life tenure and traditionally have been able to run their courts as they see fit. Disciplinary measures are not at all common, and federal judges have little fear of impeachment. In short, they have a good deal of freedom to make their own decisions and to respond to upper-court rulings in their own way.

The discretion exercised by a lower-court judge may also be a product of the higher court's decision itself. Let us look at a couple of examples. Following the famous school desegregation decision in 1954, the Supreme Court heard further arguments on the best way to implement its new policy. In 1955 it handed down its decision in *Brown v. Board of*

Education of Topeka II.[7] In that case the Court was faced with two major questions: (1) how soon were the public schools to start desegregating and (2) how much time should they be given to complete the process? Federal district judges given the task of enforcing the High Court's ruling were told that the public schools were to make a prompt and reasonable start and then proceed with all deliberate speed to bring about desegregation. What constitutes a prompt and reasonable start? How rapidly must a school district proceed in order to be moving with all deliberate speed? Since the Supreme Court justices did not provide specific answers to these questions, many lower-court judges were faced with school districts that continued to drag their feet while at the same time claiming they were acting within the High Court's guidelines.

A second example concerns the Supreme Court's decision in the 1962 reapportionment case, *Baker v. Carr*.[8] In that case the Court held that allegations of malapportioned state legislative districts in Tennessee presented a justiciable rather than a political question; that is, apportionment cases could properly be litigated in the courts. The case was remanded (sent back down) to the federal court for the middle district of Tennessee in Nashville for implementation. Justice Brennan's opinion for the Court concluded with the statement, "The cause is remanded for further proceedings consistent with this opinion." No guidelines were provided for the federal district judge, who was not told how rapidly to proceed nor what methods to use. Justice Clark, in a concurring opinion, pointed out that the Court "fails to give the District any guidance whatever."[9]

It is obvious, then, that federal district judges implementing either of the policies described above could exercise a wide degree of latitude and still legitimately say that they were in compliance with the Supreme Court's mandate. While not all High Court decisions allow such discretion, a good number of them do. Those opinions that are vague, ambiguous, or simply poorly written are almost certain to encounter problems during the implementation process.

A court's decision may be unclear for several reasons. Sometimes the issue or subject matter may be so complex that it is difficult to fashion a clear policy. In obscenity cases, for instance, the Supreme Court has had little difficulty in deciding that pornographic material is not entitled to constitutional protection. Defining obscenity has proven to be another story. Phrases such as "prurient interest," "patently offensive," "contemporary community standards," and "without redeeming social value" became commonplace in obscenity opinions. Obviously these terms leave a good deal of room for subjective interpretation. It is little wonder that a

Supreme Court justice admitted that he could not define obscenity but added that "I know it when I see it." [10]

Policies established by collegial courts are often ambiguous because the majority opinion is written to accommodate several judges. At times such opinions may read more like committee reports than forceful, decisive statements. Another situation that often occurs in a collegial setting is that the majority opinion is accompanied by several concurring opinions. When this happens, lower-court judges are left without a clear-cut precedent to follow. The death penalty cases serve as an example. In 1972 the Supreme Court struck down the death penalty in several states, but for a variety of reasons. Some justices opposed the death penalty per se, on the ground that it constituted cruel and unusual punishment in violation of the Eighth Amendment to the Constitution. Others voted to strike down the state laws because they were applied in a discriminatory manner.[11] The uncertainty created by the 1972 decision affected not only lower-court judges but also state legislatures. There was a rash of widely divergent death penalty statutes passed by the states as well as a considerable amount of new litigation.

A lower-court judge's discretion in the implementation process may also be affected by the manner in which a higher court's policy is communicated. Quite obviously, the first step in implementing a judicial policy is actually to learn of the new appellate court ruling. Although we probably assume that lower-court judges automatically are made aware of a higher court's decision, such is not always the case. Certainly the court from which a case has been appealed will be informed of the decision. In our example above, for instance, the federal district court for the middle district of Tennessee was told of the Supreme Court's decision in *Baker v. Carr* because its earlier decision was reversed, and the case was remanded to it for further action. However, no systematic, formal effort is made to inform other courts of the decision nor to see that lower-court judges have access to a copy of the opinion. Instead, the decisions that contain the new judicial policy are simply made available to the public in printed form, and judges are expected to read them if they have the time and inclination.

Although opinions of the Supreme Court and lower federal courts are available in a large number of courthouse, law school, and university libraries, that does not guarantee that they will be read and understood. The problem is especially acute for judges in rural areas. One study reported that copies of the *United States Reports,* which contain Supreme Court decisions, are available in only three cities in the entire state of Wyoming.[12] Further complicating things is the fact that many lower-level state judges, such as justices of the peace and juvenile court judges, are nonlawyers who have little interest or skill in reading complex judicial decisions.[13] Finally, even those judges who have an interest in higher-court decisions and the ability to understand them do not have adequate time to keep abreast of all the new opinions.

Given the problems described above, how do judges become aware of upper-court decisions? One way is through lawyers presenting cases in the lower courts. It is generally assumed that the opposing attorneys will present relevant precedents in their arguments before the judge. As we noted in Chapter 3, those judges who are fortunate enough to have law clerks may also rely upon them to search out recent decisions from higher courts.

Thus some higher-court policies are not quickly and strictly enforced simply because lower-court judges are not aware of them. Even those which they are aware of may not be as clear as a lower-court judge might like. Either reason contributes to the discretion exercised by lower-court judges placed in the position of having to implement judicial policies.

Interpretation by Lower Courts

A recent study notes that "important policy announcements almost always require interpretation by someone other than the policy maker." [14] This is certainly true in the case of judicial policies established by appellate courts. Thus the first exercise of a lower-court judge's discretion may be to interpret what the higher court's decision actually means.

Let us look for a moment at an example from a famous Supreme Court decision concerning what types of speech are protected by the Constitution. In a 1919 case the Court announced that "the question in every case is whether the words used are used in such circumstances and are of such a nature as to create a clear and present danger that they will bring about the substantive evils that Congress has a right to prevent." [15] With that statement the Court announced what is known as the "clear-and-present-danger" doctrine. Although it may seem simple in the abstract to say that a person's right to speak is protected unless the words create a "clear and present danger," lower-court judges do not decide cases in the abstract. They must fit higher-court policy decisions to the concrete facts of an actual case. Place yourself in the position of a lower-court judge deciding a case shortly after the announcement of the clear-and-present-danger policy. Assume that you were presiding over the trial of an individual who, in the course of a speech to a group of onlookers on a busy street corner in a large city, advocated violent overthrow of the United States government. You might well have to answer one or more of the following questions in your own mind as you tried to interpret the clear-and-present-danger doctrine: (1) How well defined must the danger be in order for it to be clear? (2) How imminent must the danger be in order for it to be present? (3) Is the danger in question one the government has a right to prevent? (4) Did the speech actually bring about any danger? (5) At what point is the government allowed to intervene or stop the speech? As you can see, interpreting what is meant by the clear-and-present-danger policy is no simple task. In fact, modern courts grapple with the free-speech question just as did the courts in 1919.

The manner in which a lower-court judge interprets a policy established by an upper court depends upon many factors. We have already noted that many policies are simply not clearly stated. Thus reasonable people may disagree over the proper interpretation. Even policy pronouncements that do not suffer from ambiguity, however, are sometimes interpreted differently by different judges.

A judge's own personal policy preferences will also have an effect upon the interpretation he or she gives to an upper-court policy. We saw in Chapters 4, 5, and 6 that judges come to the courts with their own unique background characteristics. Some are Republican, while others are Democrats; one judge may be liberal, whereas another is conservative. They come from different regions of the country. Some have been prosecutors; others have been primarily defense lawyers or corporate lawyers. In short, their backgrounds may influence their own particular policy preferences. Thus the lower-court judges, given their wide latitude anyway, may read their own ideas into an upper-court policy. The result is that a policy may be enthusiastically embraced by some judges yet totally rejected by others.

Strategies Employed by Lower Courts

We have seen that appellate court policies are open to different interpretations; let us now turn our attention to the actual strategies employed by the implementing judges. Those who favor and accept a higher court's policy will naturally try to enforce it and perhaps even expand upon it. On the other hand, a judge who does not like an upper court's policy decision may well implement it sparingly or only under duress.

Let us first examine the strategies that may be employed by a judge who basically disagrees with a policy established by an upper court. One rarely used strategy is defiance, whereby a judge simply does not apply the higher court's policy in a case before a lower court. A recent study of judicial implementation offers this example:

> Desegregation brought out considerable trial court defiance; in one extreme case, a Birmingham, Alabama, municipal judge not only refused to follow Supreme Court decisions desegregating municipal

facilities but also declared the Fourteenth Amendment unconstitutional.[16]

Such outright defiance is highly unusual, since there are other strategies that are not quite so extreme. For example, a study of the libel decisions of the U.S. courts of appeals between 1964 and 1974 did not find a single case of noncompliance with Supreme Court mandates.[17] Another study, focusing on compliance with the Supreme Court's *Miranda* decision, found only one instance of noncompliance among 120 cases decided by the courts of appeals in 1968.[18]

Another strategy often employed by judges not favorably inclined toward an upper-court policy is simply to avoid having to apply the policy. Sometimes a case may be disposed of on technical or procedural grounds so that the judge does not have to rule on the actual merits of the case. It may be determined, for example, that the plaintiff does not have standing to sue or that the case has become moot because the issue was resolved before the trial commenced. Lower-court judges sometimes avoid accepting a policy by declaring a portion of the upper-court decision to be "dicta." *Dicta* refers to the part of the opinion that does not contribute to the central logic of the decision. It may be useful as guidance but is not seen as binding. Obviously, what constitutes dicta is open to varying interpretations.

A final strategy often employed by judges who are in basic disagreement with a judicial policy is to apply it as narrowly as possible. One method of accomplishing this is for the lower-court judge to rule that a precedent is not controlling because there are factual differences between the higher-court case and the case before the lower courts. In other words, because the two cases may be distinguished, the precedent does not have to be followed. Let's look at an example.

In its *Miranda* decision the Supreme Court held that suspects taken into custody must be advised of their constitutional rights and that any confession made by a suspect who has not been so advised is invalid. A leading judicial scholar notes that some judges saw *custody* as the key word, and he provides several examples of situations in which *Miranda* was distinguished and therefore not applied:

1. Detention and interrogation at the Mexican border leading to a seizure of heroin and cocaine held not custodial.
2. A request for proof of ownership of a car on the street held not custodial.
3. Questioning of an erratic driver at roadside, with lack of *Miranda* warnings, did not void a conviction, although the policeman did intend to arrest, because he had not told driver he was free to go.

4. Questioning of the wife of a stabbing victim at the station house, when the interrogation had not focused on her, held noncustodial.[19]

Not all lower-court judges are opposed to a policy announced by a higher court. Some judges, as we have noted earlier, have risked social ostracism and various kinds of harassment in order to implement policies they believed in but that were not popular in their communities.[20]

A judge who is in basic agreement with an upper-court policy is likely to give that policy as broad an application as possible. In fact, the precedent might be expanded to apply to other areas. Let's look at one instance of judges expanding a precedent.

In *Griswold v. Connecticut* the Supreme Court held that a Connecticut statute forbidding the use of birth control devices was unconstitutional because it infringed upon a married couple's constitutional right to privacy.[21] In other words, the Court said that a decision whether to use birth control devices was a personal one to be made without interference from the state. Five years later a three-judge federal district court expanded the Griswold precedent to justify its finding that the Texas abortion statute was unconstitutional.[22] The court ruled that the law infringed upon the right of privacy of an unmarried woman to decide, at least during the first trimester of pregnancy, whether to obtain an abortion. Thus the lower court actually went further than the Supreme Court in striking down state involvement in such matters.

Influences on Lower-Court Judges

It should be quite evident by now that lower courts are not slaves of the upper courts when it comes to implementing judicial policies, but instead have a high degree of independence and discretion. At times the lower courts must decide cases for which there are no precise standards from the upper courts. Whenever this occurs, lower-court judges must turn elsewhere for guidance in deciding a case before them.

A recent study notes that lower-court judges in such a position "may take their cues on how to decide a particular case from a wide variety of factors including their party affiliation, their ideology, or their regional norms." [23] Several analyses, for example, point out that differences between Democratic and Republican lower-court judges are especially pronounced when Supreme Court rulings are ambiguous, when there is a transition from one Supreme Court period to another, or when the issue area is so new and controversial that more definite standards have not yet been formulated.[24]

Regional norms have also been mentioned prominently in the literature as having an influence on lower-court judges when they interpret and apply upper-court decisions.[25] One study found, for example, that "federal judges tend to be more vigilant in enforcing national desegregation standards in remote areas than when similar issues arise within the judge's immediate work/residence locale." In other words, the prevailing local norms may mean that "when faced with desegregating his own community a judge may be more concerned with public reaction than when dealing with an outlying area." [26]

To this point we have examined only one actor in the implementation process—the lower-court judge. It is now time to turn our attention to others in the political system who influence the way judicial policies are implemented. We begin our discussion with Congress because it is the body that most often registers and mirrors public reactions to judicial policies.[27]

Congressional Influences
On the Implementation Process

Once a judicial decision is made, Congress can offer a variety of responses. It may aid the implementation of a decision or hinder it. In addition, it can alter a court's interpretation of the law. Finally, Congress can mount an attack on individual judges. Naturally the actions of individual members of Congress will be influenced by their partisan and ideological leanings.

In the course of deciding cases, the courts are often called upon to interpret federal statutes. On occasion the judicial interpretation may differ from what a majority in Congress intended. When that situation occurs, the statute can simply be changed in new legislation that in effect overrules the court's initial interpretation. Still, the vast majority of the federal judiciary's statutory decisions are not touched by Congress. A study focusing on the Supreme Court's labor and antitrust decisions in the 1950-1972 period found that only 27 of the 222 decisions were the objects of reversal attempts in Congress, and that only nine of those attempts were successful.[28]

Besides ruling on statutes, the federal courts interpret the Constitution. There are two methods Congress can use to reverse or alter the effects of a constitutional interpretation it does not like. First, Congress can respond with another statute. After the Supreme Court struck down government prohibitions on abortion, Congress passed the Hyde Amendment and other laws restricting the use of federal funds for elective and therapeutic abortions. The Court, in later cases, indicated that the congressional action was constitutionally permissible.[29]

Second, a constitutional decision can be overturned directly by an amendment to the U.S. Constitution. Although many such amendments have been introduced over the years, it is not easy to obtain the necessary two-thirds vote in each house of Congress to propose the amendment and then achieve ratification by three-fourths of the states. In fact, only four Supreme Court decisions in the entire history of the country have been overturned by constitutional amendments. The Eleventh Amendment overturned *Chrisholm v. Georgia* (dealing with suits against a state in federal court); the Thirteenth Amendment overturned *Scott v. Sandford* (dealing with the legality of slavery); the Sixteenth Amendment overturned *Pollock v. Farmer's Loan and Trust Co.* (pertaining to the constitutionality of the income tax); and the Twenty-sixth Amendment overturned *Oregon v. Mitchell* (giving 18-year-olds the right to vote in state elections).

Congressional attacks on the federal courts in general and on certain judges in particular are another method of responding to judicial decisions. Sometimes these attacks are in the form of verbal denouncements that allow a member of Congress to let off steam over a decision or series of decisions. For example, a member of the House once expressed his disapproval of the Supreme Court by declaring that it was "a greater threat to this Union than the entire confines of Soviet Russia." [30]

Congress can also control the federal courts by limiting their jurisdiction. As we noted in Chapter 1, the appellate jurisdiction of the Supreme Court is regulated by Congress. The courts of appeals and federal district courts are of course created by Congress and therefore at its mercy as far as jurisdiction is concerned.

Another formidable weapon Congress can use is the power of the purse. Although the salary of a sitting federal judge cannot be diminished, Congress does not have to grant salary increases. In addition, Congress establishes the operating budget of the federal courts and can show its displeasure in the amount of money it chooses to appropriate for court operations.

Federal judges may be impeached and removed from office by Congress. Although the congressional bark may be worse than its bite in the use of this weapon, it is still a part of its overall arsenal.

Finally, the confirmation process offers a chance for an attack on the courts. As a new federal judicial appointee goes through hearings in the Senate, individual senators sometimes use the opportunity to denounce individual judges or specific decisions.

It should be noted, however, that Congress and the federal courts are not natural adversaries even though it occasionally may appear that way. Retaliations against the federal judiciary are fairly rare, and often the two branches work in harmony toward similar policy goals. For example, Congress played a key role in the implementation of the Supreme Court's school desegregation policy by enacting the Civil Rights Act of 1964, which empowered the Justice Department to initiate suits against school districts and gave the Department of Health, Education, and Welfare authority to terminate federal funds when school districts were not in compliance with federal district court desegregation orders. The 1964 Civil Rights Act, then, placed Congress on record as calling for a policy of racial equality and also served notice that "Congress joined the Supreme Court in deciding that public school integration should be public policy." [31] Such support from Congress was significant because it has been noted that the chances of compliance with a policy are increased when there is unity between branches of government.[32]

A recent study lends support to the notion that passage of the 1964 Civil Rights Act was an important step in the implementation of a policy of racial equality. The authors examined minority discrimination cases heard by federal district courts during the 10-year period 1960-1969 and found that the cases decided in 1965-1969 (after passage of the 1964 Civil Rights Act) were significantly more liberal than those decided in 1960-1964.[33]

Executive Influences
On the Implementation Process

In this section we examine the influence of the president, as well as various officials, agencies, and departments in the executive branch, on the implementation of judicial policies. Our first look will be at the chief executive.

At times the president may be called upon directly to implement a judicial decision. Such an example occurred in the famous Nixon tapes case, which arose during the investigation into the coverup of the break-in at the Democratic party headquarters in the Watergate Hotel.[34] As the investigation unfolded, it became apparent that the coverup led directly to high government officials working close to the president. It was also revealed during a Senate committee investigation into the matter that President Nixon had installed an automatic taping system in the Oval Office. Leon Jaworski, who had been appointed special prosecutor to investigate the Watergate affair, subpoenaed certain tapes that he felt might provide evidence needed in his prosecutions of high-ranking officials. President Nixon refused voluntarily to turn over the tapes on grounds of executive privilege and the need for confidentiality. The Supreme Court's decision—which, ironically, was announced on the day that the Judiciary Committee in the House of Representatives began holding hearings on whether to impeach Nixon—instructed the president to surrender the subpoenaed tapes to Judge John J. Sirica, who was handling the trials of the government officials. President Nixon did, of course, comply with the High Court's directive and thus implemented a decision that led to his downfall. Within two weeks he resigned from the presidency, in August 1974.

Even when not directly involved in the enforcement of a judicial policy, the president may still be able to influence its impact. Because of the stature of the position and the visibility that accompanies it, a president simply by words and actions may encourage support for, or resistance to, a new judicial policy. For instance, it has been argued that President Eisenhower's lack of enthusiasm for the *Brown v. Board of Education* decision and "his unwillingness to condemn southern resistance in more than a pro forma fashion encouraged Arkansas Governor Orval Faubus to block integration of Little Rock Central High School in 1957." [35] As a consequence, Eisenhower was later forced to send federal troops to Little Rock to enforce the district court's integration order. Sending in troops of course made President Eisenhower's participation in the implementation process more direct.

A president can propose legislation aimed at retaliating against the courts. President Franklin D. Roosevelt, for instance, urged Congress to increase the size of the Supreme Court so he could "pack" it with justices who supported New Deal legislation. President Reagan has adopted this tactic in another way. He has been a consistently strong supporter of constitutional amendments to overturn the Supreme Court's school prayer and abortion decisions.

The appointment power also gives the president an opportunity to influence federal judicial policies. Although the White House shares the power to appoint federal judges with the Senate, evidence points to the fact that the president dominates the process at the Supreme Court and courts of appeals levels. As we noted in Chapter 4, on the other hand, senatorial courtesy is a major consideration in the appointment of federal district judges.

During his campaign for the presidency in 1968, Richard Nixon made the Supreme Court an issue by criticizing the Warren Court for its liberal decisions and activist approach. He promised that, if elected, he would appoint "strict constructionists" to the Supreme Court and lower federal courts. In his first year in office Nixon appointed Warren Burger as chief justice and Harry Blackmun as an associate justice. However, the Senate rejected two consecutive nominees (Clement Haynsworth and G. Harrold Carswell) before approving Blackmun. Two years later Nixon was able to appoint another pair of justices—Lewis Powell and William Rehnquist.

How successful was Nixon in accomplishing his goal of altering the policy direction of the Supreme Court? One student of the transition from the Warren Court to the Burger Court says:

> The Burger Court, even before it consolidated its position and reversed precedents directly, showed through both doctrine and results considerable withdrawal from and undercutting of Warren Court policies affecting the entire range of civil liberties problems but particularly noticeable in the criminal procedure and free speech areas.[36]

Thus President Nixon was generally able to accomplish his goal for the Supreme Court. Also, the uncertainty and ambiguity in Supreme Court precedents brought about by the transition from the Warren Court to the Burger Court left the lower federal courts with more discretion. A study of the federal district courts, for example, says:

> With the advent of the Burger Court, the trial court jurists could no longer count on the Supreme Court for as clear and unambiguous legal guidelines as they had received from the Warren Court's more stable majority. With the decline of the fact-law congruence after 1968 the trial court judges became more free to take their decision-making cues from personal-partisan values rather than from guidelines set forth by the High Court. Consequently, the level of partisan voting increased markedly.[37]

Presidents have long realized that lower federal judges are important in the judicial policy-making process. For this reason, as we noted in Chapter 4, many chief executives have shown an interest in appointing lower court judges who share their basic ideologies and values.[38] A study of the opinions of federal district judges appointed by Presidents Wilson through Ford confirms that "to a noticeable and substantively significant degree, the appointing president does have an ideological impact on the output of the trial court judiciary." [39] Another study focused on support for criminal defendants in decisions handed down by the federal district appointees of Presidents Nixon, Johnson, and Kennedy. The authors noted that presidential influence is shaped by several legal and extralegal factors, some beyond White House control. Still, they concluded that "the value basis of presidential appointment is reflected in the subsequent policy choices of district court appointees." [40]

A president can also influence judicial policy making through the activities of the Justice Department, a part of the executive branch that we discussed briefly in Chapter 3. The attorney general and staff subordinates can emphasize specific issues according to the overall policy goals of the president. Recall, for example, that the 1964 Civil Rights Act authorized the Justice Department to file school desegregation suits. This allowed the executive branch to become more actively involved in implementing the policy goal of racial equality. The other side of the coin, however, is the fact that the Justice Department may, at its discretion, deemphasize specific policies by not pursuing them vigorously in the courts. The Nixon administration was accused of applying the brakes to the momentum that had developed in the effort to desegregate southern public schools.[41]

As we noted earlier, the president is not the only actor in the executive branch involved in the implementation process. Many judicial decisions are actually implemented by the various departments, agencies, bureaus, and commissions that abound in the executive branch. Let us look at an example of a Supreme Court decision that called upon the United States Air Force to play the major implementation role. That case was *Frontiero v. Richardson.*[42]

The *Frontiero* case called into question congressional statutes that provided benefits for married male members of the Air Force but did not provide similar benefits for married female members. Under the laws, a married Air Force serviceman who lived off the base was entitled to an allowance for living quarters regardless of whether his wife was employed or how much she earned. Married female members of the Air Force, on the other hand, were not entitled to such an allowance unless their husbands were physically or mentally incapable of self-support and dependent on their wives for more than half their support. Lieutenant Sharron Frontiero challenged the policy on the ground that it constituted sexual discrimination in violation of the Fifth Amendment. Her suit was filed in a federal district court in Alabama on December 23, 1970. It was not until April 5, 1972, that the three-judge district court announced its decision upholding the Air Force policy. Lieutenant Frontiero appealed to the Supreme Court, which overturned the lower-court decision on May 14, 1973. The Air Force was then required to implement a policy it had fought for nearly three years.

Other Implementors

To this point we have concentrated primarily upon lower-court judges, Congress, the president, and others in the executive branch as interpreters and implementors of judicial policies. There are, of course, many other actors involved in the implementation process.[43]

While our focus thus far has been on various federal officials, it should be noted that implementation of judicial policies is often performed by state officials as well. Many of the Supreme Court's criminal due process decisions, such as *Gideon v. Wainwright* and *Miranda v. Arizona*, have been enforced by state court judges and other state officials. State and local police officers, for instance, have played a major role in implementing the *Miranda* requirement that criminal suspects must be advised of their rights. The *Gideon* ruling that an attorney must be provided at state expense for indigent defendants in felony trials has been implemented by public defenders, local bar associations, and individual court-appointed lawyers.

While space does not permit us to discuss every state and local public official in the implementation process, one group of individuals has been so deeply involved in implementing judicial policies that we feel compelled to deal with them here, if only briefly. These implementors are the thousands of men and women who constitute school boards throughout the country.

Two major policy areas stand out as having embroiled school board members in considerable controversy as they faced the inevitable task of trying to carry out Supreme Court policy. First, when the High Court ruled in 1954 that segregation has no place in the public schools, it was school boards and school superintendents, along with federal district judges, who bore the brunt of implementing that decision.[44] Their role in this process has affected the lives of literally millions of schoolchildren, parents, and taxpayers all over America.

The second area that has involved school boards is the Supreme Court's policies on religion in the public schools. In *Engel v. Vitale* the Court held unconstitutional a New York requirement that a state-written prayer be recited daily in the public schools.[45] Some school districts responded to the decision by requiring instead the recitation of a Bible verse or the Lord's Prayer. Their reasoning was that since the state did not write the Lord's Prayer or the Bible, they were not violating the Court's policy. A year later the Supreme Court struck down these new practices, pointing out that the constitutional violation lay in endorsing the religious activity and did not depend on whether the state had written the prayer.[46] Some school districts continued to evade the spirit, if not the letter, of the High Court's policy by requiring a period of silent meditation during which students could pray if they wished. The Alabama silent meditation law was declared void by the Supreme Court June 4, 1985, because students were instructed that they could use the time for prayer. This action was said to unconstitutionally endorse religion as a "favored practice." The Court indicated, however, that "moment of silence" laws not endorsing prayer would pass constitutional muster.[47]

Both of these policy areas involve basically private citizens—school board officials—in implementing controversial, emotion-charged policies that they may neither clearly understand nor agree with. The lack of understanding of the Supreme Court's school prayer decisions, for example, led some school districts to take no action at all while other school boards placed a ban on all religious activities.[48]

The Impact of Judicial Policies

Thus far, we have focused primarily on the implementation of judicial policies by various government officials. This is entirely appropriate, since court decisions are often specifically directed at other public policy makers. However, as a recent study of the Supreme Court tells us, "the ultimate importance of the Court's decisions rests primarily on their impact outside government, on American society as a whole." [49] We will explore briefly a few policies that have had significant effects on "society as a whole": the courts' role in developing a policy of racial equality, legislative reapportionment, criminal due process, and abortion.

Racial Equality

Not long ago, one team of judicial impact scholars said:

Perhaps the judiciary's biggest impact on modern America came in the *Brown* decision, which initiated the drive for racial equality. However, it took the active participation of Congress and the president to sustain this effort and ensure substantial implementation of such policies. The state of race relations in America might be quite different if the courts had ignored the issue, but it also might be different if Congress and the president had not joined the effort.[50]

Quite clearly, the United States could not have achieved as much as it has in the quest for racial equality had Congress and the president stayed out of the picture. However, as the statement correctly points out, it was the courts that initiated the pursuit for a national policy of racial equality. Thus one of the most important ways the federal judiciary can influence policy is to place issues on the national political agenda.

In the beginning, the court decisions were often vague, leading to evasion of the new policy. The Supreme Court justices and many lower federal judges were persistent in decisions following *Brown* and in this way kept the policy of racial equality on the national political agenda; their persistence paid off with passage of the 1964 Civil Rights Act, ten years after *Brown*. That act, which had the strong support of Presidents

Kennedy and Johnson, squarely placed Congress and the president on record as being supportive of racial equality in America.

One other aspect of the federal judiciary's importance in the policy-making process is illustrated by *Brown* and the cases that followed it. Although the courts stood virtually alone in the quest for racial equality for several years, their decisions did not go unnoticed. It is argued that "the psychological impact of the decision far exceeded its immediate legal consequences. *Brown* stood as a symbol to blacks and whites alike that racial equality now had an institutional champion at the highest level." Spurred on by this knowledge, civil rights activists engaged in sit-ins, freedom marches, freedom rides, demonstrations, and other types of protests. Such actions "stirred up so much attention and emotion that the other branches of government could no longer avoid a major policymaking role." [51]

While no one would argue that the United States has achieved complete racial equality, some gains have been made. The federal courts are not totally responsible for those gains, of course, but they have played a major role in their achievement.

Reapportionment

Prior to the involvement of the federal judiciary in the drawing of legislative districts, malapportionment was widespread throughout the states. The problem of malapportionment, which occurs when legislative districts with different populations have the same number of legislators, had become especially acute by the early 1960s because multitudes of people had, for many years, been moving from rural areas to urban areas. Failure of the state legislatures to take these population shifts into account meant that rural areas with small populations were able to elect many more legislators than the heavily populated urban areas.

In 1962, in the famous *Baker v. Carr* decision, the Supreme Court ruled that malapportionment presented a judicial question. The remedy eventually called for by the Supreme Court was reapportionment. However, as we noted early in this chapter, the case was remanded to the federal district court with no clear guidelines as to how the High Court's decision was to be implemented.

The Supreme Court, as it frequently does, developed more specific guidelines for the lower federal courts in subsequent cases.[52] In these follow-up decisions the Court instituted the "one-person, one-vote" principle for districts pertaining to both houses of a state legislature and for congressional districts. The one-person, one-vote ideal is achieved, of course, by creating districts that are as nearly equal in population as

215

possible. With considerable effort on the part of federal district judges, the state legislatures were eventually brought into compliance with the one-person, one-vote principle. Today, census updates dictate that state legislatures go through the reapportionment process periodically.

In one sense, then, the policy goal of the federal courts was realized. Changes in the makeup of state legislatures and the U.S. House of Representatives occurred. Furthermore, urban and suburban areas gained strength at the expense of rural areas in the legislative bodies.

In another way, however, the courts' reapportionment policy has not had the effect some expected. Many believed that state expenditures for such things as aid to the cities, public education, public welfare, and urban renewal would increase considerably. Examined from this perspective, we must conclude that the impact of reapportionment on the states has been rather modest.[53]

Criminal Due Process

Judicial policy making in this area is most closely associated with the Warren Court period. Speaking of this era, a former solicitor general said, "Never has there been such a thorough-going reform of criminal procedure within so short a time." [54] The Warren Court decisions were aimed primarily at changing the procedures followed by the states in dealing with criminal defendants. By the time Warren left the Supreme Court, new policies had been established to deal with a wide range of activities. Although a complete list of the Court's decisions is too lengthy to discuss here, among the more far-reaching were *Mapp v. Ohio, Gideon v. Wainwright,* and *Miranda v. Arizona.*[55]

The *Mapp* decision extended the exclusionary rule, which had applied to the national government for a number of years, to the states. This rule simply required state courts to exclude from trials evidence that had been illegally seized by the police. Although some police departments, especially in major urban areas, have tried to establish specific guidelines for their officers to follow in obtaining evidence, such efforts have not been universal. Because of variations in police practices and differing lower-court interpretations of what constitutes a valid search and seizure, implementation of *Mapp* has not been consistent throughout the country.

Perhaps even more important in reducing the originally perceived impact of *Mapp* has been the lack of solid support for the exclusionary rule among the Supreme Court justices. The decision was not a unanimous one to begin with, and over the years some of the justices, notably Chief Justice Warren Burger, have been openly critical of the exclusionary rule. Furthermore, Burger Court decisions have broadened the scope of legal searches, thus limiting the applicability of the rule. As we saw earlier in this chapter, ambiguity and absence of clear guidelines from the High Court increase the discretion of lower-court judges who are asked to implement a policy.

The *Gideon v. Wainwright* decision held that indigent defendants must be provided attorneys when they go to trial in a felony case in the state courts. Many states routinely provided attorneys in such trials even before the Court's decision. The other states began to comply in a variety of ways. Public defender programs were established in many regions. In other areas local bar associations cooperated with judges to implement some method of complying with the Supreme Court's new policy.

The impact of *Gideon* is clearer and more consistent than that of *Mapp*. One reason, no doubt, is the fact that many states had already implemented the policy called for by *Gideon*. In other words, it was simply more widely accepted than the policy established by *Mapp*. The policy announced in *Gideon* was also more sharply defined than the one in *Mapp*. Although the Court did not specify whether a public defender or a court-appointed lawyer must be provided, it is still quite clear that the indigent defendant must have the help of an attorney. It should also be noted that the Burger Court has not retreated from the Warren Court's policy of providing an attorney for indigent defendants as it did in the search and seizure area addressed by *Mapp*. All these factors add up to a more recognizable impact for the policy announced in *Gideon*.

In *Miranda v. Arizona* the Supreme Court went a step further and ruled that police officers must advise suspects taken into custody of their constitutional rights, one of which is to have an attorney present during questioning. Suspects must also be advised that they have a right to remain silent and that any statement they make may be used in court; that if they cannot afford an attorney, one will be provided at state expense; and that they have the right to stop answering questions at any time. These requirements are so clearly stated that police departments have actually copied them down on cards for officers to carry in their shirt pockets. Then, when suspects are taken into custody, the police officers simply remove the card and read the suspects their rights.

If we measure compliance simply in terms of whether police officers read the *Miranda* rights to persons they arrest, then we would have to say that there has been a high level of compliance with the Supreme Court policy. Some researchers, however, have questioned the impact of *Miranda* because of the method by which suspects may be advised of their rights. It is one thing to simply read to a person from a card, while it is quite another to explain what is meant by the High Court's requirements and then try to make the suspect understand them. Looked at in this manner, the impact of the policy announced in *Miranda* is not quite as clear.

The Burger Court has not shown an inclination to lend its solid support to the Warren Court's *Miranda* policy. Although *Miranda* has not been overruled, its impact has been limited somewhat. In the *Harris v. New York* case, for example, the Burger Court ruled that statements made by an individual who had not been given the *Miranda* warning could be used to challenge the credibility of his testimony at trial.[56]

In sum, we would emphasize that the impact of the Supreme Court's criminal justice policies has been rather mixed. The reason for this assessment must be attributed to several factors. In some instances vagueness or ambiguity is a problem. In other cases it may be less than solid support for the policy among justices or eroding support as one Court replaces another. All these variables translate into greater discretion for the implementors.

Abortion

In *Roe v. Wade* the Supreme Court ruled (1) that a woman has an absolute right to an abortion during the first trimester of pregnancy; (2) that a state may regulate the abortion procedure during the second trimester in order to protect the mother's health; and (3) that during the third trimester the state may regulate or even prohibit abortions, except where the life or health of the mother is endangered.[57]

The reaction to this decision was immediate, and primarily negative.[58] It came in the form of letters to individual justices, public speeches, the introduction of resolutions in Congress, and the advocacy of "right to life" amendments in Congress. As might be expected given the controversial nature of the Court's decision, hospitals did not wholeheartedly offer to support the decision by changing their abortion policies. In fact, one study, using a national sample of hospitals, found that less than one-half changed their abortion policies following the Supreme Court's decision in *Roe*.[59]

Response to the Court's abortion policy was not short-lived. It has not only continued but has moved into new areas. State legislatures have enacted numerous laws aimed at regulating abortion in one way or another, some of which have passed constitutional muster, while others have not. Interest groups representing both sides of the issue are active participants in elections. The 1984 presidential election saw the two major party platforms take opposing stands on the abortion issue. The Democratic platform expressed support for *Roe v. Wade,* while the Republicans called for a constitutional amendment to protect the right to life of unborn children.

Although the abortion controversy now exists in many political arenas, Congress continues to be a hotbed of activity. Unable to secure passage of a constitutional amendment to overturn the Court's abortion decision, antiabortion forces have used another approach. For several years they successfully obtained amendments to appropriations bills preventing the expenditure of federal funds for elective abortions. In 1980 the Supreme Court, in a five-to-four vote, upheld the constitutionality of such a prohibition.[60]

What we have seen, then, is a limited impact for a judicial policy decision that, on its face, appears to confer an absolute right to an abortion on demand during the first trimester of pregnancy. As our discussion indicates, the *Roe v. Wade* decision did not have the solid backing of all the branches of the government. Not only did Congress not support the policy, it intentionally took steps to limit its impact. Similarly, other actors in the implementation process, such as state legislatures, presidents, and hospitals, have failed to lend their support to the High Court's decision. Thus *Roe v. Wade*'s impact has not been as great as many feared (or hoped, perhaps) that it would be.

Conclusions

There is no doubt that some judicial policies have a greater impact on society than others. Because many reasons for this situation have been offered throughout this chapter, an extended discussion of them is not needed here. Instead, we simply want to offer some concluding thoughts about the ability of federal courts to effectuate changes in society.

Quite clearly, the federal judiciary plays a greater role in developing the nation's policies than the constitutional framers envisioned. On the other hand, the courts are not as powerful as the rhetoric of some politicians would have us believe. The judiciary is but one of three coequal branches of the national government and is subject to the checks and balances that may be exercised by Congress or the president. The legal and democratic subcultures that have been discussed throughout the book also serve to limit the federal courts' policy-making powers.

Within this complex framework of competing political and social demands and expectations, however, there *is* a policy-making role for the federal courts. Because the other two branches of government are sometimes not receptive to the demands of certain segments of society, the only alternative for those individuals or groups is to turn to the courts. Civil rights organizations, for example, made no real headway until they found the Supreme Court to be a supportive forum for their school desegregation efforts. They were then able to use the *Brown* and other decisions as a springboard to attack a variety of areas of discrimination. Thus a champion at a high government level may offer hope to individuals and interest groups.

As civil rights groups attained some success in the federal courts, others were encouraged to employ litigation as a strategy. For example, several scholars tell us that women's rights supporters followed a pattern established by minority groups when they began taking their grievances to the courts.[61] In this manner, what began as a more narrow pursuit for racial equality was broadened to a quest for equality for other disadvantaged groups in society.

Clearly, then, the federal courts can announce policy decisions that attract national attention and perhaps stress the fact that other policy makers have failed to act. In this way the judiciary may invite the other branches to exercise their policy-making powers. Follow-up decisions indicate the judiciary's determination to pursue a particular policy and help keep alive the invitation for other policy makers to join in the endeavor.

All things considered, the federal courts seem best equipped to develop and implement narrow policies that are less controversial in nature. The policy established in the *Gideon* case provides a good example. The decision that indigent defendants in state criminal trials must be provided with an attorney did not meet any strong outcries of protest. Furthermore, it was a policy that primarily required the support of judges and lawyers; action by Congress and the president was not really necessary. A policy of equality for all segments of society, on the other hand, is so broad and controversy-laden that it must move beyond the judiciary. As it does so, the courts become simply one part, albeit an important part, of the policy-making process.

Summary

We began this chapter by pointing out that judicial decisions are not self-executing. The federal courts depend upon a variety of individuals, both inside and outside the judicial branch, to carry out their rulings.

Lower-court judges are prominent in the implementation process. Our discussion of their role in carrying out decisions of higher courts emphasized the discretion they exercise. Factors that account for the flexibility that rests with the lower-court judge include the centralization of the federal judicial system, ambiguity or vagueness in higher-court rulings, and poor intercourt communication. The chapter examined, as well, the strategies that balking lower-court judges may employ in resisting appellate court decisions they dislike.

Congress and the president may also be involved in the implementation process. Each of these two branches can react either positively or negatively to a court decision. The wide range of influences the president and Congress exert in enforcing a judicial decision were described in some detail.

It was also noted that some policies call upon state officials to take part in the implementation process. State court judges, for example, played the major role in enforcing the Warren Court's criminal due process decisions. Local school boards have also been called upon to carry out Supreme Court policies.

The chapter concluded with a discussion of the impact on society of several important federal court policies. Explanations were offered as to why some policies have a more obvious impact on society than others; most important, perhaps, is that if a ruling—like the Supreme Court's favorable decision on abortion—faces opposition, Congress and other implementors are likely to drag their feet. A final section of the chapter offered some concluding thoughts on the role of federal courts in bringing about changes in society. It noted that the judiciary can act as a kind of beacon for traditionally underrepresented groups seeking to achieve their goals.

Notes

1. *Gideon v. Wainwright,* 372 U.S. 335 (1963).
2. For a good description of the bureaucratic theory, see Walter F. Murphy, "Chief Justice Taft and the Lower Court Bureaucracy: A Study in Judicial Administration," *Journal of Politics* 24 (1962): 453-476.
3. Richard J. Richardson and Kenneth N. Vines, *The Politics of Federal Courts* (Boston: Little, Brown, 1970), 144.
4. Lawrence Baum, "Implementation of Judicial Decisions: An Organizational Analysis," *American Politics Quarterly* 4 (1976): 91.
5. The desegregation policy was announced in *Brown v. Board of Education of Topeka,* 347 U.S. 483 (1954). For a study of the lower federal courts involved in implementing *Brown,* see Jack W. Peltason, *Fifty-Eight Lonely Men* (New York: Harcourt, Brace and World, 1961).
6. For an excellent account of the school desegregation struggle in Georgia, see Harrell R. Rodgers, Jr., and Charles S. Bullock III, *Coercion to Compliance* (Lexington, Mass.: Lexington Books, 1976).
7. *Brown v. Board of Education of Topeka II,* 349 U.S. 294 (1955).
8. *Baker v. Carr,* 369 U.S. 186 (1962).
9. Ibid., 237, 251.

10. The statement was made by Justice Potter Stewart in *Jacobellis v. Ohio,* 378 U.S. 184 (1964).

11. *Furman v. Georgia,* 408 U.S. 238 (1972). A good account of the various views held by the justices, as well as the behind-the-scenes events leading to the final decision, may be found in Bob Woodward and Scott Armstrong, *The Brethren: Inside the Supreme Court* (New York: Simon and Schuster, 1979), 205-220.

12. See Stephen L. Wasby, "The Communication of the Supreme Court's Criminal Procedure Decisions," *Villanova Law Review* 18 (1973): 1090.

13. For a good discussion of this point with pertinent examples, see Charles A. Johnson and Bradley C. Canon, *Judicial Policies: Implementation and Impact* (Washington, D.C.: CQ Press, 1984), 55-56.

14. Ibid., 29.

15. *Schenck v. United States,* 249 U.S. 47 (1919).

16. Johnson and Canon, *Judicial Policies,* 40.

17. See John Gruhl, "The Supreme Court's Impact on the Law of Libel: Compliance by Lower Federal Courts," *Western Political Quarterly* 33 (1980): 517.

18. See Donald R. Songer, "The Impact of the Supreme Court on Outcomes in the U.S. Courts of Appeals: A Comparison of Four Issue Areas" (Paper delivered at the 55th Annual Meeting of the Southern Political Science Association, Birmingham, Alabama, November 1983), 6. The *Miranda* decision is *Miranda v. Arizona,* 384 U.S. 436 (1966).

19. Stephen L. Wasby, *The Impact of the United States Supreme Court: Some Perspectives* (Homewood, Ill.: Dorsey Press, 1970), 158.

20. See Peltason, *Fifty-Eight Lonely Men,* and Richardson and Vines, *The Politics of Federal Courts,* 98-99.

21. *Griswold v. Connecticut,* 381 U.S. 479 (1965).

22. *Roe v. Wade,* 314 F. Supp. 1217 (1970).

23. Ronald Stidham and Robert A. Carp, "U.S. Trial Court Reactions to Changes in Civil Rights and Civil Liberties Policies," *Southeastern Political Review* 12 (1984): 7.

24. See, for example, Kathleen L. Barber, "Partisan Values in the Lower Courts: Reapportionment in Ohio and Michigan," *Case Western Reserve Law Review* 20 (1969): 406-407; Robert A. Carp and C. K. Rowland, *Policymaking and Politics in the Federal District Courts* (Knoxville: University of Tennessee Press, 1983), chap. 2; C. K. Rowland and Robert A. Carp, "A Longitudinal Study of Party Effects on Federal District Court Policy Propensities," *American Journal of Political Science* 24 (1980): 301; and Ronald Stidham, Robert A. Carp, and C. K. Rowland, "Women's Rights Before the Federal District Courts, 1971-1977," *American Politics Quarterly* 11 (1983): 214.

25. See, for example, Peltason, *Fifty-Eight Lonely Men;* Kenneth N. Vines, "Federal District Judges and Race Relations Cases in the South," *Journal of Politics* 26 (1964): 338-357; Richardson and Vines, *The Politics of Federal Courts,* 93-100; and Micheal W. Giles and Thomas G. Walker, "Judicial

Policy-Making and Southern School Segregation," *Journal of Politics* 37 (1975): 917-936.

26. Giles and Walker, "Judicial Policy-Making and Southern School Segregation," 931.

27. For a good study of the relationship between Congress and the Supreme Court, see John R. Schmidhauser and Larry L. Berg, *The Supreme Court and Congress: Conflict and Interaction, 1945-1968* (New York: Free Press, 1972).

28. Beth M. Henschen, "Statutory Interpretations of the Supreme Court: Congressional Response," *American Politics Quarterly* 11 (1983): 441-458.

29. See *Maher v. Roe,* 432 U.S. 464 (1977) and *Harris v. McRae,* 448 U.S. 297 (1980).

30. Quoted in Lawrence Baum, *The Supreme Court,* 2d ed. (Washington, D.C.: CQ Press, 1985), 217.

31. James E. Anderson, David W. Brady, and Charles S. Bullock III, *Public Policy and Politics in America* (North Scituate, Mass.: Duxbury Press, 1978), 5.

32. See Wasby, *The Impact of the United States Supreme Court,* 256.

33. See Stidham and Carp, "U.S. Trial Court Reactions to Changes in Civil Rights and Civil Liberties Policies," 13-14. A liberal opinion was defined as one that favored the minority litigant or supported the demise of racial, social, and political discrimination.

34. *United States v. Nixon,* 418 U.S. 683 (1974).

35. Johnson and Canon, *Judicial Policies,* 160.

36. Stephen L. Wasby, *The Supreme Court in the Federal Judicial System* (New York: Holt, Rinehart and Winston, 1978), 10.

37. Carp and Rowland, *Policymaking and Politics in the Federal District Courts,* 37.

38. For a discussion of this point, see Ronald Stidham, Robert A. Carp, and C. K. Rowland, "Patterns of Presidential Influence on the Federal District Courts: An Analysis of the Appointment Process," *Presidential Studies Quarterly* 14 (1984): 548-560.

39. Ibid., 554.

40. See C. K. Rowland, Robert A. Carp, and Ronald Stidham, "Judges' Policy Choices and the Value Basis of Judicial Appointments: A Comparison of Support for Criminal Defendants Among Nixon, Johnson, and Kennedy Appointees to the Federal District Courts," *Journal of Politics* 46 (1984): 898.

41. See Rodgers and Bullock, *Coercion to Compliance,* 20. Also see Leon E. Panetta and Peter Gall, *Bring Us Together: The Nixon Team and the Civil Rights Retreat* (Philadelphia: Lippincott, 1971).

42. *Frontiero v. Richardson,* 411 U.S. 677 (1973).

43. A recent study, for example, analyzes judicial implementation and impact from the standpoint of the roles of four populations: an interpreting population, an implementing population, a consumer population, and a secondary population. See Johnson and Canon, *Judicial Policies.*

44. See Rodgers and Bullock, *Coercion to Compliance,* and Giles and Walker, "Judicial Policy-Making and Southern School Segregation."

45. *Engel v. Vitale,* 370 U.S. 421 (1962).

46. See *Abington School District v. Schempp,* 374 U.S. 203 (1963).

47. *Wallace v. Jaffree* 472 U.S. (1985).

48. For good studies of the responses of school boards to the Court's school prayer decisions, see Kenneth Dolbeare and Phillip Hammond, *The School Prayer Decisions: From Court Policy to Local Practice* (Chicago: University of Chicago Press, 1971); William Muir, *Prayer in the Public Schools: Law and Attitude Change* (Chicago: University of Chicago Press, 1967); Richard Johnson, *The Dynamics of Compliance* (Evanston, Ill.: Northwestern University Press, 1967); and Robert Birkby, "The Supreme Court and the Bible Belt: Tennessee Reaction to the *Schempp* Decision," *Midwest Journal of Political Science* 10 (1966): 304-319.

49. Baum, *The Supreme Court,* 226.

50. Johnson and Canon, *Judicial Policies,* 269.

51. Ibid., 257, 258.

52. See *Gray v. Sanders,* 372 U.S. 368 (1963); *Wesberry v. Sanders,* 376 U.S. 1 (1964); and *Reynolds v. Sims,* 377 U.S. 533 (1964).

53. See Roger A. Hanson and Robert E. Crew, Jr., "The Policy Impact of Reapportionment," *Law and Society Review* 8 (1973): 69-94; Eric Uslaner, "Comparative State Policy Formation, Interparty Competition and Malapportionment," *Journal of Politics* 40 (1978): 409-432; and Douglas G. Feig, "Expenditures in American States: The Impact of Court-Ordered Reapportionment," *American Politics Quarterly* 6 (1978): 309-324.

54. Archibald Cox, *The Warren Court* (Cambridge, Mass.: Harvard University Press, 1968), 74.

55. *Mapp v. Ohio,* 367 U.S. 643 (1961); *Gideon v. Wainwright,* 372 U.S. 335 (1963); and *Miranda v. Arizona,* 384 U.S. 436 (1966).

56. *Harris v. New York,* 401 U.S. 222 (1971).

57. *Roe v. Wade,* 410 U.S. 113 (1973).

58. For a good case study of the impact of *Roe v. Wade,* including reactions to the decision, see Johnson and Cannon, *Judicial Policies,* 4-14. Our discussion draws heavily on this study.

59. See Jon R. Bond and Charles A. Johnson, "Implementing a Permissive Policy: Hospital Abortion Services After *Roe v. Wade,*" *American Journal of Political Science* 26 (1982): 1-24.

60. See *Harris v. McRae,* 448 U.S. 297 (1980).

61. See Richard C. Cortner, "Strategies and Tactics of Litigants in Constitutional Cases," *Journal of Public Law* 17 (1968): 287-307; Jo Freeman, *The Politics of Women's Liberation* (New York: David McKay, 1975); Leslie Friedman Goldstein, "Sex and the Burger Court: Recent Judicial Policy Making Toward Women," in *Race, Sex and Policy Problems,* ed. Marian Lief Palley and Michael B. Prestion (Lexington, Mass.: Lexington Books, 1979), 103-113; and Karen O'Connor, *Women's Organizations' Use of the Courts* (Lexington, Mass.: Heath, 1980).

Policy Making by Federal Judges: An Attempt at Synthesis

8

"An education," the saying goes, "is what you have left after you've forgotten what you've learned." This text has presented you with many facts, theories, statistics, and examples about the federal court system. But as time goes on and the myriad of facts and illustrations are largely forgotten, what *education* ought you to have about the operation and policy making of U.S courts? It is the purpose of this chapter to pull out of the previous seven chapters certain key ideas and significant themes that we would like you to remember long after most factual tidbits have faded from memory.

By this time it is surely clear that the decisions of federal judges and justices affect all our lives. Whether it be the norm enforcement rulings or the broader policy-making decisions, the output of federal courts permeates the warp and woof of the body politic in the United States. No one can have a full and accurate understanding of the American political system without being cognizant of the work of the men and women who wear the black robe. As we look at the matter of decision making by the federal judiciary, we think there are two basic questions that are worthy of consideration. First, what are the conditions that cause judges to engage in policy making and to do so boldly? Second, does the literature give any clues as to the substantive direction of this policy making—that is, will it be conservative or liberal, supportive of or antagonistic toward the status quo? In seeking answers to these two basic questions, we have synthesized four sets of variables that shed some light in this realm: (1) the nature of the case or issue presented to the court, (2) the values and orientations of the judges, (3) the nature of the judicial decision-making process, and (4) extraneous variables that serve to implement and sustain judicial decisions.

The Nature of the Case or Issue

One critical variable that clearly affects the degree to which (and sometimes the direction in which) federal jurists influence our lives rests with the type of dispute or controversy that might serve as grist for the judicial mills. If it is the sort of issue that judges can resolve with room for significant maneuver, the impact of the case on public policy may be impressive. Conversely, if federal jurists are forbidden to enter a certain decision-making realm or may enter with only limited options, the policy impact will be nil. There are several aspects of this general proposition, as we shall indicate.

Jurisdiction

In Chapter 2 we outlined the jurisdiction of the three levels of the federal judiciary. A knowledge of this is important in and of itself, but it takes on a second meaning in the context of this discussion—namely, that judges may not make policy in subject areas over which they have no legal authority. The controversy between the United States and the Soviet Union over the deployment of nuclear weapons in space is of great significance to the American people—and indeed our very lives may be dependent on its successful resolution—but judges will not affect this matter because they have no jurisdiction over war-and-peace disputes between America and its adversaries. Conversely, the federal courts will have considerable policy impact over matters of racial segregation and disputes over reapportionment because such disputes fall squarely within the legal jurisdiction of the U.S. judiciary.

While the federal courts do have some leeway in determining whether or not they have jurisdiction over a particular subject matter, for the most part jurisdictional boundaries are set forth in the Constitution and by acts of Congress. In this same context Congress's power to create and restrict the courts' jurisdiction can often affect greatly the *direction* of judicial decision making. For example, in the Voting Rights Act Congress has granted citizens the right to sue local governments in federal courts if those governments alter the contours of electoral districts so as to dilute significantly the voting strength of minorities. By giving courts jurisdiction in this area and by telling judges in effect how to decide the cases (by establishing the decision-making goals), Congress has obviously had a major impact on judicial policy making. Likewise, the current threat by some members of Congress to remove certain matters from federal court jurisdiction, such as the power to use busing as a tool of desegregation, has policy-making potential of equal magnitude.

Judicial Self-Restraint

The nature-of-the-case variable is also related to whether a controversy falls into one of those forbidden realms into which the "good judge" ought not to set foot. One judge might well like to sink his judicial teeth into a particular matter that is crying for adjudication, but if the litigant has not yet exhausted all legal or administrative remedies, the jurist will have to stay his hand. Another judge might well like to overturn a particular presidential action because she thinks it "smacks of fascism," but if no specific portion of the Constitution has been violated, she will have to express her displeasure in the voting booth—not in the courtroom. As we have indicated, the various maxims of judicial self-restraint may come from a variety of sources, including the Constitution, tradition, and acts of Congress; some have been imposed by the judges themselves. But whatever their source, they serve to channel the potential areas of judicial policy making. Judges would have little success in attempting to adjudicate matters that would soon bring reversal, censure, or organized opposition from those who are in a position to "correct" a judge who has strayed from the accepted pathway of judicial behavior.

Norm Enforcement Versus Policy Making

Throughout this book we have discussed judicial behavior as being that of both norm enforcement and significant policy making. Most cases, as we have noted, fall into the former category—particularly for the lower federal judiciary. That is, for the majority of cases, judges routinely cite the applicable precedents, yield to the side with the weightiest evidence, and apply the statutes that clearly control the given fact situation; discretion is at a minimum. For these routine cases judges are not so much making policy as they are applying and enforcing *existing* norms and policy. In addition to norm enforcement, however, judges are presented with cases in which their room to maneuver—that is, their potential to make policy—is much greater. Such opportunities exist at all levels of the federal judiciary, but appellate judges and justices probably have more options for significant policy making than do their colleagues on the trial court bench. We would also recall that since the late 1930s, it has been Bill of Rights issues rather than labor and economic questions that have provided judges with the greatest opportunities for significant policy making.

In exploring this overall subject, we identified several situations (or case characteristics) that greatly enhance the judge's capacity to make policy rather than merely to enforce existing policy. One such opportunity occurs when the legal evidence is contradictory or equally strong on both sides. That is, it is not uncommon for judges to preside over a case for which the facts and evidence are about equally compelling or for which there are about an equal number of precedents that would sustain a finding for either party. Being pulled in several directions at once may not be an entirely comfortable position, but it does allow the jurists freer rein to strike out on their own than if prevailing facts and law impelled them toward one position.

Likewise judicial policy making can flower when jurists are asked to resolve new types of controversies for which statutory law and past judicial precedents are virtually absent. For example, when the federal courts were asked whether artificially created life forms could be patented, there was no way they could avoid making policy. (Even the refusal to decide is a decision, as the existentialists have long argued.) Thus some cases by their very nature invite judicial policy making, while others carry with them no such invitation. Of course, judges differ in their perceptions of whether or not there is an opportunity in a given case for creative, innovative decision making. To some extent such differences are a function of the judges themselves—a point we shall address momentarily. But our contention here is that whether a case is of the garden-variety norm enforcement genre or whether it invites major judicial policy making depends to a large degree on the nature of the controversy itself.

Summary

In considering whether and in what direction federal judges' decisions will significantly affect our lives, we can say this: the nature of the case itself is a vital component in this line of inquiry. Judges can make policy only in those areas over which the Constitution and the Congress have granted them jurisdiction and only in a manner consistent with the norms of judicial self-restraint. Also, if the controversies presented to the judges provide them with some room to maneuver—such as many current civil rights and liberties issues do—there will likely be more policy making than if the cases were tightly circumscribed by clearly controlling precedents and law.

The Values and Orientations of the Judges

A second set of variables to be considered if we want to know about judicial policy making and about the direction it will take involve the judges themselves. What are their background characteristics? How were they appointed and by whom? What are their judicial role conceptions? By learning something about the values and orientations of the men and women who are tapped for judicial service, we are better able to explain and predict what they will do on the bench.

We have looked at judicial background characteristics in a variety of contexts in this book. Here we shall examine several that have particular relevance vis-à-vis judicial policy making and its direction.

Judges as a Socioeconomic Elite

In Chapter 4 we made much of the fact that America's federal jurists come from a very narrow segment of social and economic strata. To an overwhelming degree they are offspring of upper- and upper-middle-class parents and come from families with a tradition of political, and often judicial, service. They are the men and women to whom our system has been good, who fit in, who have "made it." The mavericks, malcontents, and ideological extremists are discreetly weeded out by the judicial recruitment process.

What does all this suggest about judicial policy making and its direction? Given the striking similarity of the federal jurists and the backgrounds from which they come, their overall policy making is generally going to be within fairly modest, conventional, and ideologically moderate boundaries. While many judges have a commitment to reform and will use their policy making opportunities to this end, still it is to adjust and enhance a way of life that they basically believe in. Seldom bitten is the hand of the socioeconomic system that feeds them. Although an occasional maverick may slip in or develop within the judicial ranks, most judges are basically conservative in that they hold dear the traditional institutions and rules of the game that have brought success to them and their families. While America's elite has its fair share of both liberals and conservatives, it does not contain many who would use their discretionary opportunities to alter radically the basic social and political system.

Judges as Representatives of Their Political Parties

While the nature of the judicial recruitment process gives virtually all U.S. judges a similar and fairly conventional cast, still there are differences. The (prior) political party affiliation of jurists does alter the way they exercise their policy-making discretion when the circumstances of a case give them room for maneuver. As we have noted, judges and justices who come from the ranks of the Democratic party have been somewhat more liberal than their colleagues from Republican ranks. This has meant, for one thing, that Democrats on the bench are more likely to favor government regulation of the economy—particularly when such regulation appears to benefit the underdog or the worker in disputes with management. In criminal justice matters, Democratic jurists are more disposed toward the motions made by defendants. Finally, in questions involving civil rights and liberties, the Democrat on the bench tends to establish policies that favor a broadening position.

In this same context we stress the important policy link between the partisan choice made by voters in a presidential election, the judges whom the chief executive appoints, and the subsequent policy decisions of these jurists. When voters make a policy choice in electing a conservative or a liberal to the presidency, they also have a discernible impact upon the judiciary as well. Despite the many participants in the judicial selection process and the variety of forces that would thwart policy-oriented presidents from getting "their kind of people" on the bench, it is still fair to say that to an impressive degree presidents tend to get the type of men and women they want on the federal judiciary.

In a speech made just prior to the 1984 presidential election, conservative Supreme Court justice William Rehnquist discussed this phenomenon with unusual candor. Although he was speaking primarily about the Supreme Court, his remarks pertain to the entire U.S. judiciary. There is "no reason in the world," said Rehnquist, why President Reagan should not attempt to "pack" the federal courts. The institution has been constructed in such a way that the public will, in the person of the president, have something to say about the membership of the Court and thereby indirectly about its decisions. Thus, Rehnquist felt, presidents may seek to appoint people who are sympathetic to their political and philosophical principles. After calling new judicial appointments "indirect infusions of the popular will," Rehnquist added that it "should come as no surprise" that presidents attempt to pack the courts with people of similar policy values, but "like murder suspects in a detective novel, they must have motive and opportunity." [1]

Judges as Manifestations of 'Localism'

Another aspect of the values and orientations of the judges themselves has an impact upon their policy-making process: the attributes and mores that the judges carry with them from the region in which they grew up or in which they hold court. For both trial and appellate jurists we have documented a wide variety of geographical variations in the way they view the world and react to its demands. On a regional basis, for example, we noted that on many policy issues northern jurists have been more liberal than their colleagues in the South. Not only does judicial policy-making vary from one region of the land to another, but studies reveal that each of the circuits tends to be unique in the way its appellate and trial court judges administer the law and make decisions. The presence of significant state-by-state differences in U.S. trial judge behavior is further evidence that judges bring with them to the bench certain local values and orientations that subsequently affect their policy-making patterns. Finally, we showed that judges in larger cities (particularly in the South) tend to be somewhat more liberal than their colleagues in smaller towns and in rural districts. This evidence, too, bespeaks the impact of localism on the decision-making values of the jurists.

Judges' Conceptions of Their Judicial Roles

In our discussion of this phenomenon we noted three basic ways in which judges conceive of their roles vis-à-vis the policy-making process. At one end of the spectrum are the "law makers," who take a rather broad view of the judicial role. These jurists, often referred to as "activists" or "innovators," contend that they can and sometimes must make significant public policy when they render many of their decisions. At the other end of the spectrum are the "law interpreters," who take a very narrow view of the judicial function. Sometimes called "strict constructionists," they believe that norm enforcement rather than policy making is the only proper role of the judge. In between are the "pragmatists," or "realists," who contend that judging is primarily a matter of enforcing norms but that on occasion they can and must formulate new judicial policy.

Understanding the role conception that a judge brings to the bench (or develops on the bench) will not tell us much about the substantive direction of his or her policy making: it is possible to be a conservative activist just as well as a liberal activist. One can go out on a judicial limb and give the benefit of the doubt to the economic giant or to the underdog, to the criminal defendant claiming police brutality or to the police officer urging renewed emphasis on law and order. But a knowledge of the judges' role conceptions will tell us a good deal about whether they are more inclined to defer to the norms and policies set by others or to strike out occasionally and make policy on their own.

Summary

Let us recapitulate for a moment. In attempting to learn about policy making by judges and its substantive direction, we have set forth a second factor that helps channel our thinking—namely, the values and orientations that the judges bring with them to the bench. Here we have suggested four items that are particularly relevant in this regard: (1) that America's judges come from the establishment's elite, a fact that serves to discourage radical policy making; (2) that judges' policy making is reflective of their partisan orientations and that of the president who nominated them; (3) that policy decisions manifest the local values and attitudes that judges possess when they first put on the black robe; and (4) that judges will engage in more policy making if they bring to the bench a belief that it is right and proper for judges to act in this manner.

The Nature of the Judicial Decision-Making Process

Knowing how judges think and reason, how they are influenced in their decision-making process, provides us with a good clue about policy making by U.S. judges. While this factor is inexorably intertwined with the first two we have outlined here, it is distinct enough to warrant a separate discussion. The account in Chapter 5 of the legal subculture examined the nature of the legal reasoning process that is at the very heart of the system of jurisprudence in America. We noted that this is essentially a three-step process described by the doctrine of precedent as follows: (1) similarity is seen between cases, (2) the rule of law inherent in the first case is announced, and (3) the rule of law is made applicable to the second case. Adherence to past precedents, to the doctrine of *stare decisis,* is also part and parcel of the legal reasoning process. Skillfully shaping and crafting the wisdom of the past, as found in previous court rulings, and applying it to contemporary problems is what this time-honored process is all about.

Decision making on collegial courts contains some dimensions not inherent in the behavior of trial judges sitting alone. In Chapter 6 we examined several approaches that judicial scholars have used to get a theoretical handle on the way appellate court judges and justices think and act. One of these is small-group dynamics, an approach that sees the output of the appellate judiciary as strongly influenced by three general phenomena: persuasion on the merits, bargaining, and the threat of sanctions.

The first of these, persuasion, lies at the heart of small-group dynamics. It means quite simply that because of their training and values, judges are receptive to arguments based on sound legal reasoning, often spiced with relevant legal precedents. Both hard and anecdotal evidence exists to indicate that judicial policies are indeed influenced in the refining furnace of the judicial conference room.

Bargaining, too, molds the content and direction of judicial policy outputs. The compromises that are made among jurists—during the decision-making conference and while an opinion is being drafted—to satisfy the majority judges are almost always the product of bargaining. It's not that judges say to one another: "If you vote for my favorite judicial policy position, I'll vote for yours." Such is fantasy. Rather, a justice might phrase a "bargaining offer" more like this—say in a case dealing with the right of students to appeal adverse disciplinary rulings from a state university to the federal courts: "I don't agree with your opinion as it now stands permitting students to appeal *all* adverse disciplinary decisions to the local federal district court. That's just too liberal for me, and I don't approve of interfering in university affairs to that degree. However, I could go along with a majority opinion that permitted appeals in *really se-rious* disciplinary matters that might result in the permanent suspension of a student." The first justice must then decide how badly the colleague's vote is needed—badly enough to water down the opinion to include only cases dealing with permanent suspension rather than all cases, as in the original opinion? Such is the grist for the bargaining mill that spews forth judicial policies.

The sanctions that we discussed include a variety of items in the genteel arsenal of judicial weaponry. A judge's threat to take a vote away from the majority and dissent may cause the majority judges to alter the content of a policy decision. A judge's willingness to write a strong, biting dissent is another sanction that occasionally causes a unity-conscious majority to consider policy changes in an opinion. The threat to go public is a third tactic that judges use in collegial courts to alter the policy course of other jurists. Public exposure of an objectionable internal court practice or stance is probably the least pleasant of the sanctions. Finally, we noted that the chief justice of the United States and the counterparts at the appellate and trial court levels all have singular opportunities to guide and shape the policy decisions of the courts. The stature and options that are part of their unique leadership positions provide them an opportunity for crafting court policy if they have the desire and innate ability to make the most of it.

Besides small-group dynamics we also looked at an approach to appellate court decision making known as attitude and bloc formation analysis. This school of thought sees judges as possessing a stable set of attitudes that guide their policy choices. Such attitudes exist on dimensions like civil rights and liberties, social issues (matters of voting and ethnic status), and economic questions dealing with the equal distribution of wealth. Justices with similar attitudes on these several dimensions tend to vote in a similar manner on cases and thus form into voting blocs. Scholars have used the techniques of content analysis of opinions (to find and measure attitudes), scaling, and bloc analysis to test this theory. Their research has borne some impressive fruit because it has been possible to demonstrate that members of the appellate judiciary do decide cases in accordance with consistent underlying value dimensions and that voting blocs do form and behave according to predictable patterns.

Fact pattern analysis competes effectively with the small-group approach and with attitude and bloc analysis to account for appellate judge behavior. As we have seen in Chapter 6, the fact pattern approach would explain the individual behavior of appellate court judges in terms of their response to key facts inherent in the cases. Unlike traditional scholars, who postulate that judges respond only to the *legal* facts of a case, the fact pattern school argues that the jurists are alert to a wide variety of quite extrajudicial factors, such as the race and gender of a defendant, or whether a petitioner's attorney was court-appointed or privately retained. This approach does not assume the existence (or nonexistence) of consistent patterns in the acceptance of facts or in decisions based on facts. Finally, the fact pattern scholars have used sophisticated mathematical equations to weight the key facts they have identified and have learned the various fact combinations that have the maximum (and minimum) effect on each justice. The fruits of these exhaustive labors have been impressive.

What does this third general factor—the nature of the judicial decision-making process—tell us about judicial policy making and its substantive direction? We would offer two observations about this. First, most policy making by judges is likely to be slow and incremental. Indeed, this is exactly what one would expect from a reasoning process that relies so heavily on respecting *past* precedents and that places such emphasis on stability and continuity. The decision-making process of American judges does not lend itself to radical and abrupt departures from past precedents and behavior. Yet change does occur and new policies are made. But legal history suggests that American jurists have often "reformed to preserve," and that is a principle often associated with conservatism.

Second, an understanding of the judicial thought process and of the small-group dynamics of collegial courts does not in itself tell us anything about the substantive direction of a court's policy making. However, knowing which judges and justices are masters at persuasion, bargaining, and the use of sanctions does give us some insight into explaining and predicting the content of judicial policy decisions. If on a given court it is the conservatives who have developed a mastery of these tactics, then the bettor would do well to wager a few dollars on more conservative judicial decisions; vice versa if it is the liberals who have honed their interactive spears to the sharpest points.

The Impact of Extraneous Influences

At this point there should be little doubt that the making and implementation of judicial policy decisions are influenced by a variety of actors and forces quite outside the courtroom. It is not just judges and law clerks, leather-bound casebooks and arguments by silk-tongued lawyers that go into the shaping and carrying out of judicial decisions. Into the calculus must also go such unwieldy variables as these: the values and ability of the president, the will of Congress, the temper of public opinion, the strength and ideological orientation of key interest groups, and the attitudes and good will of those called on to implement judicial decisions in the "real world."

The presidential input into the making and implementation of key judicial decisions is considerable. Selected as a policy choice of the citizenry in the past presidential election, the chief executive has the opportunity to fill the federal courts with men and women who share the basic political and judicial philosophies of the administration. Once on the court, judges may be encouraged or discouraged in their policy making by the words and deeds emanating from the White House. For instance, the willingness of Presidents Eisenhower and Kennedy to use federal troops to help enforce judicial integration orders must have encouraged subsequent policy decisions in this realm; conversely, the public statements of Presidents Nixon and Reagan about judges having gone too far in tampering with our local schools must have caused many federal judges to think at least twice before issuing new school integration orders. The overall role of the chief executive in implementing judicial policy decisions was examined more systematically in Chapter 7.

Congress, too, has its impact on the creation and nurturing of judicial policy decisions. In its power to establish most of the original and appellate jurisdiction of the federal judiciary, it has the capacity to determine the subject-matter arenas where judicial policy battles are fought. In its capacity to establish the number of courts and the financial support they will have, Congress can show its approval or displeasure at the third branch of government. By accepting or rejecting presidential nominees to the courts, the Senate helps to determine who the judicial decison makers will be and hence the value orientations of these jurists. Finally, the implementation of many key judicial policy decisions is absolutely dependent on legislation that Congress must pass to make the ruling a meaningful reality for those affected by it. Had not Congress passed several key bills to implement the courts' desegregation orders (discussed in Chapter 7), integration of the public schools would be little more than a nice idea for those whom the rulings were intended to benefit.

Public opinion also has a role to play in this policy-making process—not an outrageous prospect for a nation that calls itself a democracy. In rendering key policy decisions, judges can hardly be oblivious to the mood and values of the citizenry of which they themselves are a part. And indeed in many policy areas (such as obscenity, desegregation, and legislative apportionment) judges have actually been ordered by the Supreme Court to take the local political and social climate into consideration as they tender their rulings. In the implementation of court decisions, the support or opposition of the public is often a key variable in determining whether or not the judge's orders are carried out in the spirit as well as the letter of the law.

Interest-group activity is another thread in the tapestry of judicial policy making. Such organizations often provide the president with the names of individuals whom they support for judicial office, and they lobby against those whose judicial values they consider suspect. They often provide the vehicle for key judicial decisions by instigating legislation, by sponsoring test cases, and by giving legal and financial aid to those litigants whose cases they favor. At the implementing stage we have seen (in Chapter 7) how they can thwart or help carry out more effectively judicial decisions.

The final group of extraneous forces are those individuals and organizations who are expected to implement the judicial policy decision on a day-by-day basis out on the street: the police officer who is asked to be *sure* that the accused understand their legal rights; the physician who must certify that a requested abortion is *really* in the mental health interests of the pregnant woman; the personnel officer at a state institution who could readily find some technicality for refusing to hire a minority applicant; or the censor on the town's movie review board who is told that nudity and obscenity are not synonymous but who doesn't want to believe it. It is the values, motivations, and actions of individuals such as these that we must consider if we are to understand fully the judicial policy making process. Their good-faith support of a judicial policy decision is vital to making it work; their indifference or opposition will cause the judge's ruling to die aborning.

It was our intention in this chapter to get some grip on the slippery handle of policy making by federal judges. While many more questions have been raised than answered, perhaps we know a little better now at least where to search for some answers. If we want to learn the conditions that allow for bold policy making and if we want some clue as to the direction that policy making will take, here is where we must focus our attention: on the nature of the case or controversy that can properly be brought into federal court; on the values and orientations of the jurists who preside over these courts; on the precise nature of the decision-making process of American judges; and, finally, on a variety of extraneous individuals and groups whose values filter into the American judicial process from beginning to end.

Notes

1. "Rehnquist Says It's OK for a President to Pack High Court," *Houston Chronicle,* October 19, 1984, 1:3.

Selected Bibliography

Books

Abraham, Henry J. *The Judicial Process*. 4th ed. New York: Oxford University Press, 1980.

Ball, Howard. *Courts and Politics: The Federal Judicial System*. Englewood Cliffs, N.J.: Prentice-Hall, 1980.

Baum, Lawrence. *The Supreme Court*. 2d ed. Washington, D.C.: CQ Press, 1985.

Berkson, Larry C., and Susan B. Carbon. *The United States Circuit Judge Nominating Commission: Its Members, Procedure and Candidates*. Chicago: American Judicature Society, 1980.

Birkby, Robert H. *The Court and Public Policy*. Washington, D.C.: CQ Press, 1983.

Carp, Robert A., and C. K. Rowland. *Policymaking and Politics in the Federal District Courts*. Knoxville: University of Tennessee Press, 1983.

Chase, Harold W. *Federal Judges: The Appointing Process*. Minneapolis: University of Minnesota Press, 1972.

Dolbeare, Kenneth, and Phillip Hammond. *The School Prayer Decisions: From Court Policy to Local Practice*. Chicago: University of Chicago Press, 1971.

Early, Stephen T., Jr. *Constitutional Courts of the United States*. Totowa, N.J.: Littlefield, Adams, 1977.

Eisenstein, James. *Counsel for the United States: U.S. Attorneys in the Political and Legal Systems*. Baltimore: Johns Hopkins University Press, 1978.

Fish, Peter G. *The Politics of Federal Judicial Administration*. Princeton, N.J.: Princeton University Press, 1973.

Frank, Jerome. *Courts on Trial: Myth and Reality in American Justice*. Princeton, N.J.: Princeton University Press, 1950.

Selected Bibliography

Frank, John P. *Marble Palace.* New York: Knopf, 1968.

Frankfurter, Felix, and James M. Landis. *The Business of the Supreme Court.* New York: Macmillan, 1928.

Friesen, Ernest C., Jr., Edward C. Gallas, and Nesta M. Gallas. *Managing the Courts.* Indianapolis: Bobbs-Merrill, 1971.

Glick, Henry R. *Courts, Politics, and Justice.* New York: McGraw-Hill, 1983.

Goldman, Sheldon. *Constitutional Law and Supreme Court Decision-Making.* New York: Harper & Row, 1982.

Goldman, Sheldon, and Thomas P. Jahnige. *The Federal Courts as a Political System.* 3d ed. New York: Harper & Row, 1985.

Goulden, Joseph C. *The Benchwarmers: The Private World of the Powerful Federal Judges.* New York: Weybright and Talley, 1974.

Grossman, Joel B. *Lawyers and Judges: The ABA and the Politics of Judicial Selection.* New York: Wiley, 1965.

Henderson, Dwight F. *Courts for a New Nation.* Washington, D.C.: Public Affairs Press, 1971.

Howard, J. Woodford, Jr. *Courts of Appeals in the Federal Judicial System.* Princeton, N.J.: Princeton University Press, 1981.

Jackson, Donald Dale. *Judges.* New York: Atheneum, 1974.

Jacob, Herbert. *Justice in America.* 4th ed. Boston: Little, Brown, 1984.

Johnson, Charles A., and Bradley C. Canon. *Judicial Policies: Implementation and Impact.* Washington, D.C.: CQ Press, 1984.

Johnson, Richard. *The Dynamics of Compliance.* Evanston, Ill.: Northwestern University Press, 1967.

Kitchin, William. *Federal District Judges.* Baltimore: Collage Press, 1978.

Levi, Edward H. *An Introduction to Legal Reasoning.* Chicago: University of Chicago Press, 1948.

Mason, Alpheus T. *Harlan Fiske Stone: Pillar of the Law.* New York: Viking Press, 1956.

McLauchlan, William P. *Federal Court Caseloads.* New York: Praeger, 1984.

Milner, Neal. *The Court and Local Law Enforcement.* Beverly Hills, Calif.: Sage, 1971.

Muir, William. *Prayer in the Public Schools: Law and Attitude Change.* Chicago: University of Chicago Press, 1967.

Murphy, Walter F. *Elements of Judicial Strategy.* Chicago: University of Chicago Press, 1964.

Murphy, Walter F., and C. Herman Pritchett, eds. *Courts, Judges, and Politics.* 3d ed. New York: Random House, 1979.

Nagel, Stuart S. *The Legal Process from a Behavioral Perspective.* Homewood, Ill.: Dorsey Press, 1969.

Oakley, John Bilyeu, and Robert S. Thompson. *Law Clerks and the Judicial Process*. Berkeley, Calif.: University of California Press, 1980.

O'Connor, Karen. *Women's Organizations' Use of the Courts*. Lexington, Mass.: Heath, 1980.

Peltason, Jack W. *Fifty-Eight Lonely Men*. New York: Harcourt, Brace and World, 1961.

Pritchett, C. Herman. *The Roosevelt Court: A Study of Judicial Votes and Values, 1937-1948*. New York: Macmillan, 1948.

Richardson, Richard J., and Kenneth N. Vines. *The Politics of Federal Courts*. Boston: Little, Brown, 1970.

Rodell, Fred. *Nine Men*. New York: Random House, 1955.

Rodgers, Harrell R., Jr., and Charles S. Bullock III. *Coercion to Compliance*. Lexington, Mass.: Heath, 1976.

Rohde, David W., and Harold J. Spaeth. *Supreme Court Decision Making*. San Francisco: Freeman, 1976.

Schmidhauser, John R. *Judges and Justices: The Federal Appellate Judiciary*. Boston: Little, Brown, 1979.

_____. *The Supreme Court: Its Politics, Personalities, and Procedures*. New York: Holt, Rinehart and Winston, 1960.

Schubert, Glendon. *The Judicial Mind Revisited*. New York: Oxford University Press, 1974.

_____. *Judicial Policy Making*. Glenview, Ill.: Scott, Foresman, 1974.

_____. *Quantitative Analysis of Judicial Behavior*. New York: Free Press, 1959.

Seron, Carroll. *The Roles of Magistrates in Federal District Courts*. Washington, D.C.: Federal Judicial Center, 1983.

Simon, James F. *In His Own Image*. New York: McKay, 1973.

Vago, Steven. *Law and Society*. Englewood Cliffs, N.J.: Prentice-Hall, 1981.

Wasby, Stephen L. *The Impact of the United States Supreme Court: Some Perspectives*. Homewood, Ill.: Dorsey Press, 1970.

Wheeler, Russell R., and Howard R. Whitcomb, eds. *Judicial Administration: Text and Readings*. Englewood Cliffs, N.J.: Prentice-Hall, 1977.

Williston, Samuel. *Life and Law*. Boston: Little, Brown, 1940.

Wirt, Frederick M. *Politics of Southern Equality: Law and Social Change in a Mississippi County*. Chicago: Aldine, 1970.

Woodward, Bob, and Scott Armstrong. *The Brethren: Inside the Supreme Court*. New York: Simon and Schuster, 1979.

Wright, Charles Alan. *Handbook of the Law of Federal Courts*. 2d ed. St. Paul, Minn.: West, 1970.

Articles

Adamany, David W. "Legitimacy, Realigning Elections, and the Supreme Court." *Wisconsin Law Review* (1973): 790-846.

------. "The Party Variable in Judges' Voting: Conceptual Notes and a Case Study." *American Political Science Review* 63 (1969): 57-74.

Armstrong Virginia C., and Charles A. Johnson. "Certiorari Decisions by the Warren & Burger Courts: Is Cue Theory Time Bound?" *Polity* 15 (1982): 141-150.

Atkins, Burton M., and William Zovoina. "Judicial Leadership on the Court of Appeals: A Probability Analysis of Panel Assignment on Race Relations Cases on the Fifth Circuit." *American Journal of Political Science* 18 (1974): 701-711.

Baar, Carl. "Federal Judicial Administration: Political Strategies and Organizational Change," pp. 97-109 in *Judicial Administration: Text and Readings*. Ed. Russell R. Wheeler and Howard R. Whitcomb. Englewood Cliffs, N.J.: Prentice-Hall, 1977.

Baum, Lawrence. "Implementation of Judicial Decisions: An Organizational Analysis." *American Politics Quarterly* 4 (1976): 86-114.

------. "Policy Goals in Judicial Gatekeeping: A Proximity Model of Discretionary Jurisdiction." *American Journal of Political Science* 21 (1977): 13-35.

Birkby, Robert. "The Supreme Court and the Bible Belt: Tennessee Reaction to the *Schempp* Decision." *Midwest Journal of Political Science* 10 (1966): 304-319.

Bond, Jon R. "The Politics of Court Structure: The Addition of New Federal Judges, 1949-1978." *Law & Policy Quarterly* (1980): 181-188.

Bond, Jon R., and Charles A. Johnson. "Implementing a Permissive Policy: Hospital Abortion Services After *Roe v. Wade*." *American Journal of Political Science* 26 (1982): 1-24.

Brenner, Saul. "Fluidity on the United States Supreme Court: A Reexamination." *American Journal of Political Science* 24 (1980): 526-535.

Broach, Glen T., et al. "State Political Culture and Sentence Severity in Federal District Courts." *Criminology* 16 (1978): 373-382.

Canon, Bradley C., and S. Sidney Ulmer. "The Supreme Court and Critical Elections: A Dissent." *American Political Science Review* 70 (1976): 1215-1218.

Carp, Robert, and Russell Wheeler. "Sink or Swim: The Socialization of a Federal District Judge." *Journal of Public Law* 21 (1972): 359-393.

Casper, Jonathan D. "The Supreme Court and National Policy Making." *American Political Science Review* 70 (1976): 50-63.

Cook, Beverly Blair. "Public Opinion and Federal Judicial Policy." *American Journal of Political Science* 21 (1977): 567-600.

Dahl, Robert A. "Decision-Making in a Democracy: The Supreme Court as a National Policy-Maker." *Journal of Public Law* 6 (1957): 279-295.

Dolbeare, Kenneth M. "The Federal District Courts and Urban Public Policy: An Exploratory Study (1960-1967)," pp. 373-404 in *Frontiers of Judicial Research.* Ed. Joel B. Grossman and Joseph Tanenhaus. New York: Wiley, 1969.

Feig, Douglas G. "Expenditures in American States: The Impact of Court-Ordered Reapportionment." *American Politics Quarterly* 6 (1978): 309-324.

Flanders, Steven, and Jerry Goldman. "Screening Practices and the Use of Para-Judicial Personnel in a U.S. Court of Appeals," pp. 241-258 in *Judicial Administration: Text and Readings.* Ed. Russell R. Wheeler and Howard R. Whitcomb. Englewood Cliffs, N.J.: Prentice-Hall, 1977.

Funston, Richard. "The Supreme Court and Critical Elections." *American Political Science Review* 69 (1975): 795-811.

Gibson, James L. "From Simplicity to Complexity: The Development of Theory in the Study of Judicial Behavior." *Political Behavior* 5 (1983): 7-50.

Goldman, Sheldon. "Conflict on the U.S. Courts of Appeals 1965-1971: A Quantitative Analysis." *University of Cincinnati Law Review* 42 (1973): 635-658.

_____. "Reagan's Judicial Appointments at Mid-Term: Shaping the Bench in His Own Image." *Judicature* 66 (1983): 335-347.

_____. "Should There Be Affirmative Action for the Judiciary?" *Judicature* 62 (1979): 488-496.

_____. "Voting Behavior on the United States Courts of Appeals, 1961-1964." *American Political Science Review* 60 (1966): 370-385.

_____. "Voting Behavior on the United States Courts of Appeals, Revisited." *American Political Science Review* 69 (1975): 491-506.

Gottschall, Jon. "Carter's Judicial Appointments: The Influence of Affirmative Action and Merit Selection on Voting on the U.S. Courts of Appeals." *Judicature* 67 (1983): 165-173.

Gruhl, John. "The Supreme Court's Impact on the Law of Libel: Compliance by Lower Federal Courts." *Western Political Quarterly* 33 (1980): 502-519.

Grunbaum, Werner F. "A Quantitative Analysis of the 'Presidential Ballot' Case." *Journal of Politics* 34 (1972): 223-243.

Handberg, Roger, and Harold F. Hill, Jr. "Court Curbing, Court Reversals, and Judicial Review: The Supreme Court Versus Congress." *Law and Society Review* 14 (1980): 309-322.

Hanson, Roger A., and Robert E. Crew, Jr. "The Policy Impact of Reapportionment." *Law and Society Review* 8 (1973): 69-94.

Henschen, Beth M. "Statutory Interpretations of the Supreme Court: Congressional Response." *American Politics Quarterly* 11 (1983): 441-458.

Howard, J. Woodford, Jr. "On the Fluidity of Judicial Choice." *American Political Science Review* 62 (1968): 43-57.

Johnson, Charles A. "Judicial Decisions and Organizational Change: A Theory." *Administration and Society* 11 (1979): 27-51.

Kort, Fred. "Quantitative Analysis of Fact-Patterns in Cases and Their Impact on Judicial Decisions," pp. 330-334 in *American Court Systems*. Ed. Sheldon Goldman and Austin Sarat. San Francisco: Freeman, 1978.

Kuklinski, James H., and John E. Stanga. "Political Participation and Government Responsiveness: The Behavior of California Superior Courts." *American Political Science Review* 73 (1979): 1090-1099.

Lamb, Charles M. "Warren Burger and the Insanity Defense: Judicial Philosophy and Voting Behavior on a U.S. Court of Appeals." *American University Law Review* 24 (1974): 91-128.

Lawlor, Reed C. "Personal Stare Decisis." *Southern California Law Review* 41 (1967): 73-118.

Murphy, Walter F. "Chief Justice Taft and the Lower Court Bureaucracy: A Study in Judicial Administration." *Journal of Politics* 24 (1962): 453-476.

Neiser, Eric. "The New Federal Discipline Act: Some Questions Congress Didn't Answer." *Judicature* 65 (1981): 142-160.

Newland, Chester A. "Press Coverage of the United States Supreme Court." *Western Political Quarterly* 17 (1964): 15-36.

Puro, Steven. "United States Magistrates: A New Federal Judicial Officer." *Justice System Journal* 2 (1976): 141-156.

Rohde, David W. "Policy Goals, Strategic Choice and Majority Opinion Assignments in the United States Supreme Court." *Midwest Journal of Political Science* 16 (1972): 652-682.

Rowland, C. K., and Robert A. Carp. "A Longitudinal Study of Party Effects on Federal District Court Policy Propensities." *American Journal of Political Science* 24 (1980): 291-305.

Rowland, C. K., Robert A. Carp, and Ronald Stidham. "Judges' Policy Choices and the Value Basis of Judicial Appointments: A Comparison of Support for Criminal Defendants Among Nixon, Johnson, and

Kennedy Appointees to the Federal District Courts." *Journal of Politics* 46 (1984), 886-902.

Schmidhauser, John R. "Judicial Behavior and the Sectional Crisis of 1837-1860." *Journal of Politics* 23 (1961): 615-640.

———. "The Justices of the Supreme Court: A Collective Portrait." *Midwest Journal of Political Science* 3 (1959): 1-57.

Schubert, Glendon. "Jackson's Judicial Philosophy: An Exploration in Value Analysis." *American Political Science Review* 59 (1965): 940-963.

Slotnick, Elliot E. "The Changing Role of the Senate Judiciary Committee in Judicial Selection." *Judicature* 62 (1979): 502-510.

———. "The Chief Justice and Self-Asignment of Majority Opinions." *Western Political Quarterly* 31 (1978): 219-225.

———. "Federal Appellate Judge Selection: Recruitment Changes and Unanswered Questions." *The Justice System Journal* 6 (1981): 283-305.

———. "Judicial Selection Systems and Nominations Outcomes: Does the Process Make a Difference?" *American Politics Quarterly* 12 (1984): 222-240.

———. "The Paths to the Federal Bench: Gender, Race and Judicial Recruitment Variation." *Judicature* 67 (1984): 371-388.

———. "Reforms in Judicial Selection: Will They Affect the Senate's Role? Part II." *Judicature* 64 (1980): 114-131.

———. "Who Speaks for the Court? Majority Opinion Assignment from Taft to Burger." *American Journal of Political Science* 23 (1979): 60-77.

Songer, Donald R. "Concern for Policy Outputs as a Cue for Supreme Court Decisions on Certiorari." *Journal of Politics* 41 (1979): 1185-1194.

Stidham, Ronald, and Robert A. Carp. "U.S. Trial Court Reactions to Changes in Civil Rights and Civil Liberties Policies." *Southeastern Political Review* 10 (1984): 3-27.

———. "Trial Courts' Responses to Supreme Court Policy Changes: Three Case Studies." *Law and Policy Quarterly* 4 (1982): 215-235.

Stidham, Ronald, Robert A. Carp, and C. K. Rowland. "Patterns of Presidential Influence on the Federal District Courts: An Analysis of the Appointment Process." *Presidential Studies Quarterly* 14 (1984): 548-560.

———. "Women's Rights Before the Federal District Courts, 1971-1977." *American Politics Quarterly* 11 (1983): 205-218.

Tanenhaus, Joseph. "The Cumulative Scaling of Judicial Decisions." *Harvard Law Review* 79 (1966): 1583-1594.

Tanenhaus, Joseph, et al. "The Supreme Court's Certiorari Jurisdiction: Cue Theory," pp. 111-132 in *Judicial Decision-Making*. Ed. Glendon Schubert. New York: Free Press, 1963.

Tate, C. Neal. "Personal Attribute Models of the Voting Behavior of U.S. Supreme Court Justices: Liberalism in Civil Liberties and Economic Decisions, 1946-1978." *American Political Science Review* 75 (1981): 355-367.

Ulmer, S. Sidney. "The Analysis of Behavior Patterns in the United States Supreme Court." *Journal of Politics* 22 (1960): 629-653.

_____. "The Decision to Grant Certiorari as an Indicator to Decision 'on the Merits.'" *Polity* 4 (1972): 429-447.

_____. "The Discriminant Function and a Theoretical Context for Its Use in Estimating the Votes of Judges," pp. 335-369 in *Frontiers of Judicial Research*. Ed. Joel B. Grossman and Joseph Tanenhaus. New York: Wiley, 1969.

_____. "Selecting Cases for Supreme Court Review: An Underdog Model." *American Political Science Review* 72 (1978): 902-910.

_____. "Supreme Court Behavior in Racial Exclusion Cases: 1935-1960." *American Political Science Review* 56 (1962): 325-330.

_____. "Toward a Theory of Sub-Group Formation in the United States Supreme Court." *Journal of Politics* 27 (1965): 133-152.

Wasby, Stephen L. "The Communication of the Supreme Court's Criminal Procedure Decisions." *Villanova Law Review* 18 (1973): 1086-1118.

Government Publications

The Third Branch. Washington, D.C.: Administrative Office of the United States Courts and the Federal Judicial Center. Monthly.

Index

Abington School District v. Schempp - 224

Abortion decisions of courts - 28, 158, 159, 179-180, 184-187, 206, 207, 210, 218-221, 236

Abraham, Henry J. - 59, 131, 132, 167

Adamany, David W. - 31, 35, 36, 168

Adams, John - 6, 15, 24

Administrative Office Act of 1939 - 67, 73

Administrative Office of the U.S. Courts - 61, 66-68, 70, 72, 75, 83, 86

Advisory opinions - 48-50, 59, 137

Alberts v. California - 171

American Bar Association (ABA)
  philosophical orientation - 107-108
  in selection of judges - 91, 95, 102, 106-108, 115

American Jewish Congress - 155

Amici ("friends of the court") - 155

Anderson, James E. - 223

"Anticipatory socialization." *See* Socialization of judges

Appellate court decisions, implementation of. *See* Implementation of appellate court decisions

Appellate jurisdiction
  of appeals courts - 18-20, 41-42, 59, 208, 235
  of Supreme Court - 10-11, 18, 28, 43-45, 208, 235

Appointments, judicial
  ideologically based - 112, 113, 116, 118-121, 128-130, 211, 230, 235
  recess - 103-104

Armstrong, Scott - 88, 132, 180, 196-197, 222

Armstrong, Virginia C. - 196

Armstrong v. Board of Education of Birmingham - 197

Articles of Confederation
  lack of federal judiciary - 1-2

Asbestos Case Management Conference - 72

Assistant U.S. attorneys - 26, 83, 84-85, 104-105. *See also* U.S. attorneys

Atkins, Burton M. - 197

Attitude theory and bloc-formation analysis - 189-193, 233-234

Attorney general - 85, 102, 104-105, 106, 107, 142, 211-212

Baar, Carl - 87

Background of judges
  appeals courts - 15-16, 91-95, 96-98, 113, 129-130
  district courts - 24, 90-93, 96-98, 113, 129-130
  influence on judicial behavior - 121-125, 141-166, 204, 206-207, 227-232
  relation of background studies to attitude analysis - 190-191
  Supreme Court - 4-5, 89-90, 96-98, 119, 129-130

Bailiffs - 83

Baker v. Carr - 34, 55, 60, 170, 201, 202, 215, 221

Ball, Howard - 88, 130-131

Bankruptcy courts - 29-30, 71, 127

Bankruptcy Reform Act of 1978 - 29-30

Barber, Kathleen L. - 222
Bargaining, and collegial court decision
making - 13, 179-181, 232-233, 234
Bartlett, D. Brock - 113
Baum, Lawrence - 34, 170, 221, 223-224
Bayh, Birch - 110
Behavior, judicial, circuit-by-circuit vari-
ations - 148-151, 153, 231. *See also*
Background of judges; Decision-making,
judicial
Berg, Larry L. - 223
Berkson, Larry C. - 131
Bill of Rights. See specific constitutional
provisions and categories of civil liberties
Birkby, Robert H. - 34, 224
Black, Hugo
conference behavior - 186-187
judicial disability - 128
Ku Klux Klan membership - 150
Blackmun, Harry
appointment to Court - 210
conference behavior - 186-187
decision in *Roe v. Wade* - 180, 184
Blacks
as judges - 91-98, 104, 109-110, 112,
113, 143
as subjects of decisions. See Racial
equality; School desegregation
Blair, John - 4-5
Bloc analysis - 189-193, 234
"Blue slip" - 103, 109-110
Bond, Jon R. - 131, 224
Bonner v. City of Prichard, Alabama -
169
Bradley, Joseph P. - 181
Brady, David W. - 223
Brandeis, Louis - 79, 99
Brennan, William
capital punishment - 179
judicial socialization - 123
Nixon tapes case - 182
opinion in *Baker v. Carr* - 201
Brenner, Saul - 197
Broach, Glen T. - 170
Brown, John - 127
Brown v. Board of Education (1954) - 8-
9, 10, 19, 34, 138, 157, 158, 160, 170,
182, 186, 210, 219, 221
Brown v. Board of Education (1955) -
200-201, 214-215, 221
Buchanan, James - 91

Bullock, Charles S. III - 170, 221, 223-
224
Bureaucratic theory of judicial hierarchy
- 200
Burger, Warren
appointment to Court - 9, 103, 149,
210
conference behavior - 186-187
as court of appeals judge - 21
decision in *Roe v. Wade* - 184
exclusionary rule - 216-217
family background - 90
judicial administration - 65
relationship with colleagues - 183-184
Burger Court
comparison with Warren Court - 9, 45,
162-163, 175-176, 210-211, 216-218
intracourt relations - 175-176, 184-187
policies - 45, 157, 162-163, 175-176,
211, 216-218
Burton, Harold - 119
Byrd, Robert - 107

C scale, use in analysis of court decisions
- 193
Callahan, Robert Dale - 50
Cameron, Ben J. - 22, 188
Campbell, Angus - 168
Canon, Bradley C. - 35-36, 222-224
Carbon, Susan B. - 131
Cardozo, Benjamin - 79, 99, 123
Carp, Robert A. - 35-36, 87-88, 130-132,
168-171, 222-223
Carswell, G. Harrold - 99, 107-108, 150,
210
Carter, Jimmy
Bankruptcy Reform Act - 29
circuit judge nominating commissions -
104, 108
courts of appeals appointments - 91-95
district court appointments - 90-93
judicial appointment criteria - 113
lack of Supreme Court vacancies - 113
liberalism of district court appointees -
120-121
Caseloads
of appeals courts - 17, 41-42, 73-74, 86
of district courts - 38-41, 63, 73-74, 86
of Supreme Court - 43-45, 86
Casper, Jonathan D. - 31, 35-36
Chandler, Stephen S. - 126

Chase, Harold W. - 131
Chief judge
  of appeals courts - 22, 65, 124, 126-
    127, 187-188, 233
  of district courts - 124, 233
Chief justice. *See also* individual names
  conference leadership - 12, 185-187,
    233
  duties and powers - 6-7, 12-13, 64-66,
    70, 185-187, 233
  history of office - 4-8
  opinion assignment - 6, 12, 184, 186,
    233
Chisholm v. Georgia - 5, 34, 208
Circuit Court Act of 1802 - 16
Circuit courts - 15-17
Circuit Judicial Conferences
  agendas of - 72
  as forum of interaction between district
    and appellate judges - 72, 86
Circuit Judicial Councils - 72-74, 75, 86,
  126
Citizenship. *See* Diversity of citizenship
  cases
Civil liberties. *See also* Racial equality
  as court concern - 8-10, 32-33, 117-
    121, 123, 143-145, 147-148, 150-152,
    156, 163, 175-176, 211
  impact of court decisions - 8-9, 20, 27-
    28
Civil Rights Act of 1964 - 28, 209, 212,
  214
Civil Rights Act of 1968 - 46
Clark, Charles - 22
Clark, Jesse E. - 82
Clark, Tom - 119, 201
Class actions - 49
Clear-and-present-danger doctrine - 203-
  204
Clerks of court - 71, 82, 126
Cobb, Howell - 91
Committee on the Federal Judiciary of
  the ABA. *See* American Bar Association
Common law tradition - 47, 137
Communication of appellate court policy
  decisions - 202-203
Compliance by lower courts with Su-
  preme Court decisions. *See also* Imple-
  mentation of appellate court decisions
  examples of compliance - 206
  strategies of noncompliance - 204-206

Computers
  use by court personnel - 22
  use by judicial behavioralists - 191, 195
Conferences
  appeals courts - 22-23, 178-185, 232-
    234
  Supreme Court - 11-13, 175-187, 188-
    189, 232-234
Conference of Senior Circuit Judges - 64
Congress
  attacks on courts - 15, 207-209, 218-
    219, 226-227
  comparison with courts - 10, 30-33,
    54-55, 62-63, 143
  effect on courts' agenda, caseloads and
    jurisdiction - 2-3, 6, 8, 11, 15-16, 18,
    23-25, 28-30, 37-59, 62-65, 68, 75,
    98, 142, 159, 208, 226-227, 235
  impeachment of judges - 125-127, 208
  influence on court decisions - 8, 30-33,
    159-161, 165, 166
  influence on implementation of court
    decisions - 159-161, 165, 207-209,
    214-215, 220-221, 235-237
Conservatism, judicial, defined - 117,
  190, 192, 193, 229, 234
Constitution, U.S. *See also* Judicial review
  provisions concerning courts - 2, 3, 29,
    37-41, 43-48, 98, 125, 185
  as source of law or jurisdiction - 37-41,
    43-48, 49, 50, 55, 58, 208, 226
Constitutional amendments, used to overturn Court decisions - 208, 218-219
Constitutional Convention, and creation
  of federal judiciary - 2
Constitutional courts - 13, 28-30, 43, 62,
  127
Constitutional provisions. *See also* specific
  issues
  commerce clause - 7, 58
  necessary-and-proper clause - 7
  supremacy clause - 3
  1st Amendment - 8, 23, 50, 51, 56, 57,
    164-165, 203-204, 213-214
  4th Amendment - 13, 216-217
  5th Amendment - 38, 212
  6th Amendment - 26, 38, 52, 199, 217-
    218
  7th Amendment - 26
  8th Amendment - 51, 179, 202

Index

9th Amendment - 180
11th Amendment - 5, 208
13th Amendment - 208
14th Amendment
  due process - 8, 13, 27, 143-145,
    180, 206
  equal protection - 10, 21, 55, 163,
    212
  privileges and immunities - 51, 143-
    145
15th Amendment - 135-136
16th Amendment - 208
26th Amendment - 208
Content analysis - 190-191, 193, 234
Cook, Beverly Blair - 87
Coolidge, Calvin
  association with Taft - 106
  liberalism of district court appointees -
    118
Cooper, Irving Ben - 104
Cortner, Richard C. - 224
Court of Appeals Act of 1891 - 63
Court of Appeals for the Federal Circuit -
  17, 29
Court of Claims - 17, 29
Court of Customs and Patent Appeals -
  17
Court of International Trade - 29
Court of Military Appeals - 29
"Court-packing" plan - 8, 66, 210
Cox, Archibald - 224
Cox, William Harold - 109, 188
Crew, Robert E., Jr. - 224
Criminal defendants. *See* Procedural
  rights of criminal defendants
Cue theory - 174-176
Cushing, William - 4-5, 187

Dahl, Robert A. - 31, 35
Daley, Richard J. - 105
Danaher, John A. - 183
Danelski, David J. - 196-197
Decision-making, judicial
  on collegial courts - 173-196
  as determined by democratic subculture
    - 141-161, 161-165
  as determined by judge's role concep-
    tion - 165-166
  as determined by legal subculture -
    133-141, 161-165

Decision-making environment, trial and
  appellate courts contrasted - 133-135,
  173
Democratic subculture
  components of - 133, 141-161, 166
  as predictor of judicial behavior - 161-
    165, 219-221
Dewey, Charles A. - 128-129
Dewey, Thomas E. - 129
"Dicta" - 205
Disability of judges. *See* Retirement and
  removal of judges
Disciplinary action against judges. *See*
  Impeachment and removal of judges
Discuss list - 12, 186
Dissents and dissenting opinions - 6, 12,
  123, 181-183, 184-185, 186, 233
Diversity of citizenship cases - 40, 59, 154
Doe v. Bolton - 184
Dolbeare, Kenneth M. - 36, 224
Douglas, Paul - 105
Douglas, William O.
  conference behavior - 186-187
  decision in *Roe v. Wade* - 184
  judicial disability - 127-128
Downey, Martin - 100

E scale, use in analysis of court decisions -
  193
Early, Stephen T., Jr. - 34, 35
Eastland, James - 109, 114-115
Ecole Nationale de la Magistrature - 122
Economic policy
  as court concern - 8, 117-121, 143-145,
    146-148, 150-152, 156, 160, 163,
    175-176, 190, 227
  impact of court decisions - 8, 160
Eisenhower, Dwight D.
  enforcement of *Brown v. Board of Edu-
    cation* - 160, 210
  judicial appointment criteria - 112, 119
  judicial appointment success rate - 115
  and liberal federal judiciary - 116
Eisenstein, James - 88
En banc proceedings - 22-23, 74, 151-152
Engel v. Vitale - 34, 213, 224
Epstein, Leon - 169
Error correction by appellate courts - 19,
  20, 25, 124, 134
Evarts Act (1891) - 17

Evasion of court rulings. *See* Compliance by lower courts with Supreme Court decisions
Evers v. Jackson Municipal Separate School District - 138-139, 167
Exclusionary rule - 216-217
Exhaustion of remedies - 53-54, 138, 227
Ex Parte McCardle - 47, 59

Factor analysis - 192
Fact pattern analysis - 193-195, 234
Fairman, Charles - 197
Farley, James A. - 119, 132
Faubus, Orval - 160, 210
Federal Bureau of Investigation, role in judicial selection process - 102, 105
Federal Communications Commission (FCC) - 21
Federal Courts Improvement Act (1982) - 17
Federal Judicial Center - 65, 68-72, 77, 83, 86
Federal Magistrates Acts of 1968, 1976, and 1979 - 74-78
Federalism - 3-4, 7-8, 43-45, 148
Feig, Douglas G. - 224
Fenton, J. H. - 169
Field, Stephen J. - 181
Fish, Peter G. - 86-87
Flanders, Steven - 88
Ford, Gerald
  courts of appeals appointments - 91-95
  district court appointments - 90-93, 114
  liberalism of district court appointees - 120, 211
Fortas, Abe - 115
Frank, Jerome - 167
Frank, John P. - 34
Frankfurter, Felix
  law clerks - 78-79
  political thicket - 55
  praised by Senator Hruska - 99
  voting behavior - 194
Freedom of expression - 8, 56, 144, 163, 203-204, 211
Freedom of religion - 8-9, 50, 51, 57, 144, 157, 158, 159, 160-161, 210, 213-214
Freeman, Jo - 224
Freshman socialization. *See* Socialization of judges

Friesen, Ernest C., Jr. - 87
Frontiero, Sharron - 212
Frontiero v. Richardson - 212, 223
Funston, Richard - 35-36
Furman v. Georgia - 222

Gall, Peter - 223
Gallas, Edward C. - 87
Gallas, Nesta M. - 87
Geographic representation and influences on courts - 4-5, 15, 19, 32, 38, 62-63, 142, 148-156, 161-165, 166. *See also* Background of judges; Urban-rural variations in judicial behavior
Gibbons v. Ogden - 7, 34
Gibson, James L. - 197
Gideon v. Wainwright - 34, 199, 213, 216-217, 220, 221, 224
Giles, Micheal W. - 36, 222-224
Glick, Henry R. - 86-87, 170-171, 196
Godbold, John C. - 151-153
Goldberg, Arthur J. - 123
Goldberg, Irving L. - 28
Goldman, Jerry - 88
Goldman, Sheldon - 34, 87, 130, 132, 145-146, 167-169, 198
Goldstein, Leslie Friedman - 224
Gomillion, Charles - 136
Gomillion v. Lightfoot - 135-136, 167
Gottschall, Jon - 132
Goulden, Joseph C. - 130-132
Graham, Fred P. - 87
Grand jury - 26, 38, 65
Graven, Henry - 153-154
Gray, Horace - 78, 181
Gray, John Chipman - 78
Gray v. Sanders - 224
Griffin, William - 110
Griswold v. Connecticut - 57, 60, 206, 222
Grossman, Joel B. - 36, 131, 198
Gruhl, John - 222
Grunbaum, Werner F. - 198

Hadley, Charles D. - 168
Hager, Philip - 132
Hall, Peirson - 99-100
Hamilton, Alexander - 1
Hammond, Phillip - 224
Handberg, Roger - 35-36
Hanson, Roger A. - 224

Harding, Warren G.
association with Taft - 106
liberalism of district court appointees -
118
Harlan, John Marshall - 128
Harris v. McRae - 223-224
Harris v. New York - 218, 224
Harrison, Robert H. - 5
Hawkins v. Town of Shaw, Mississippi -
35
Haynsworth, Clement - 107-108, 150,
210
Henderson, Dwight F. - 35
Henschen, Beth M. - 223
Higher Education Facilities Act (1963) -
57
Hill, Harold F., Jr. - 35-36
Hinckley, Barbara - 169
Holmes, Oliver Wendell
evolution of the law - 140-141
law clerks - 78-79
Hoover, Herbert
liberalism of district court appointees -
118
rejection of Supreme Court nominee -
115
Howard, J. Woodford, Jr. - 34-35, 87-
88, 130, 132, 167-171, 196-197
Hruska, Roman - 99
Hughes, Charles Evans - 8, 34
Hughes, Sarah T. - 28
Hyde Amendment on abortions - 207

Ideology in judicial appointments. *See*
Appointments, judicial
Innes, Harry - 24
Impeachment and removal of judges - 29-
30, 62-63, 125-130, 200, 208
Implementation of appellate court decisions
as influenced by Congress - 207-209,
214-215, 235-237
as influenced by the president - 209-
212, 214-215, 235-237
as influenced by other implementers -
212-214, 235-237
by lower courts - 203-207
examples of - 157-158, 160-161, 182,
199-221, 235-237
Index of interagreement, use in bloc analysis - 191

"Innovation" by judges. *See* Policymaking
Integration. *See* Black civil rights issues
Interest groups
in litigation - 155, 218-219, 220, 235-
237
in selection of judges - 105-106, 108,
115, 235-237
Iredell, James - 4-5, 15

Jackson, Donald Dale - 131, 132, 167,
197
Jackson, Robert - 82, 178
Jacob, Herbert - 35
Jacobellis v. Ohio - 171, 222
Jahnige, Thomas P. - 87
Jaworski, Leon - 209
Jay, John - 4-5, 15
Jefferson, Thomas - 6-7, 16, 187
Johnson, Andrew - 47
Johnson, Charles A. - 196, 222-224
Johnson, Frank M. - 27, 32
Johnson, Lyndon B.
appointment of Thurgood Marshall -
96
courts of appeals appointments - 91-95
district court appointments - 90-93,
105, 114-115, 145, 211
judicial appointment criteria - 113
liberalism of district court appointees -
120
as lobbyist - 107
rejection of judicial nominations - 115
Johnson, Richard - 224
Johnson, William - 187
Judge's Bench Book - 71
Judicial activism and restraint - 47-59,
113, 210, 231
Judicial administration
as furthered by court personnel - 74-86
as furthered by support agencies - 65-
74
history of - 61-63
and judicial reform - 64-68
"Judicial Behavioralists" - 141, 161, 166,
191, 192
Judicial Conference Committee on the
Budget - 66
Judicial Conference Committee on Court
Administration - 66

Judicial Conference of the United States - 30, 64-68, 72, 73, 75, 86, 127
Judicial Councils Reform and Judicial Conduct and Disability Act - 126-127
"Judicial realists" - 141, 161, 166
Judicial recruitment process - 89-111, 228-232
Judicial review - 3-11, 28-30, 30-33, 47-59, 158
Judicial self-restraint. *See* Self-restraint, judicial
Judiciary Act of 1789 - 2-3, 7, 15, 23, 28, 62-63, 84
Judiciary Act of 1801 - 16
Judiciary Act of 1925 - 19, 44, 174
Judiciary Committee, U.S. Senate - 99, 102, 103, 104, 108-110, 113, 114-115, 120
Jurisdiction. *See also* Original jurisdiction
  as affected by Congress - 7, 15-20, 28, 45-47, 48, 56, 58-59, 159, 161, 208, 226-227
  of appeals courts - 18-20, 41-42, 58-59
  concurrent - 43
  of district courts - 16, 25, 28, 29, 37-41, 43, 58-59
  of Supreme Court - 7, 10-11, 28, 43-45, 58-59
Justice Department, and selection of judges - 104-105. *See also* Assistant U.S. attorneys; Solicitor general; and U.S. attorneys
Justice, William Wayne - 27-28
Justiciability - 47, 55, 201

Kennedy, Edward - 109-110
Kennedy, John F.
  and the ABA - 107
  federal bench appointments - 104, 105, 107, 109, 114-115, 211
  enforcement of *Brown v. Board of Education* - 160
  liberalism of district court appointees - 119-120
  omnibus judgeship bill - 114
Key, V. O., Jr. - 168-169
Kitchin, William - 164, 167, 171
Klein, Joel - 81
Kort, Fred - 198
Kuklinski, James H. - 170

Ladd, Everett Carll, Jr. - 168
Lamar, Joseph R. - 181
Lamb, Charles M. - 198
Landis, James M. - 86
Lane v. Wilson - 135-136, 167
Law clerks - 22, 61, 72, 78-82, 86, 128, 177, 180, 186, 203
"Law interpreters." *See* Role conception of judges
"Law makers." *See* Role conception of judges
Law schools, as wellspring of legal subculture - 139-140, 148, 162
Lawlor, Reed C. - 198
Laxalt, Paul - 113
Leavitt, Donald - 167-168, 169, 170
Lee, Rex E. - 84, 88
Legal reasoning process - 9, 122, 135-141, 142, 147-148, 161-165, 173, 178-179, 189-190, 193-195, 227-228, 232-234
Legal subculture
  approach contrasted with fact pattern analysis - 193-195
  components of - 133, 135-141, 147, 148, 166, 178-179, 232-234
  as predictor of judicial behavior - 161-165, 219-221, 232-234
Legislative courts - 28-30, 43, 127
Levi, Edward H. - 167
Liberalism, judicial, defined - 117, 192, 193
Lincoln, Abraham - 89
Lobbying activities, judicial. *See* Interest groups
Local influences on judges. *See* Geographic representation and influences on courts; State boundaries
Local party leaders, role in judicial selection - 105
Lord, Miles W. - 30

McCardle, William - 46-47
McCree, Wade H., Jr. - 84, 88
McCulloch v. Maryland - 7, 34
McLauchlan, William P. - 59
Madison, James - 1, 6-7
Magistrates Committee of the Judicial Conference of the United States - 75
Maher v. Roe - 223
Maine, Henry Sumner - 167

Index

Mapp v. Ohio - 34, 216-217, 224
Marbury v. Madison - 6-7, 34, 158, 170, 186
Marbury, William - 6
Marshall, John
  as chief justice - 5-8, 187
  on function of appellate review - 52
  opinion in *Marbury v. Madison* - 6-7
Marshall, Thurgood
  appointment to Court - 96
  appointment to court of appeals - 109
  capital punishment - 179
  family background - 90
Martin, Donald G. - 35
Mason, Alpheus T. - 196
Mass media
  communication of decision - 13
  influence on judicial selection and on judges - 115, 121-122, 157, 190
Miller, Samuel F. - 181
Miller v. California - 170, 171
Minton, Sherman - 119
Miranda v. Arizona - 34, 205, 213, 216-218, 222, 224
Mitchell, John - 107
Mize, Sidney - 138-139
Moral Majority, as judicial lobbying group - 106
Muir, William - 224
Murphy, Frank - 123
Murphy, Walter F. - 131-132, 167, 196-197, 221
Muskrat v. United States - 59

Nagel, Stuart S. - 198
National Association for the Advancement of Colored People (NAACP) - 21, 155
National Labor Relations Board v. Jones and Laughlin Steel Corp. - 34, 170
National Organization for Women, as judicial lobbying group - 106
Neisser, Eric - 132
New Deal programs and court decisions - 8, 66, 116, 119, 163, 191, 210
New-judges bills, and presidential influence on courts - 113-114
New Judges Seminars - 70-71
Nixon, Richard M.
  and the ABA - 107-108

appointment of Warren Burger - 103, 210
courts of appeals appointments - 91-95
criticism of Warren Court - 210
district court appointments - 90-93, 99, 114, 145, 211
liberalism of district court appointees - 120
Nixon tapes case - 182, 209-210
rejection of Supreme Court nominees - 108, 210
southern school desegregation - 212
southern strategy - 149-150
Supreme Court appointments - 9, 176, 210-211
Norm enforcement by courts
  contrasted with judicial policy making - 26-28, 161-165, 200, 225, 227-228, 231
  examples of - 26, 133-135
Northern Pipeline Construction Co. v. Marathon Pipe Line Company - 35

Oakley, John Bilyeu - 87-88
Obscenity - 13, 56, 157, 164-165, 201-202, 236
"Occupational heredity" - 90-98, 229
Occupational socialization. *See* Socialization of judges
O'Connor, Karen - 224
O'Connor, Sandra Day, appointment to Court - 96, 103, 106, 108
Office of Communications of the United Church of Christ v. F.C.C. - 35
Omnibus Judgeship Act of 1978 - 25, 74, 104
Opinions
  advisory - 48-50
  announcement - 6, 23, 176
  assignment - 6, 12-13, 184, 186
  concurring and dissenting - 6, 12, 23, 123, 183, 184-185, 186, 202, 233
  per curiam - 13
  seriatim - 6
  use and purposes - 6, 158, 179, 181-183, 186
  writing and reaching agreement - 11-13, 14, 23, 78, 123, 175-185, 202, 233
Oral argument - 12, 22, 23, 80, 134
Order of the Coif - 140
Oregon v. Mitchell - 208

Original jurisdiction
  and appeals courts - 41, 59, 208,
  235
  of district courts - 16, 37-41, 43, 58-59,
  208, 235
  of Supreme Court - 10, 43-45, 59, 208,
  235
Overend, William - 60
Overton, William - 157

Pacific States Telephone & Telegraph v.
  Oregon - 60
Palley, Marian Lief - 224
Panetta, Leon E. - 223
Parker, John J. - 115
Paterson, William - 2, 187
Paterson (New Jersey) Plan - 2
Paupers' petitions - 44
Peltason, Jack W. - 36, 86, 221-222
Persuasion on the merits
  importance for collegial court decision
    making - 178-179, 232, 234
Petit jury - 26, 70, 74
Plessy, Homer - 9
Plessy v. Ferguson - 9, 34
Policy making
  by appeals courts - 20-21, 30-33,
    227
  contrasted with norm enforcement -
    26-28, 124, 161-165, 200, 225, 227-
    228, 231
  by district courts - 26-28, 30-33, 200,
    203-204, 227
  examples of - 6-11, 21, 26-28, 57-58,
    66, 199-221, 228
  factors influencing such activity - 9-10,
    16, 26-28, 30-33, 45, 51, 142-167,
    178-185, 219-221, 225-237
  links between judges, the president,
    and the citizenry - 111-121, 128-130,
    158, 211, 230, 235-237
  relation to judge's role conception -
    165-166, 228-229, 231-232
  by Supreme Court - 9-10, 16, 30-33,
    45, 57-58, 66, 124, 137, 200-202, 209,
    214-221, 227
Political party
  differences by region - 150-151
  influence on voting behavior of judges -
    121, 141-148, 163-164, 166, 206-207,
    211, 229-230

Political patronage, in staffing U.S. judiciary - 85, 99-100, 101-102, 112, 118-
  119
"Political questions" - 54-55, 59,
  138
Pollock v. Farmer's Loan and Trust Co. -
  208
Pound, Roscoe - 64
Powell, Lewis
  appointment to Court - 211
  law clerks - 81
  Nixon tapes case - 182
"Pragmatists." *See* Role conception of
  judges
Precedents, importance of. *See Stare deci-*
  sis, doctrine of
President. *See also* individual names
  attacks on courts - 8-9, 66, 210-211,
    235
  comparison with courts - 10, 30-33,
    54-55, 62-63
  influence on implementation of judicial
    decisions - 111-121, 159-161, 209-
    212, 214-215, 220-221, 235-237
  policy links with judges - 111-121,
    128-130, 142, 211, 230, 235-237
  selection of judges - 4-5, 24, 89-98,
    98-121, 129-130, 142, 147, 149-150,
    210
Presidential Election Campaign Fund
  Act of 1974 - 28
Preston, Michael B. - 224
Prisoners' petitions - 19, 40-42, 44, 59,
  77, 79
Pritchett, C. Herman - 132, 196
Probation officers - 71, 82-83
Procedural rights of criminal defendants
  as court concern - 8-9, 13, 117-121,
    143-145, 147-148, 150-152, 156, 163,
    176, 199, 205-206, 211, 212-213,
    216-218
  impact of court decisions - 8-9, 205-
    206, 212-213, 216-218, 220
Progressive Movement
  impact for judicial reform - 64-65
Public opinion
  influence on judges - 30-33, 54-55,
    111-121, 156-159, 160, 166, 206, 207,
    218-219, 236
Public policy. *See* Policy making.
Puro, Steven - 87

Index

Qualifications of judges
  formal - 98, 129
  informal - 98-102, 109-110, 129

Racial equality. *See also* School desegregation
  congressional influences - 46, 108-109,
    209
  and judicial innovation - 164
  judicial panel assignment - 22, 188
  party identification in judges - 143-147
  presidential appointments and ideology
    - 112
  regional and public opinion influences
    on judges - 150-151, 156, 157-158
  Supreme Court role - 8-10
  voting rights - 135-136
Rainey, R. Lee - 132
Randolph, Edmund - 2, 15
Randolph (Virginia) Plan - 2
Rayburn, Sam - 107
Reagan, Ronald
  courts of appeals appointments - 91-95
  district court appointments - 90-93
  Federal Courts Improvement Act - 17
  impact on the federal judiciary - 116
  judicial appointment criteria - 112-113,
    230
  liberalism of district court appointees -
    120-121
  repeal of circuit judge nominating com-
    missions - 104
  support for constitutional amendment -
    210
  Supreme Court appointment - 96, 103,
    106, 108
Reapportionment (legislative) decisions
  of courts - 9, 55, 144, 157, 201, 202,
  215-216, 236
Recess appointments. *See* Appointments,
  judicial
Reforms of judiciary - 16, 18, 61-86
Rehnquist, William
  appointment to Court - 211
  as commentator - 88, 230
  law clerks - 81-82
  Nixon tapes case - 182
Religion of judges - 89-98, 121, 143,
  146
Research Division of the Federal Judicial
  Center - 70

Retirement and removal of judges - 125-
  130
Reynolds v. Sims - 224
Richardson, Richard J. - 34-36, 135, 148,
  167-168, 221-222
Riley, William F. - 153-154
Ripley, Randall B. - 169
Ritter, Willis - 125-126
Roberson, Peggy - 130
Roberts, Owen - 8
Rodell, Fred - 34
Rodgers, Harrell R., Jr. - 170, 221, 223-
  224
Roe v. Wade - 28, 35, 158, 184, 218-219,
  222, 224
Rohde, David W. - 197-198
Role conception of judges, and decision-
  making process - 165-166, 228-229,
  231-232
Roosevelt, Franklin D.
  appointment of Harlan Fiske Stone -
    103
  and conservative federal judiciary - 116
  court administrator poposal - 66-67
  Court-packing plan - 8, 66, 210
  liberalism of district court appointees -
    118-119
*Roosevelt Court: A Study in Judicial Poli-
  tics and Values, 1937-1947* - 191
Ross v. Sirica - 197
Roth v. United States - 171
Rowland, C. K. - 35, 36, 130-131, 168-
  171, 222-223
Rule 17, governing writs of certiorari -
  174-175
Rutledge, John - 4-5

Sanctions, threat of, and collegial court
  decision making - 181-185, 232-233,
  234
Sarat, Austin - 198
Scaling of judicial decisions - 192-193,
  234
Schenck v. United States - 222
*Schlesinger v. Reservists Committee to
  Stop the War* - 59
Schmidhauser, John R. - 130-131, 167,
  169, 223
School boards, role in implementing de-
  segregation and prayer decisions - 213-
  214, 221

School desegregation
  court policies - 8-10, 19, 21, 32-33,
    117, 138-139, 157, 159-160, 182,
    200-201, 204, 207, 209, 210, 212,
    213-215, 219-220
  legislative policies - 28, 46, 159-160,
    209, 226-227, 235, 236
Schubert, Glendon - 191-192, 193, 196-
  198
Scott v. Sandford - 208
Segregation. *See* School desegregation
Self-restraint, judicial - 47-59, 113, 116,
  119, 137-138, 139, 140, 163, 166, 227
Senate, U.S., and selection of judges - 6,
  24, 30, 62, 98, 99, 102-104, 107, 108-
  111, 114-115, 120, 159, 161, 208, 235
Senatorial courtesy - 103, 105, 108-110,
  120, 210
"Senior" status for judges - 128
Seniority
  importance for Congress - 109
  importance for judicial behavior - 11,
    12
Sentencing behavior - 38, 71, 122, 153,
  158-159
Separate-but-equal doctrine - 9-10
Seron, Carroll - 87
Sharpe, Debra - 130
Simon, James F. - 169
Sirica, John J. - 210
Slotnick, Elliot E. - 131, 197
Small-group analysis
  as affected by the chief justice and chief
    judges - 185-188, 233
  aspects of - 176-185, 232-233
  empirical evidence of - 188-189
Socialization of judges - 121-125, 130,
  188
Social leadership on collegial courts - 177,
  185-187
Solicitor general - 61, 83-84
Songer, Donald R. - 196, 222
"Southern strategy" of President Nixon -
  149-150
Spaeth, Harold J. - 193, 197-198
Stancili, Nancy - 88
Standing to sue - 48-50, 137-138, 190,
  205
Stanga, John E. - 170
Stanley v. Georgia - 13, 34

Stare decisis, doctrine of - 136-137, 139,
  140, 142, 147-148, 161-165, 178, 193-
  195, 232, 234
State boundaries
  importance in federal judicial organiza-
    tion and selection - 23, 25, 62-63, 105,
    110, 114, 142, 148-151, 153-154
  as predictor of judicial voting behavior
    - 153-154
States' rights - 2, 7-8, 16
Stevens, John Paul - 120
Steward Machine Co. v. Davis - 34
Stewart, Potter
  concurring opinion in *Stanley v. Geor-*
    gia - 13
  definition of obscenity - 165, 222
  dissenting opinion in *Griswold v.*
    Connecticut - 57-58
Stidham, Ronald - 170, 222-223
Stone, Harlan Fiske
  appointment to Court - 103
  judicial socialization - 123
  law clerks - 79
  leadership - 187
Stouffer, Samuel A. - 169
"Strict constructionists." *See* Judicial activism and restraint
Structure of federal judiciary, principal
  characteristics of - 61-63, 74, 86, 97-98,
  125, 148, 200
Switzer, Carroll O. - 101-102, 112

Taft, William Howard
  judicial reform - 64-65
  judicial socialization - 123
  law clerks - 79
  retirement - 129
  in selection of judges - 106
Tanenhaus, Joseph - 36, 196, 198
Taney, Roger - 7-8
Tate, C. Neal - 168
Task leadership on collegial courts - 177,
  185-187
Tax court - 29, 41
Taylor, W. N. - 28
Third Branch - 70
Thompson, Robert S. - 87-88
Thornberry, Homer - 115
Three-judge district courts - 28, 212
Three-judge panels of appellate courts -
  22, 181, 187-188

Thurmond, Strom - 110
Tilton v. Richardson - 60
Tinker v. Des Moines Independent Community School District - 23, 35
Totenberg, Nina - 88
Truman, Harry S.
  appointment of Carroll Switzer - 101-102, 112
  judicial appointment criteria - 112
  liberalism of district court appointees - 119
  seizure of steel mills - 53
Tuttle, Elbert F. - 22, 188

Ulmer, S. Sidney - 35-36, 196, 198
U.S. attorneys - 61, 67, 83, 84-85. *See also* Assistant U.S. attorneys
U.S. Circuit Judge Nominating Commission - 104, 108
U.S. commissioners - 75
U.S. magistrates - 61, 70, 71, 72, 74-78, 86, 127
U.S. marshals - 83
United States v. Nixon - 158, 170, 186, 223
United States v. Seeger - 170
Urban-rural variations in judicial behavior - 154-156, 231
Uslaner, Eric - 224

Vago, Steven - 167
Vines, Kenneth M. - 34-36, 135, 148, 167-168, 221-222
Vinson, Fred - 119
Voting Rights Act of 1965 - 28, 40, 226

Wagner Act (1935) - 159
Wahlke, John - 169
Walker, Thomas G. - 36, 222-224
Wallace v. Jaffree - 224
Warren, Charles - 34
Warren, Earl
  as chief justice - 8-0
  Federal Judicial Center - 65

judicial socialization - 123
school desegregation - 182
Warren Court
  comparison with Burger Court - 9, 45, 175-176, 210-211, 216-218
  intracourt relations - 175-176
  policies - 8-9, 31, 45, 120, 175-176, 210, 216-218
Wasby, Stephen L. - 170, 222-223
Washington, Bushrod - 187
Washington, George
  district court appointments - 24
  impact on Supreme Court - 113
  objection to circuit riding duties - 15
  Supreme Court appointments - 4-5, 149
Wesberry v. Sanders - 224
West Coast Hotel Co. v. Parrish - 34, 170
Wheeler, Russell R. - 86-88, 132, 168-170
Whitcomb, Howard R. - 86-88
White, Byron - 182
White House staff, role in judicial selection process - 102, 103, 104, 105
Williams, John Sharp - 148
Williston, Samuel - 78, 87-88
Wilson, James - 4-5
Wilson, Woodrow, and liberalism of district court appointees - 117-118, 211
Women
  as judges - 91-98, 103, 104, 108, 109-110, 112, 113, 143
  rights of, as subject of court decisions - 212, 220
Woodward, Bob - 88, 132, 180, 196-197, 222
Wright, Skelly - 32-33
Writ of certiorari - 11, 44, 59, 80, 84, 174-176
Writ of habeas corpus - 40, 46, 164
Writ of mandamus - 7
Wyatt v. Stickney - 35

Zavoina, William - 197

8140